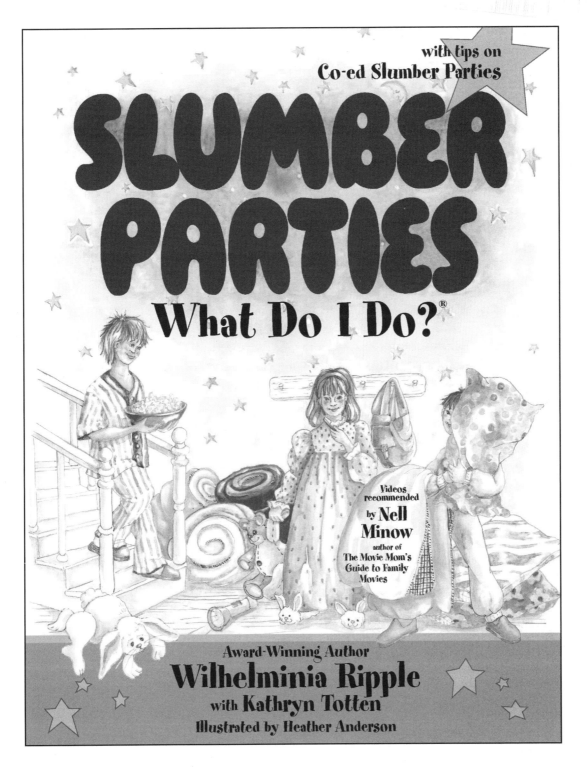

with tips on
Co-ed Slumber Parties

SLUMBER PARTIES
What Do I Do?®

Videos recommended by **Nell Minow** author of The Movie Mom's Guide to Family Movies

Award-Winning Author
Wilhelminia Ripple
with **Kathryn Totten**
Illustrated by Heather Anderson

Slumber Parties...What Do I Do?®

Authors Wilhelminia Ripple with Kathryn Totten

Oakbrook Publishing House
P.O. Box 2463
Littleton, Colorado 80161-2463
PHONE: (303) 738-1733 • **FAX:** (303) 797-1995
OR E-MAIL US AT: oakbrook@whatdoidobooks.com
WEBSITE: http://www.whatdoidobooks.com

To order: 1-888-738-1733

Publisher's Cataloging-in-Publication
(Provided by Quality Books, Inc.)

Ripple, Wilhelminia.
   Slumber parties : what do I do? / award-winning
author Wilhelminia Ripple with Kathy Totten ;
illustrated by Heather Anderson ; editor, Dianne Lorang.
—1st ed.
   p. cm. — (What do I do? series)
   Includes index.
   ISBN: 0-9649939-0-2

   1. Sleepovers. 2. Children's parties.
3. Entertaining. I. Totten, Kathy. II. Anderson,
Heather. III. Title.

GV1205.R56 2002   793.2'1
                        QB133-274

Printed and bound in the United States of America.

Printing 10 9 8 7 6 5 4 3 2 1

To my husband Mark

who has scanned all the illustrations for all the books in the
What Do I Do?® series, who continually fixes the computers and printers
when they decide to stop working (which is almost always when there is a deadline),
and who supports me even through the hard times…

and

To my children Mark, Nick, and Michelle

for having fun at their Slumber Parties (not realizing that
the ideas for those would end up in a book), for brainstorming,
creating, testing, and working on even even more ideas, and for understanding
when I needed to work and encouraging me when I didn't want to…

and

To parents

who get no sleep at Slumber Parties but keep letting their kids have them…

and

To all who believed in me!

Acknowledgments

Thanks to all the children, parents, and business owners that let me interview them:

Emily Appleby, Theresa Ayers, Teri Bavley, Dinah Benedict, Megan Bradford, Toby Bradford, Ann E. Byrnes, Todd Carpenter, Veronica Chavez, Katie Day, Anne Davidson, Todd Davidson, John Detweiler, Diamond Comic Distributors, Inc, Kaitlyn Ferber, Bobbie Gilbert, Juliana Greco, Stephanie Howe, Kelly Leins, Chris Hill, Kelly, Hill, J. Renée Howell, Drucilla F. Jones, Jessica King, Kristi Lackey, Nicole LaDuca, Jean Loth, Tom Marucco, Peggy Masek, Cassie Mason, Corina Nazzaro, Tine Norseth, Jamie O'Farrell, Karen Radeck, Matthew Radeck, Nick Ripple, Linda Robinson, Patty Savin, Mitch Schupanitz, Velvet Shogren, Laura Siegel, M. Snyder, Barbara Taylor, Marlene N. Thorpe, Robert Weatherwax and Lassie, Ashley Williams, and Barbara Young

A BIG Thank You to family and friends who shared ideas and brainstormed with me:

Maria E. Scordo Allen, Amy Arcuri, Angela Arcuri, Dolores Arcuri, Donna Arcuri, Dom Arcuri, Rose Arcuri, Sheila Arcuri, Tammy Arcuri, Shelly Beard, Nichole Franco, Kay Cassinis, Katie Dark, Christie Day, Tina Delponte, Nancy Ecker, Rebecca Gumley, Lauren Hendricks, Joanne Hill, Donna Kortman, Patrick King, Lauren MacMillan, Sabrina McCue, Samantha McCue, Tabatha McCue, Kendra and Vanessa Reiter, Amy Richardson, Mark Ripple, Michelle Ripple, Nick Ripple, Kathy Sweitzer, and Dawn Watson

Special Thanks to the following who were wonderful to work with:

Cover Design – Bobbi Shupe of E.P. Puffin & Company
Editor – Dianne Lorang of The Write Help (at www.thewritehelp.net) and author
    of *Single Women – Alive and Well!* (1stBooks Library, 2001)
Illustrator – Heather Anderson
Graphic Designer – Rebecca Finkel of F + P Graphic Design, Inc.
Production Assistants – Debbie Foster, Linne Junkin, Pam Kortman, Liz Lorang,
    Mark Ripple, Nick Ripple, and Michelle Ripple

And if I have forgotten you, "Thank You!"

About the Authors

Some call her the Martha Stewart of School Parties. **Wilhelminia "Willie" Ripple,** award-winning author of the **What Do I Do?**® series of party books, has appeared on Good Morning Texas, Denver's WB2 Morning Show (numerous times), and Denver's Channel 9 NEWS, plus been interviewed on radio. She has been featured in the *Rocky Mountain News* and *Woman's Day,* along with many other publications around the United States. With over 14 years of experience in organizing and creating party ideas, Willie currently lives in Colorado with her husband Mark and their three children.

Kathryn Totten works for the Arapahoe Library District, Colorado, organizing the award-winning children's summer reading programs and the annual storytelling festival at the district's libraries. The author of three books for children's librarians, she is a professional storyteller, sharing her original songs and stories at festivals, conferences, schools, and libraries. She lives in Colorado with her husband and family.

About "The Movie Mom"

Nell Minow is the author of *The Movie Mom's Guide to Family Movies.* Her reviews of current movies and videos are at www.moviemom.com.

To learn more about the **What Do I Do?**® series, visit our web site at:
www.whatdoidobooks.com

Table of Contents

Key To Symbols Used Throughout This Book

Knowledge Symbol
Educational facts relating to the themes, to share with everyone.

Favorite Symbol
Don't miss this game (craft, goody, drink, etc.).

Messy Symbol
Sure to cause a mess: Have paper towels ready.

Supply Symbol
Complete list of items needed for each game, craft, goody, drink, etc.

Sleeping Bag Symbol
Easy-to-copy list of all ingredients and supplies needed for each party.

Anytime Symbol
Anytime you want to have a slumber party without using a theme, use these fun ideas.

Note: Throughout the book, we will refer to both genders as "he" for the sake of consistency. "He" can be either male or female.

Introduction
How To Use This Book

***Slumber Parties…What Do I Do?*®** will help you plan Slumber Parties—for both boys and girls—that are first-rate and unforgettable. If you haven't had a Slumber Party before, or have and it wasn't what you expected, you'll be encouraged. There are plenty of games, activities, crafts, food and drink ideas, along with Video Recommendations and extra fun ideas for each chapter that will keep your guests busy all night long.

The What, Why, and How chapter will help answer all your Slumber Party questions, including those about the new rage—co-ed sleepovers. You'll find this information in The Seven Stages of Slumber Parties and Sleepovers. The Twenty Helpful Hints and Ten Don'ts for Parent will help you avoid party pitfalls and discover the details that make parties shine. Your party will be quick to plan and impress the best: *"No more fussing, no more headaches. It couldn't be easier."*

If you enjoy theme parties, there are thirteen to choose from in this book. Eight of the parties can be used for both boys and girls, ages 5 to 13. Two are tailored especially for girls, two are for boys, and one is for twins. There is even a bonus chapter for a Slumber Party for the family dog. The Table of Contents will tell you which party is for whom. A Slumber Party wouldn't be complete without an entertaining story. You can read these word-for-word or improvise and tell it how you recall. They are meant to be read early in the party because most of the games, crafts, food, and activities will tie in with the stories. Follow the Order of the Party in each chapter for smooth-sailing fun.

Here are some time guidelines that will help you plan your party. Every party has three games or activities averaging 10 to 30 minutes. Crafts also take this long. Stories are about 10 minutes long. Breakfast and dinner can take 20 to 30 minutes. (Desserts aren't included because there are Midnight Snack Attacks in each chapter.) Be sure to allow at least 20 minutes to an hour if your party is a combined birthday and Slumber Party, so you can serve cake and ice cream and then have your child open his presents. Videos are typically 1½ to 2 hours long. "The Movie Mom®" has recommended at least two to go along the Slumber Party theme in each chapter.

Since all children love to receive party favors, the crafts for each Slumber Party can double as favors. Have the kids put them in their overnight bags before everyone goes to sleep. This will prevent kids from forgetting about them in the morning when they're all sleepy. You can also opt to give out additional favors if you want, but try to keep them theme-related.

Now choose a Slumber Party theme, use all the ideas within that chapter, or mix and match, and send out your unique invitations. Include Drop-off Times and Pick-up Times, directions to your house and a phone number for a R.S.V.P.. Be creative and adapt any section of your theme to fit your Slumber Party, or add ideas of your own.

Using this book, you can do it, and everyone will stay busy and have fun—including the adults. Remember—*"No more fussing, no more headaches. It couldn't be easier."*

CHAPTER ONE

The What, Why, and How of Slumber Parties

What are important
items to bring to a
Slumber Party?

"Bring yourself."

—Stephanie Howe,
age 9
Littleton, Colorado

How many children
should you invite to a
Slumber Party?

"About five or six, not
twenty, like my sister
had. They spilled pop on
me, there was hardly any
room, and they chased
me. Some girls had to
sleep in the bathroom
and in the shower."

—Jessica King, age 8
Littleton, Colorado

What is a Slumber Party?

A Slumber Party is when children get together and spend the night at a friend's house. Another name for a Slumber Party is a sleepover, although a sleepover usually refers to a child having one friend spend the night rather than several.

Slumber Parties most often take place on weekend nights or during the summer, but they certainly aren't limited to those times.

A Slumber Party's guest list usually consists of all boys or all girls. At times, though, an occasion may call for both boys and girls to come. If you give a co-ed Slumber Party, you may want to designate different sleeping areas for boys and girls. Or you may invite both boys and girls to the party but only have one gender stay and spend the night. (See co-ed sleepovers on page 18.)

Why Have a Slumber Party?

Because they're fun! And kids have more time to be with their friends than a regular party. Most families will combine a Slumber Party with a birthday party. Another reason to throw a Slumber Party? Kids often miss their friends during summer break. Two weeks before the fall session starts makes for a great time to get reacquainted as well as stave off the summer doldrums.

How To Have a Slumber Party?

Inviting children close to the same age is almost a necessity. If your guest list has ten or more, split the group into two or more rooms. Have a quiet room (for those ready to go to sleep) and a chat room for the night owls.

Number of Guests

So how many children should you invite? A rule of thumb is the same number as your child's age. But some parents can only handle a small number of children such as three, no matter what their age. I have had over twenty at my children's Slumber Parties. The trick is in the planning. If you have lots of activities, there is no time for mischief and you will do just fine. I suggest having another adult help with a large group, and make use of those older more experienced siblings who may otherwise feel left out.

The Invitation

Be sure to list any items on the invitation you want the kids to bring, especially anything out of the ordinary. Normal things include sleeping bags, pillows, pajamas, toothbrushes, clean clothes for the morning, and stuffed toys for that touch of home.

Also include on the invitation if dinner will be served, although this and breakfast are considered standard. And let parents know if you'll be taking the children out.

Don't forget a pick-up time (for your own sanity) keeping in mind that some children may need to leave early for church or a sporting event. It may be hard to set your alarm to wake up a child when you just got to bed, but you need to be flexible—it will soon be over! (See timetable section on page 12.)

Special Concerns

Find out from parents if their children have any special needs such as medication or medical problems (such as bed-wetting, see page 13). This is especially important if a child has never been to a Slumber Party.

The first sleepover experience for some children may warrant a call to the parents because they are scared or crying. I have never had a parent upset when this happens. Most will tell you to call when they drop their children off if there are any problems. (See First Stage, "big boy/big girl," on page 16).

Fun and Games

Keeping the night packed with plenty of fun activities, which you'll find in all the parties in this book, usually keeps the kids so busy they don't have time to miss their parents or own beds. The plan is to wear them out so they'll go to sleep when you want. Ha! I wish I could promise you that will happen just by using this book. You have an okay chance if your guests are young, but beware that some kids think the idea behind a Slumber Party is to stay up all night!

If you don't plan a lot of activities for the kids, letting them entertain themselves, be sure to check in on them frequently. They are, after all, entrusted to your care.

Lights Out

There will be a handful of kids who need a light on to sleep, and another handful who need it dark. Yikes! Sometimes, if you don't bring it up you can just turn off all the lights, say goodnight, and warn them no more talking after 15 to 30 minutes. Other times, when you can't get away with just turning out the lights, leave a light on in another room and close the door almost all the way.

If anyone complains that he wants more light, tell him to wait a few minutes so his eyes can adjust. When the kids are laying out their sleeping bags, tell them what part of the room will be darker and what part of the room will be lighter (the part closest to the door).

The Morning After

When everyone has gone home the next morning, you may have a collection of "leftover" items. You can send them with your child to school, wait for the parents to call, take them to the children's homes, add the items to your rummage pile, or toss them after a week or so. It all depends on how valuable the item is, but keep in mind that one person's trash is another person's treasure.

If your Slumber Party is large, leftovers are a given. Prevent this by having the kids put their clothes in their bags after putting their pajamas on, and then telling them to check the bathrooms about half an hour before their parents are due to pick them up.

Be sure not to plan anything important the day after a Slumber Party. You and your child will be tired and need a day to rest!

How Important are Decorations?

If you're having a holiday party, you know you want to decorate and ideas come easy. The same goes for a birthday party where balloons, streamers, banners, and table décor are the norm. But Slumber Parties bring to mind sleeping bags and popcorn scattered on the floor. So should you decorate for your Slumber Party?

The idea of going to a Slumber Party is usually exciting enough for your guests, but if you want to add that extra touch, keep it simple. Putting more time and creativity into activities and food will keep you in better control of the party than a roomful of decorations. Here are some easy decorating ideas:

What are important items to bring to a Slumber Party?

"CDs, makeup, movies, and girly games, like Truth or Dare."

—Jamie O'Farrell, age 11
Littleton, Colorado

When the party's over, what do you do with things left behind, such as a sock, toothbrush, a Teddy bears, even underwear?

Call the parents to see if they are coming to get the things. If not donate to charity — Teddy bears to the police department to comfort children in crisis, Discard any toothbrushes.

—Drucilla F. Jones
Richmond, Virginia

What is your best idea for a Slumber Party favor?

"Make felt pockets to resemble sleeping bags. Use white glue to glue the sides together. Cut out children shapes in felt and glue moving eyes to them. The children tuck into the sleeping bags. You could also tuck in lollipops. You can make several of these in advance and write the names of the children on them when all of your guests have arrived. This works well when there are last minute guests and guests who cancel. Your child can help you choose the colors of felt to use for the sleeping bags and children."

—Marlene N. Thorpe
Baltimore, Maryland

- For a decoration that doubles as a game, enlarge the Slumber Party Word Search on page 92 to the size of a poster or larger. Be sure to include the words found in the sidebar. Tape it on a wall. Hang crayons or markers from the ceiling with fishing line so the kids can play the game during any free time.
- Create fun signs on your computer and glue them to colorful poster board. Hang them outside your front door or on the walls of the party room. Some fun ones could be:
  - Only Cute Boys (Girls) Allowed
  - Sleepy Heads Go Home!
  - No Snoring Allowed
  - Caution: Girls (Boys) in Pajamas on the Loose
  - What's Your Scary Story?
  - Dreams Incorporated
  - Party Yes! Slumber No!
- Or make signs that read: Reserved for (child's name). Have the kids lay these on their sleeping bags.
- Hang beads, streamers, or old sheets cut into strips in doorways.
- Make a Slumber Party autograph wall by taping up butcher paper. Have a tray of markers nearby. The kids can include drawings or poems, as long as they're tasteful.
- Hang toothbrushes and toothpaste, combs and brushes, or mini flashlights from the ceiling with fishing line.
- Decorate a table with items that go with your Slumber Party theme. If you choose the Wish Upon A Star party from this book, for example, you can have a black tablecloth sprinkled with silver star confetti. Turn off the lights and lay flashlights, turned on, around the table. Hang glow-in-the-dark stars, moons, and planets around the room.

Whatever you do, keep it simple so you can save your energy for the things that really matter—the activities, the food, and most important, your mood!

What Timetable Should You Follow?

The parties in this book include dinner menus, so if you start a party around 6:00 in the evening, you'll find that the activities and dinner can take anywhere from 3 to 4 hours, which will put you at around 9 or 10 p.m..

This is a good time to get the kids organized by having them lay out their sleeping bags and change into their pajamas. Then you can start a video and be on target to choose food from the Midnight Snack Attack for them to eat while watching a second video. Hopefully, around 2:00 in the morning, the kids will be ready to sleep.

If you want to give them some free time, eliminate one or two of the activities or a video, or start your party earlier. If you want to be watching videos later when it's dark, like in the summer, start the party later. Kids won't want to watch videos when it's still light out.

Pick-up time around 10 to 11 a.m. works great. It still gives everyone some sleep and allows time for breakfast. Beware, there will always be some kids that need to leave early to go to church, a family event, or perhaps to a game (sport) they are involved in. The hardest thing to do is to set your alarm and get up when a child has to leave 2 to 3 hours earlier than the rest of the group, especially when you just got to bed.

You'll find that your child may be invited to parties that start later, when dinner won't be served. These are usually for older kids. You'll also discover that some parties won't serve breakfast. If you plan to go somewhere right after picking up your child, either ask if he will have breakfast or bring something for him to eat in the car.

If you need to go somewhere important, think about picking your child up late the night before, because he'll get more and better sleep in his own bed. He won't be happy with you but you'll be happier with him, for sure.

What About Bed-Wetting Accidents?

Sure it can happen. Even if your child isn't a bed-wetter, one of his friends might be. This medical condition (enuresis) is as embarrassing for a child as it is frustrating for his parents. They have usually been to their doctor who told them it is an inherited problem their child will outgrow by age 5 or 6. A handful of children are affected up to adolescence. Their bladders grow large enough to get them through the night, or they don't sleep as soundly as they used to.

In the meantime, there are precautions their parents and you can take so their child can enjoy your Slumber Party along with his friends. Some people believe that limiting fluids later in the evening might help, but this is not foolproof and it's hard to control how much one child is drinking without singling him out. Still, do remind all the children to go to the bathroom before bedtime when you tell them to brush their teeth.

Other people think certain foods that may stimulate the kidneys should be avoided, such as chocolate, anything with caffeine, carbonated drinks, and citrus juices. It's your choice to not serve these at your party if you're concerned about it. Chocolate and caffeine can also keep kids up.

Another solution is to set your alarm clock for the middle of the night to take the child with the problem to the bathroom. Chances are, however, that his "body clock" will not co-operate or that other children will wake up or still be up!

It is possible that the child and his parents decide not to tell you that he wets the bed. They may have a plan worked out to cover all the "ifs, ands, or buts." If the child only wets occasionally, they may simply take measures in case going to a Slumber Party would be one of "those times." Plan A is for the child to have a reason to call his parents and leave the party early should he wet. Plan B is to lay a waterproof sheet inside the child's sleeping bag, along with an identical pair of pajamas in a plastic bag with a twist-tie. Then if the child should have an accident, he can change in the sleeping bag and put his wet pajamas and the sheet inside the plastic bag, tying it shut, and no one will be the wiser.

Another scenario is that the parents have not made plans with their child but happen to mention his problem to you when they drop him off. Or the child tells you or your child, who then tells you. You can quickly prevent any damage to the child's ego or to your carpet by cutting open a plastic garbage bag and laying it under his sleeping bag when the children are pre-occupied elsewhere. (For safety reasons, do not put it inside the bag. It is not a substitute for a waterproof sheet.) You can provide him with a change of clothing sealed inside a plastic bag as above, or give him permission to come and wake you up should he have an accident. Then if it is a sunny morning, you might suggest that all the children air out their bags.

If neither the child's parents nor you take precautions and there is an accident, do

You can't sleep because the child next to you is giggling, snoring, or talking in her sleep—what do yo do?

"Move! That solves the problem."

—Kaitlyn Ferber, age 8
Cheek, New York

assure the child that it is okay and that he is not a bad person. If it is the middle of the night, you can give him fresh clothing (a large T-shirt works well) and another sleeping bag. Blot your carpeting with cool water without making a big issue out of it. If you hear any negative remarks from the other children, tell them that accidents can happen to anyone. Don't let the others at your Slumber Party be cruel to the bed-wetter with any teasing or jokes. He could have stayed home but decided to take a chance and come to the party. Support him in that decision.

How Do Single Parents Do Slumber Parties?

Whether you're a single mom or a single dad, hosting a Slumber Party for your child can be a unique challenge. The other parents may be nervous about leaving their kids with you, especially if you're a dad hosting a girls' party or a mom hosting a boys' party. They will want to know if you're dating or living with someone, something about that person, and how that will affect their children. Although it is tempting to entertain your own guest during a Slumber Party in order to have another adult on the scene, it may be what keeps other parents from letting their children attend the party.

A good friend of mine who is single says she has to prove herself to other parents. She has to tell them how conservative she is by emphasizing she will only show age-appropriate movies, not allow any drugs or alcohol, and not tolerate any mischief of any kind.

Having to be the perfect parent, however, while hosting a Slumber Party simply adds to your stress level. There are several things you can do to help yourself cope. The first is to keep the number of children you invite small. A good rule is to have no more than you can safely fit in your car, one child per seatbelt. Not only is this how many children you can in reality handle alone for a whole night, but should you need to drive somewhere for an emergency, you won't be leaving any children in your care alone.

To further help your sense of security, you should have a back-up adult who you know is at home and available at a minute's notice—a close friend or neighbor, even one of the other parents.

Finally, have lots of activities planned. Keeping your guests busy to help them and you stay in control is even more important when you're a single parent hosting a Slumber Party. That doesn't mean you have to wrack your brain for ideas or be a cre-ative genius. This book is full of parties and ideas to keep your anxiety to a minimum, before the party as well as during it.

What If You're Concerned About Safety?

Whether you're a single parent or married parent, you might have concerns about dropping your child off for a Slumber Party, especially if you don't know the host family. You may find a two-parent household where one parent is out for the evening or away on business, when you thought both parents would be present to handle things. This may leave you feeling more uncomfortable than leaving your child with a single parent who was upfront with you about the circumstances.

Chances are, your child will be fine, but you should always have a plan should your child not feel safe. Discuss with him ahead of time your values and what is acceptable behavior for children and adults. Tell him right before the Slumber Party that he should call you immediately if he feels something is wrong, and keep yourself

What are important items to bring to a Slumber Party?

"Your favorite pajamas, toothbrush, toothpaste, clothes for the morning, a sleeping bag and a pillow, and a disposable camera to remember all of the fun memories!"

—Kelly Hill, age 10
Canton, Ohio

available with a pager or cell phone. If you have already set up a code with your child to use in an emergency, remind him what it is.

If he doesn't have access to a phone at the Slumber Party for one reason or another, give him permission to leave the house and go to a neighbor's. But emphasize that this is only for an emergency which he cannot trust the host parent or parents to handle. Even if two parents are present, your experience may have told you that two parents are not necessarily better than one. Sometimes the home is safer with one of the parents gone.

Since there are no hard and fast rules, and no two households are the same, you need to pay attention to your "gut." If you feel uneasy, whether leaving your child in the hands of one or two parents, talk to the other parents who are dropping their children off. Chat with them back at your cars or ask them to meet you around the corner if you want to keep your conversation completely private. They may know the host family better than you do and alleviate all your fears.

Or you can always address your concerns directly to the host parent or parents by asking them who will be helping with the party, how many children are coming to the party, and what kind of activities are planned, including the movies being shown. Responsible parents with nothing to hide won't be offended and you'll feel better leaving your child at their house. If you don't feel good about the situation, you can tell them nicely by saying you think it's better if your child doesn't stay. Your child will no doubt react negatively, even kicking, screaming, or crying, but wouldn't you, as his parent, rather be wrong than sorry? Of course.

Is Your Child Ready for a Slumber Party?

Take This Quiz.

It can be hard to tell if your child is ready to have or go to a Slumber Party. Some children can be ready as early as 4 years old while others aren't ready until age 10. Here is a quiz to help you make this decision:

> Does your child follow directions?
>
> Is your child cooperative?
>
> Does your child get along with other children?
>
> Does your child ask for help (from other children or adults) if needed?
>
> Does your child go to bed without feeling scared?
>
> Can your child be away from Mom and Dad?
>
> Has your child ever spent the night away from home and you—at Grandma's house, at camp, or on vacation with family or friends?
>
> Does your child have any medical conditions such as allergies to food or pets?
>
> Does your child think he can handle a Slumber Party?

Now here are some questions for you, the parent:

> Do you think your child can handle a Slumber Party?
>
> Do you know the children coming to your party or the family having the Slumber Party?
>
> Does your child show some independence?
>
> Will you be available to pick up your child from the Slumber Party if needed?
>
> Are you willing to let your child have or go to a Slumber Party?

If most or all of your answers are "yes," then your child is ready to have or go to

What reasons have children used to go home early?

"The child hasn't had much exposure to sleeping away from home. He is scared of the dark or spooky stories."

—Patty Savin
Queensbury, New York

a Slumber Party. Certain questions such as "Do you know the family?" can be tough to answer. Yes, you may know the child giving the party really well, or one parent from that family but not the other parent. Be sure you're comfortable with all the family members, their home, and their neighborhood.

Ask to stop by for a visit to meet everyone including their pets. Ask to be shown around the house, both inside and out, the basement, the garage, even a storage shed or attic! Don't feel uncomfortable if you see any possible problems concerning your child's safety or welfare. If you still can't decide, always go with your gut. Those feelings are there for a reason!

If you do decide to let your child go to the Slumber Party but you're still unsettled about it, call every few hours to check up on him or stop back by the house. Bring him something as your excuse, something you thought he forgot such as a toothbrush. Most kids forget theirs anyway. *Caution:* Your child may want to come home once he sees you, but there is a good chance he'll surprise you by asking you why you're there and telling you to go away!

If you're giving the Slumber Party, encourage the other parents to visit you beforehand and during the party. And always, always exchange phone numbers where you and the other parents can be reached—pagers and cell phones are a great way to stay in touch, just in case!

The Seven Stages of Slumber Parties and Sleepovers

If you're new to the concept of Slumber Parties and sleepovers, here is a quick summary of what to expect from children at different ages. Even if you're not new to your child giving and going to Slumber Parties, these seven stages will still help you. Keep in mind that children mature at different rates and never seem to follow the norm.

First Stage (big boy/big girl)

Your child will typically want to go on his first sleepover when he is 5 to 7 years old. He thinks he can be away from home without any problem. This seems young, but your child is simply trying to be a big boy or girl.

His first try may be a Slumber Party or spending the night at a friend's house. The result is often the same: He ends up coming home before the sleepover is over, usually around bedtime. He misses his parents, his house, his bed, or his routine. He might cry or just ask to leave.

Of course, not every child will follow this pattern. Some do quite well, making it all the way through the night. And some children are better than others because they have had more experience being apart from their parents, for example, staying with grandparents or aunts and uncles when their parents are on vacation or out of town for other reasons. Those children may have cried and wanted to go home but couldn't.

Second Stage (I did it!)

No matter what your child's age, he has gotten through the second stage of sleepovers when he stays through the night, whether at a Slumber Party or just at a friend's house. He may have tried a sleepover before and come home early.

Typically, he does best if he stays with a friend, cousin, or neighbor first before tackling the bigger group and stranger house. A wise parent will encourage a one-on-one sleepover before saying "yes" to a regular Slumber Party. If the child gets through a night with one friend, especially more than once, he is probably ready to move on to a Slumber Party.

Whether he makes it through a one-on-one sleepover or a Slumber Party, he will be proud of himself. He will think, I did it! He'll think it was easy and had so much fun that he'll say he can't wait until the next time.

Third Stage (doesn't miss home at all...)

Your child will hit the third stage of sleepovers in second to fifth grade. He gets invited over to a friend's house for a Slumber Party for a birthday or other special occasion and doesn't think anything of it. The last thing on his mind is missing you, his house, his bed, or his routine.

It is now cool to sleep on the floor and be with all his friends. The kids ride down the banister on their sleeping bags, pull the cushions off the couch and jump on them, and have lots of pillow fights, making them fall asleep more quickly than in the next stage. They aren't up to the all-nighters yet like their big brothers and sisters.

Fourth Stage (all-nighters and the opposite sex)

When your child is in sixth to eighth grade, it really matters to him what grade he is in and who is in his class or classes. In other words, it is no longer cool to go to a Slumber Party with kids from a different grade.

Where the goal used to be to stay at the party all night, the goals are now to stay up all night, watch all the late night TV shows, and chat with the opposite sex on the phone or the Internet.

So expect your child to fall asleep between 3 and 5 a.m. and be very grouchy when he comes home, needing to sleep some more. Some parents think that making them stay up all day will teach them a lesson, but it won't. You'll only suffer more.

Keep in mind that Slumber Parties at this stage are a sort of bonding process with friends. This is why sleepovers become more frequent, sometimes every weekend. And your child will not want you to pick him up until as late as 3:00 in the afternoon, so he can sleep in and hang out some more.

Besides watching TV and talking with the opposite sex, what do kids do to stay awake all night? Boys play video games and look for mischief. Girls try on clothes and do each other's hair and makeup. Both sexes like to go "teepeeing" if they get the chance.

Some parents are totally against what they consider a type of vandalism while others will stock the family car with toilet paper and take the kids themselves. If you're the latter type of parent, never force a child to go teepeeing if they don't want to. Let him stay at the house with another adult, but don't be gone for too long. That would be inconsiderate.

Whatever type of parent you are, conservative or fun-loving, emphasize to your child to always wear a seatbelt while in a moving vehicle, to be considerate of neighbors who are sleeping, and to be prepared to clean up any mess he makes teepeeing.

If the kids haven't played Truth or Dare, Light as a Feather, Stiff as a Board, or Capture the Flag at an earlier age, they will now. They will pull harmless pranks, like calling an anonymous phone number and asking the person at the other end if his

How do you comfort a frightened child?

"Before bedtime, I make sure all the children know where my room is and that they can get me at any time. I also offer the comfort of sleeping close to a phone so they know their parents are only buttons away. A night light is good too."

—Laura Siegel
Englewood, Colorado

How do you comfort a frightened child?

"I am against Slumber Parties for kids under age 11. I do not want to sit up all night with someone else's child or have them want to go home at 3 a.m.."

—Toby Bradford
Watkins, Colorado

refrigerator is running. (If you don't know the joke, ask your child.) There is really no stopping them, if you want them to be kids and have fun.

On the other hand, some kids try forms of entertainment that can be considered on the "dark side," such as Ouija™ Boards, Magic 8-Balls, and Séances. Allowing these may bother the children and upset their parents. Consider having strict rules against such activities and making sure the kids adhere to your rules by doing spot checks during the night.

Fifth Stage (sneaking around)

By the time your child is in eighth to tenth grade, he will use sleepovers to sneak out of the house to meet members of the opposite sex at their houses, in parks, or in parking lots.

They can get away with this because their friends have a later curfew than your child or you only think your child is staying where he'd be. He may have called you from one friend's house to ask if he can stay there, then they have gone to another friend's house and called the first friend's parents to ask if they can stay there, and so on until they get to a house where the parents either have no rules or are away for the weekend.

One way to make sure your child is where he said he'd be is to call back and speak to a parent, even if the kids say the parents are sleeping. This may very well prevent an unsupervised co-ed sleepover with sex, drugs, and alcohol. Of course, children don't need sleepovers to partake in these serious and dangerous activities, but it is an easy way for them to hide what they're doing from their parents.

Whether kids are staying at your house or elsewhere, you need to be vigilant of what they are doing. That means staying up late and checking up on them by talking to other parents. It means being a parent when you're tired of being a parent on top of doing whatever else has been on your plate that week.

In other stages, you only lost sleep when you hosted a Slumber Party. Hang in there, this stage will pass almost as quickly as your baby started sleeping through the night, and it is as important to be there for him now as you were back then.

Sixth Stage (co-ed sleepovers)

When your child reaches the eleventh and twelfth grades, he wants to be with his group of friends, which includes boys and girls. Co-ed sleepovers are a means to that end, and can be safer for teens than roaming the streets and hanging out.

While some parties are organized for after school events such as formal dances, complete with planned activities, food, and parental supervision, others, called "lockdowns" or "lockins," are sponsored by sport teams or church groups. You can probably trust your child's welfare to the adults in charge of these activities.

The co-ed sleepovers at homes after proms, for example, are great alternatives to the children renting hotel rooms, which has become a common practice. A home with adults present is easier to swallow than visions of your first unsupervised co-ed party. The kids usually listen to music, watch videos, play games, and fall asleep in their jeans.

As in all the other stages, it is up to you to check on the situation before allowing your child to participate, and possibly calling to make sure that your child is where he said he'd be, and doing what he said he'd be doing. If need be, give him a cell phone and insist he keep it on. Wherever the party is, whatever the occasion, make sure there is at least one adult present and no alcohol or drugs.

Because the teens at this age are also driving, it is a good idea for the host parents

Have you ever had a co-ed Slumber Party?

"I didn't realize I had a co-ed Slumber Party until I actually thought about it. My idea was to let my daughter have three or four friends sleep over and my son have three or four friends, too, but it was on the same night. Why lose two nights of sleep instead of one!"

—Kelly Leins
Littleton, Colorado

Would you let your child go to a co-ed Slumber Party? Why or why not?

"Absolutely not! It's just an open door to teenage problems."

—M. Snyder
Littleton, Colorado

to "check" the kids' car keys and licenses at the door. This keeps them from going else-where. Checking names off of a guest list at the door can also prevent party crashers who may bring unwanted trouble. Beware that kids will find a way around these tactics, so once again, you may have to pull an all-nighter yourself, whether you're the host parent or your child is at a party.

If you just don't want your child going to a co-ed sleepover, you can insist he come home at a certain time, which means you may have to do the driving where there are curfew laws or if you think he will be too tired to drive safely.

As with the Slumber Parties when your child was younger, breakfast for a co-ed sleepover is on the menu and a big part of the fun. Either the host parents or the teens make it, or the kids go out alone on their way home. At this point, in the daylight, they are tired and have proven themselves trustworthy.

Seventh Stage (unsupervised co-ed sleepovers)

Close to when your child graduates from high school, he may want to partake in unsupervised co-ed sleepovers at hotels, campgrounds, or homes where the parents are away. If you're like a lot of parents, you may react with "Not while I'm alive!" But if your child tells you the situation, once again, it is just a way for him to be with his group of friends. He probably isn't sneaking around and may have tried or done all the things you are worried about anyway.

It is also a way for him to say, "I'm an adult now and responsible for myself." If your child is under 18 years old, however, you are still legally accountable for any entanglements he may have with the law. To prevent problems, some parents have their children sign contracts promising not to drink and drive. This will not necessarily stop that from happening, but it does keep the doors of communication open.

Your child needs to know you care enough to be concerned about him and his friends. You need to tell him what your values and expectations are and what will happen if he disappoints you. And he needs to know that you mean what you say. You have to be prepared to follow through with any consequences should he deserve them.

Chances are if you're the type of parent who is involved in your child's life from the early years on, such as reading a book like this in order to help him have a terrific Slumber Party, he knows you care and he will, in turn, care enough to follow your advice.

Remember, he is just about ready to go out into the world on his own, without your supervision. Just like the first time he went to a friend's house for a Slumber Party or sleepover, he will be trying something new. And he will need you to call, to talk to, and to come home to. It may not seem like it anymore, but you are still his security in an uncertain world.

In the end, if you did your homework, discussed things with other parents, made your decisions according to your values and whether or not your child is responsible, then set down ground rules and been vigilant through all the stages of Slumber Parties and sleepovers, your job is done, for the moment, and you can finally get some rest!

How do you separate the boys from the girls at a co-ed Slumber Party?

"On YMCA camping trips, we put the boys in one tent and the girls in another, with counselors of the same sex in each tent."

—Tom Marucco, Aurora, Colorado

Why go through the trouble of having a co-ed Slumber Party?

"It goes back to preparing kids for the world they will be entering after graduation, whether it's work or an apartment or going to college. Suddenly in August or September, they will be faced with many new experiences, not all of which will be good. If the kids are going to mess up, I want them to do it in high school when I see them daily. They are in an environment of supportive adults (teachers and friends' parents), not in college or in an apartment."

—J. Renée Howell Centennial, Colorado

Ten Don'ts for Parents Hosting Slumber Parties

1. Don't let the dog and cat run freely during the party. Some kids will be scared of them or allergic to them. And you don't want them eating the munchies.

2. Don't make the kids clean their messes, such as vacuuming up spilled popcorn. Drinks, on the other hand, need to be mopped up pronto.

3. Don't forget to tell the kids any house rules you have.

4. Don't let the kids put cellophane on the toilet seat.

5. Don't let other girls freeze other's training bras.

6. Don't let the kids go "teepeeing" unless it is a planned activity and the parents at the "victim's" house have given you permission.

7. Don't let the kids leave the house unsupervised.

8. Don't forget to take plenty of photos and videos.

9. Don't forget to keep your cool at 2:00 in the morning.

10. Don't plan anything important for you or your child the day after your Slumber Party. You'll both be too tired!

Twenty Helpful Hints for Slumber Parties

1. Read the entire Introduction and the What, Why, and How chapter for important information in all aspects of Slumber Parties and sleepovers.

2. It's okay to mix age groups when kids are younger, but it's not cool when they're older.

3. Try to get to know your guests and their families before the party.

4. Find out where the parents will be in case you need to call. This is where cell phones and pagers come in handy, as long as they are not turned off.

5. Be sure to show all your guests where the bathrooms are.

6. Most kids will just wake their friends up if there is a problem, but in case there is an emergency, they need to know where your bedroom is, too.

7. Tell the kids about any off-limit areas in your house and use locks if needed.

8. Check the temperature in the house for extremes of hot and cold to make sure the kids will be comfortable. Never leave a freestanding heater in the room they will sleep. Instead, get out extra blankets or clothes, or turn up the house heat, even if that means opening your bedroom window.

9. Before you go to bed, show the kids how to use the TV, VCR, and DVD player. Better to teach them than have them trying to figure it our on their own, possibly hurting your system or themselves.

10. At dinnertime, have hot dogs, peanut butter, or carrot sticks handy for the picky eaters.

11. Leave food out for night owls and early risers.

12. Have water and cups available at all times.

13. A craft is a good way to start your party. Latecomers can always jump in and hurry their craft along or work on it later. It's not as bad as missing a game or dinner.

14. Take advantage of the crafts for the parties in this book. They are meant to double as favors, saving you time and money.

15. Use extreme care when using tools for crafts such as glue guns and x-acto® knives.

16. Since some of the ideas require preparation before the party, read through all the directions well in advance.

17. If there is time, read some of the Knowledge Facts (found in the sidebars) to the kids.

18. Have a box full of things for the night owls and early risers to do if you prefer they not turn on the TV. Some good items are board games, playing cards, books and magazines, and paper and markers.

19. A half hour before their parents are due to pick them up, have the kids check all around for their belongings.

20. Read the hundreds of Helpful Hints in the entire **What Do I Do?**® series of party books. They'll help you with games, crafts, food and drinks, and how to handle groups of children who just want to have fun!

CHAPTER TWO

Passion for

A perfect party to add pizzazz to that extra-special occasion! Tell the girls to come prepared for plenty of purple surprises, beginning with making their own Purple Letter Shirts before getting gorgeous at the Magical Purple Beauty Salon. For dinner, present them with some-thing kids are passionate about—Cheesy Pizza Bagels and pop (grape, of course). They'll love making and baking the Star Boy Cookies to eat while you read them "The Purple Mist" story. After a video or two, along with a purple Midnight Snack Attack, they're sure to dream in purple. Wake them up in the morning with a Purple Fruit Tray and Other Yummy Stuff. Use purple plates, purple napkins, purple streamers, purple balloons...make everything as purple as possible, for a party they're tickled "purple" about.

Passion for Purple Invitation

Order of Passion for Purple Party

Paint the Purple Letter Shirts

Dinner (Cheesy Pizza Bagels)

Make and Bake Star Boy Cookies (to serve with story)

Read "The Purple Mist Story" (serve cookies and Purple Mist Drink)

Do the Magical Purple Beauty Salon

Get on pajamas and lay out sleeping bags

Watch videos with Midnight Snack Attack

Sleep

Breakfast (Purple Fruit Tray and Other Yummy Stuff)

Brush teeth, get dressed, and pack

Play the Purple Word Race

Say good-bye!

Supplies

Makes 12

Newspaper

⅛ cup purple acrylic paint

⅛ cup water

Small bowl

Small spoon

½ teaspoon

Twelve 4 x 5½-inch blank notecards with envelopes

Drinking straws

Copy paper

Scissors

Glue

Purple pen

Optional: 9 x 12-inch white construction paper

Directions

1. Cover your work area with newspaper.

2. Pour the paint and water into the bowl, and mix with the spoon.

3. Pour ½ teaspoon of thinned paint in the center front of a notecard.

4. Aim a drinking straw at the paint and blow, rotating the card to create a spider-like design. Let dry.

5. Repeat steps #3 and #4 for all the cards.

6. Make copies of the invitation. Cut to fit inside of a notecard, then glue in place.

7. Fill in the details with a purple pen!

Optional: In place of using notecards, for each invitation, fold a 9 x 12-inch sheet of white construction paper in half, then in half again.

Variation: Rather than copying, cutting, and gluing, simply write out the invitation on each notecard and fill in the details.

Passion for Purple Slumber Party!

Purple food and purple drinks,
Purple games to play.
We'll see purple all night long!
Won't you come and stay?

Party Given By: _____

Special Occasion: _____

Day and Date: _____

Drop-off Time: _____

Pick-up Time: _____

Address and Directions: _____
_____

Phone Number: _____

Please call and let me know if you can come!
And wear something purple!

Purple Letter Shirts

Supplies

Sponge letters
(found at craft stores)

White T-shirts (one per girl)

8½ x 11-inch piece cardboard
(one per girl)

Purple fabric paint

Paper plate (one per girl)

Optional: Purple ribbon
and scissors

Directions

1. Before the party, think of a word or phrase, such as "purple" or "purple passion," that has one letter per each girl coming to the party. Purchase the sponge letters needed to spell out your word or phrase.

2. Pre-wash and dry the T-shirts. Slide a cardboard piece inside each shirt, positioning it under the chest and smoothing out any wrinkles. Lay flat.

3. Squeeze paint onto each plate, enough to cover a sponge letter. Have each girl carefully dip one letter into the paint, then onto the chest of her shirt. Explain the need to carefully lift the letters straight up off the shirts so they won't smudge.

4. Let the shirts dry overnight. Have the girls put them on in the morning and line up to spell out your word or phrase. Take a picture and make a copy for each girl.

Tip: If you can't find sponge letters, use dehydrated or expandable sponges, also found at craft stores. Simply trace the letters (using a stencil) onto the sponges, cut them out, soak in water to expand, then let dry.

Optional: Before the party, paint the shirts yourself, let them dry, roll them up separately, and tie purple ribbons around them.

Age Adjustment: Younger children may need an older child or adult to help sponge their letters onto their shirts.

Besides taking photos, how would you record memories of your Slumber Parties?

"Have the children put their handprints and names on T-shirts. Videotape or record on a cassette player the children answering questions about their favorite parts of the party, worst parts, and so on."

—Jean Loth
East Troy, Wisconsin

Cheesy Pizza Bagels

Ingredients and Supplies

Makes one
Knife
Bagel
2 tablespoons
  pizza sauce

Assorted pizza
  toppings
⅓ cup shredded
  mozzarella cheese

½ teaspoon Italian
  seasoning
Star kiss fruit
  (one for every
  three girls)

Directions

1. Slice the bagel in half and spread pizza sauce on both sides.

2. Add pizza toppings and cheese, then sprinkle Italian seasoning over those.

3. Broil until the cheese is melted and brown.

4. Slice the star kiss fruit and serve with the pizza.

Make and Bake Star Boy Cookies

Serve these with "The Purple Mist Story"

Ingredients and Supplies

Makes approximately 15
2¾ tablespoons
  shortening
½ cup brown sugar
  (packed firmly)
¾ cup molasses
⅓ cup water
Mixer and bowl

3½ cups flour
½ teaspoon salt
1 teaspoon baking
  soda
½ teaspoon of each:
  ground allspice,
  ground cloves,
  ground cinnamon,
  and ground ginger

Medium bowl
Spoon or spatula
Plastic wrap
Rolling pin
5-inch gingerbread
  boy cookie cutter
Greased cookie
  sheets

Directions

1. Cream the shortening, brown sugar, molasses, and water together in mixer bowl.

2. Put the flour, salt, baking soda, allspice, cloves, cinnamon, and ginger together in a medium bowl and stir.

3. Mix the flour mixture into the shortening mixture.

4. Cover the dough with plastic wrap and put in the refrigerator for 2 hours.

5. Preheat oven to 350°. Roll the dough ½ inch thick on a lightly floured counter. (It helps to flour the rolling pin.)

6. Cut with the cookie cutter (also floured) and place on greased cookie sheets a couple of inches apart.

7. Bake for 10 minutes or until lightly brown. No need to decorate.

Purple Mist Drink with Dry Ice

Serve this with "The Purple Mist Story"

Ingredients and Supplies

Mixing spoon
Equal parts grape juice and club soda
Plastic container

Punch bowl
Ladle
Dry ice and container
Clear plastic cups

Directions

1. Mix grape juice and club soda together in plastic container.

2. Freeze approximately 3 hours until "misty."

3. Put frozen juice into punch bowl and chop slightly with ladle.

4. Activate dry ice in container near the punch bowl to create fog. (Learn more about dry ice in sidebar.)

5. Serve Purple Mist in plastic cups.

Using Dry Ice

You can purchase dry ice (solid carbon dioxide) at grocery stores, ice cream shops, or butcher shops. Most ask that you order it at least 1 to 3 weeks ahead of time and pick it up the day you need it. A small block (3 to 5 pounds), which comes wrapped in paper, is plenty. It can be chopped into smaller pieces, but must always be handled with gloves so it won't "burn" your skin. (Tongs also work well.)

To "activate" the dry ice, place it in a container with warm water. A "mist" will form immediately, rising up and out of the container. You can use a fan to direct the mist where you want it. After about 15 minutes, the water will start to freeze and the dry ice will stop "bubbling." (Using salt water can make the mist last longer.) Replace the cold water with warm water.

Dry ice can also be added directly to a punch bowl, but be sure that no pieces end up in anyone's drink! A good safety net is to wrap the dry ice with cheese-cloth before putting it in the punch.

The Purple Mist Story

There was a new girl in school who was having a hard time getting to know anyone. No one invited her to eat lunch at their table. No one asked her to join them on the playground. No one seemed to notice she was there at all. Then one day before school, when she was standing alone outside, a boy came up to her and gave her a note. He smiled, pressed it into her hand, stood there for a moment, then walked away. She didn't open the note then, because the bell rang and she had to go in. But later, when she had time at her desk after finishing an assignment, she opened it.

"Will you have a Coke with me after school?" the note read. The boy hadn't signed it. He hadn't told her how she could find him to answer "yes" or "no," or where to meet him. And she didn't see him at school all day. But she made up her mind that if she saw him after school, she would have a Coke with him. He had been the first person to notice her. She really wanted a friend.

After school, the new girl waited around awhile hoping the boy would find her. But after about 15 minutes, when almost everyone had left, she decided to go home. "It must have been a joke," she thought. "That boy didn't really like me after all. He was just teasing me." A tear slipped down her cheek. She brushed it away quickly and blew a puff of hot breath, determined not to cry. She started walking fast, with her jaw tipped up and her lips pressed tight. "Maybe no one wants to get to know me in this town, but what do I care?"

When she came to a tree-covered section of the sidewalk, she saw first a shadow, then a figure step out in front of her. Even with the dark shade across his face, she recognized the boy. She just stopped and stared at him a minute, before, that is, walking right past him. But he walked right beside her, matching his steps to hers. "Want to have a Coke?" he asked, as he nodded toward a gas station. The girl sighed, decided not to be mad at him, and followed him to the gas station. He bought two pops from the vending machine, and they sat on the curb and drank them.

Then they walked and talked for quite awhile before the girl said, "I should be going home." The boy took her hand and asked, "Will you have a Coke with me tomorrow?" She nodded yes. As the boy turned and walked away, she noticed a faint purple glow around him, but she thought it was from the sunset.

But then, when she woke up the next morning, her fingernails were long, shiny, and purple. And she knew they weren't from the sunrise! They looked like she had gotten an expensive manicure. She liked them, of course, but had no idea how they got that way. A couple of girls at school complimented her on her nails, and then sat by her at lunch.

She did not see the boy at school, but he found her again when she was walking home. They stopped for a Coke again, and talked and walked again for a long time. The girl enjoyed having a friend. When the wind blew her blonde hair in her face, the boy brushed it away. When it was almost dark, he said good-bye, and she saw the same purple glow around him as he walked away.

In the morning, the girl was surprised to see a purple streak in her hair where the boy had touched it. She had been able to hide her fingernails, but how would she ever explain this to her parents? She could not figure it out. At school, quite a few kids waved and called her by name. She felt brave enough to answer a question in class, and the teacher praised her answer. The girl had a cheerful crowd at her lunch table.

She almost forgot about her special friend all day, but wondered once why she never saw him at school. She walked part way home with some girls, but when they turned to go another way, the boy stepped out from some bushes. She was glad to see him, and they spent a long time together again.

This time, though, when it was starting to get dark, he got very quiet and looked sad. "I'm going away tonight," he told her. The girl asked where, but he would not say. He only pointed up. There was one star out, blinking faintly in the gray sky. "That star, is that it? You're not trying to tell me you come from space, are you?"

The boy walked a few steps, turned toward her, and blew her a kiss. His breath looked faintly purple, and she was sure she felt it lightly touch her forehead. There seemed to be a fog, a mist, gathering around the boy's feet. It was getting darker, and the mist looked purple in the setting sun. It became so thick she could no longer see the boy at all. All she saw was purple mist. "Good-bye, star boy," she whispered.

Even though she knew she would not see the boy the next day, she felt strangely happy all evening. In the morning, she wasn't really shocked when there was a permanent purple star on her forehead. She didn't think she could wash it off, but she tried anyway.

Days and weeks and years went by. She never saw the star-boy again. She never talked about him to her other friends. For the rest of her life, she had purple fingernails, a purple streak in her blonde hair, and a purple star on her forehead. And, for the rest of her life, she always had plenty of friends.

—*Kathryn Totten,* storyteller/author

Magical Purple Beauty Salon

Supplies

Purple nail polish

Purple neon temporary hair color (sold in spray cans)

Purple star stickers (one per girl)

Optional: Purple face paint and paint brush

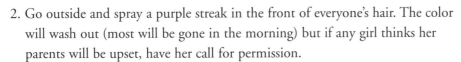

Directions

1. Have the girls take turns polishing their nails purple.

2. Go outside and spray a purple streak in the front of everyone's hair. The color will wash out (most will be gone in the morning) but if any girl thinks her parents will be upset, have her call for permission.

3. Stick a purple star on each girl's forehead.

Note: Blonde hair colors easily while brown hair will need more color.

Optional: Pull each girl's hair away from her face, paint a purple star on her forehead, and let it dry.

Age Adjustment: For younger children, have an older child or adult polish the girls' nails.

Did you know there are other names for purple, such as violet, heliotrope, plum, hyacinth, lavender, magenta, lilac, raisin, orchid, fuchsia, dahlia, amethyst, mauve, and royal?

Midnight Snack Attack

Purple jelly beans

Grape Popsicles®

Grape gelatin

Purple milkshakes

Bubble Tape® Gushing Grape™ gum

Grape Nerds®

What are important items to bring to a Slumber Party?

"Ear plugs, just in case a kid is snoring."

—Jessica King, age 8 Littleton, Colorado

Video Recommendations

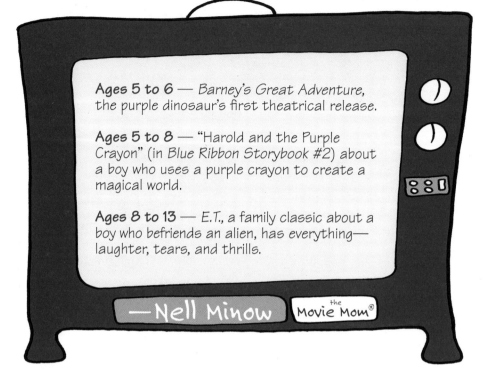

Ages 5 to 6 — *Barney's Great Adventure,* the purple dinosaur's first theatrical release.

Ages 5 to 8 — "Harold and the Purple Crayon" (in *Blue Ribbon Storybook #2*) about a boy who uses a purple crayon to create a magical world.

Ages 8 to 13 — *E.T.,* a family classic about a boy who befriends an alien, has everything— laughter, tears, and thrills.

—Nell Minow the Movie Mom®

Purple Fruit Tray and Other Yummy Stuff

Ingredients and Supplies

Plums

Grapes

Blueberries

Two platters

Kellogg's™ Frosted Pop-Tarts® Wild Berry

Blueberry muffins

Blueberry cereal bars

Directions

1. Arrange plums, grapes, and blueberries on one of the platters.

2. On the other platter, arrange the Pop-Tarts®, muffins, and cereal bars.

The Purple Word Race

Supplies

Paper (one piece per girl)

Purple crayon (one per girl)

Directions

1. Give the girls the paper and crayons.

2. Have them write the word PURPLE down the left side of the paper, spreading the letters out.

3. Next to the letters, have them write as many words as they can think of that start with those letters. For example, "P" is for "pony" and "pen."

4. Allow them 5 minutes. The one with the most words wins.

The crayon color Purple Heart ranked third in the Crayola® color census 2000. It received 6900 votes. Check out the website at www.crayola.com.

Twenty Extra Fun Ideas

1. Tell your guests to wear purple pajamas, then take a group photo.

2. Have a hairstyling contest using purple ribbons, bows, and such.

3. Do makeovers using purple eye shadow and lipstick.

4. Mix up purple shakes with grape juice and vanilla ice cream.

5. Have a purple plum eating contest! (Don't forget the purple napkins!)

6. Have a purple bubble gum blowing contest.

7. Hold a scavenger hunt to see who can collect the most purple items.

8. Conjure up a new language with words that rhyme with purple.

9. Name all the shades of purple in a large box of sixty-four crayons.

10. Ask what color goes best with purple? Worst?

11. Watch a TV show and count the purple things.

12. Flip through a catalog and count the purple items.

13. Ask if purple is prettier than pink? Why or why not?

14. Bounce a purple balloon around until it pops!

15. Create purple puppets with purple felt, yarn, and whatever else you can find.

16. Stir different colors of paint together until you come up with purple.

17. Mold purple candles with different shades of purple wax.

18. Ask what are you particularly passionate about? Explain to younger children what the word "passionate" means.

19. Use purple plates, napkins, cups, even plastic ware.

20. Be sure to purchase purple prizes!

How does an adult or parent get through the night?

"I was lucky enough to be invited to help with a child's first Slumber Party. As a first time chaperon, I discovered the most important items for me to bring were a good attitude and a sense of humor. That's the only way anyone could have survived."

—Juliana Greco
Canton, Ohio

Passion for Purple Invitation

Newspaper
⅛ cup purple acrylic paint
⅛ cup water
Small bowl
Small spoon
½ teaspoon
Twelve 4 x 5½-inch
   blank notecards with
   envelopes
Drinking straws
Copy paper
Scissors
Glue
Purple pen
*Optional: 9 x 12-inch white
   construction paper*

Purple Letter Shirts

Sponge letters
   (found at craft stores)
White T-shirts
   (one per girl)
8½ x 11-inch piece
   cardboard (one per girl)
Purple fabric paint
Paper plate (one per girl)
*Optional: Purple ribbon
   and scissors*

Cheesy Pizza Bagels

Knife
Bagel
2 tablespoons pizza sauce
Assorted pizza toppings
⅓ cup shredded
   mozzarella cheese
½ teaspoon Italian
   seasoning
Star kiss fruit (one
   for every three girls)

Make and Bake Star Boy Cookies

2¾ tablespoons shortening
½ cup brown sugar
   (packed firmly)
¾ cup molasses
⅓ cup water
Mixer and bowl
3½ cups flour
½ teaspoon salt
1 teaspoon baking soda
½ teaspoon of each:
   ground allspice,
   ground cloves,
   ground cinnamon, and
   ground ginger
Medium bowl
Spoon or spatula
Plastic wrap
Rolling pin
5-inch gingerbread boy
   cookie cutter
Greased cookie sheets

Purple Mist Drink with Dry Ice

Mixing spoon
Equal parts grape juice
   and club soda
Plastic container
Punch bowl
Ladle
Dry ice and container
Clear plastic cups

Magical Purple Beauty Salon

Purple nail polish
Purple neon temporary
   hair color (sold in
   spray cans)
Purple star stickers
   (one per girl)
*Optional: Purple face
   paint and paint brush*

Purple Fruit Tray and Other Yummy Stuff

Plums
Grapes
Blueberries
Two platters
Kellogg's™ Frosted
   Pop-Tarts® Wild Berry
Blueberry muffins
Blueberry cereal bars

Midnight Snack Attack

Purple jelly beans
Grape Popsicles®
Grape gelatin
Purple milkshakes
Bubble Tape® Gushing
Grape™ gum
Grape Nerds®

The Purple Word Race

Paper (one piece per girl)
Purple crayon
   (one per girl)

Don't forget the camera and film

CHAPTER THREE

CARTOONIVAL

A party that every child can really relate to! Everyone likes cartoons and everyone likes a carnival, so cartoons at a carnival may just be your ticket to local fame. Start by asking your guests to wear cartoon character T-shirts and to bring cartoon character pajamas, slippers, and slumber bags. Be a super hero like those in "The Twisted Slipper Mystery: A Cartoonival Adventure" and rent a cartoon character costume for yourself to be part of the action. Plaster your home with cartoon characters, from the plates, napkins, and cups to Mylar balloons. You'll have as much fun planning your Cartoonival as the children will love it!

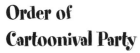

Order of Cartoonival Party

Do The the Cartoonival Puppet Show

Dinner (Carnival Foot Longs and Carnival Corn with Icy Slippery Drinks)

Play the three Midway Games

Get on pajamas and lay out sleeping bags

Read "The Twisted Slipper Mystery: A Cartoonival Adventure"

Make the Comic Creations

Watch videos with Midnight Snack Attack

Sleep

Breakfast (Create-a-Pancake)

Brush teeth, get dressed, and pack

Say good-bye!

Cartoonival Invitation

Supplies

Makes 12

Twelve 4 x 5-inch blank notecards with envelopes

Black permanent marker (fine tip)

Copy paper

Scissors

Glue stick

Optional: Cartoon character sticker (one per envelope)

Directions

1. On the front of a notecard, draw three conversation balloons, one coming from the left side, one from the right, and one from the bottom.

2. Write the following messages in the balloons: In the left, Hey! Where did everyone go? In the right, To the Cartoonival. And in the bottom, What are we waiting for? Repeat for each invitation.

3. Repeat steps #1 and #2 for each notecard.

4. Make copies of the invitation. Cut to fit inside the notecard, then glue in place.

5. Fill in the details.

Optional: Seal with a cartoon character sticker.

Cartoonival Slumber Party!

Bring your favorite cartoon collectible to share!
All the cartoon stars will be there. Don't miss the fun!

Party Given By: _____

Special Occasion: _____

Day and Date: _____

Drop-off Time: _____ Pick-up Time: _____

Address and Directions: _____

_____

Phone Number: _____

Please call to let me know if you can come!

Cartoonival Puppet Show

Supplies

Tube socks (one per child)
Lots of felt (assorted colors)
Lots of pom-poms
  (assorted colors)
Pipe cleaners (assorted colors)

Moving eyes (all sizes)
Assorted feathers
Fabric scraps
Scissors (several pair)
Fabric glue (several bottles)

What are is your best ideas for a Slumber Party favors?

"Face masks, the type that cover just your eyes and nose, and Chinese yo-yos have have worked for every type of party I've given."

—Bobbie Gilbert
Sulphur, Louisiana

Directions

1. Give each child a tube sock and have him choose a character for his puppet, such as Cool Cat, Super Strong Mouse, Crying Crocodile, Spacey Astronaut, Smart Dog that Solves Crimes, Crazy Bird, or Nervous Timid Monster.

2. Have the children use the supplies, scissors (if necessary), and glue to make faces on the toe end of their tube socks. Suggest they give their puppets at least one identifying feature. For example, a dog might have long droopy ears.

3. Let the children slide their puppets over their hands and practice making them walk, talk, fly, sing, or whatever their characters might do. Urge them to use funny voices, even ones that would not make sense for their characters.

4. Divide the children into two teams and tell them to make up a cartoon story with their teams. (Some ideas are below.) Have them practice their stories once or twice, and then later that night, after you read "The Twisted Slipper Mystery: A Cartoonival Adventure," let the teams perform for the other.

Cartoon Story Ideas

1. Animals fall off a bridge into a river, but the super hero saves them

2. A monster is afraid of everything, but his friends teach him to be brave

3. A cat tries many tricks to catch a mouse, but the mouse always gets away

4. An astronaut gets lost on his way to the moon

5. A dog catches the crooks who stole a famous painting from the museum

6. Baby sibling swallows everything in sight, but finally swallows something REALLY big

Tip: The back of a couch works well for a puppet stage.

Note: Allow about an hour to make puppets, but be flexible. Some kids will surprise you and be done in 15 minutes.

Carnival Foot Longs and Carnival Corn

Ingredients and Supplies

Sweet corn in husk (one per child)

Barbecue grill

Foot long hot dogs (one per child)

Large saucepan

Foot long buns (one per child)

Paper towels

Butter (melted)

Tall thin container

Ketchup

Mustard

Chopped onions

Pickles

Salt and pepper

Option #1: Regular hot dogs and buns

Option #2: Frozen corn on the cob and wooden skewers

Directions

1. Peel back husks on corn, remove all the silk, lay husks back over the corn, and cook on a barbecue grill until golden brown. Do not burn.

2. Put the foot longs into boiling water and cook about 8 minutes. Put into the buns, then steam by wrapping each in a paper towel and microwaving for 30 seconds.

3. Peel back husks on the corn again (like a peeled banana) then dip the corn into the melted butter in a tall container.

4. Let the children fix up their own foot longs and corn with the condiments of their choice.

Option #1: If you can't find foot longs and/or buns, use regular hot dogs and buns.

Option #2: Frozen corn on the cob and wooden skewers.

How did Cartoonival get its name?

"In 1990, I volunteered to be the chairperson for the school carnival. I got together a committee and we played around with several different themes. We liked the idea of a cartoon theme, thinking it would work well for elementary-age kids. One committee member had connections in the movie industry and was able to get us lots of cartoon items. I played with the the words "cartoon" and "carnival" on paper and came up with my new word "Cartoonival" —for cartoons at a carnival!"

— Author Wilhelminia Ripple Littleton, Colroado

Icy Slippery Drinks

Ingredients and Supplies

Ice

Snow cone machine or ice shaver

Ice cream scoop

Paper cones

Flavored syrup

Spoon straws

Directions

1. Shave the ice in the snow cone machine or ice shaver.

2. Scoop ice into one paper cone at a time.

3. Pour flavored syrup over ice. Serve with a spoon straw.

Note: Snow cone items can be purchased at party rental companies, or discount stores.

Flavored Syrup Grape

Midway Games

Play these games together for a carnival atmosphere, outside if possible. If you have access to canopies, use them for Head-to-Toes (see sidebar), Dress-Up Tent, What's Wrong, Doc?, and Orange, Apple, Banana Slot Machine. Allow about an hour to play these games. You may need to encourage the children to play all of the games. They might have so much fun at one that they forget to play the others. Give each child about 40 tickets. After playing the games, have the children write their names on any left-over tickets and put them into a "popcorn hat." To make one, glue popcorn all over a hat and let dry. (A top hat works best.) Draw a winner to wear the hat while watching videos. *Caution:* Tell the kids not to eat the popcorn as it has glue on it.

Play Head-to-Toes

You may have been at an event where they play Head-to-Toes as a fundraiser. They sell you a strip of tickets the length of someone's height from Head-to-Toes. The taller someone is, the more tickets you get for a set price, such as $5. So you pick the tallest person you can find, even someone just walking by the ticket table. After the money is counted, a ticket is drawn. The winner gets half the money and the other half goes to the organization holding the event.

You can play a similar version at your party, the prize being the "popcorn hat." Charge each child 3 tickets for a strip of tickets, measured from Head-to-Toes of the tallest party guest they can find. The children put their names on each ticket on their strips and put them into the popcorn hat, along with their left-over tickets from the Midway Games, for the drawing for the hat. You don't raise any funds, but you do get the excitement of children as they anticipate the winner!

Dress-Up Tent

Supplies

Poster board (any color)
Colored markers
Carnival tickets
  (found at party stores)
Tent
Rope and hangers

Clothes and accessories
  (that make up cartoon
  characters)
Small tables and chairs
Optional: Full-length mirror

Directions

1. Create a poster board sign with the name of the game and how many tickets it will cost. Charge 15 tickets for a complete outfit and 5 tickets for a single item.

2. Put the tent up outside. Drape a rope inside to hang clothing on. Set up some small tables and chairs.

3. Display the clothing and accessories on the tables, chairs, and hangers, leaving at least one chair for children to sit on if needed. Group some items together for a sample of a complete outfit, just as one would see at a costume store.

4. Let the kids come into the tent, try items on, and then purchase their items. They can wear their outfits or items all night long, but tell them if there are things you will need back in the morning.

Tip: This game is more fun if you have lots of dress-up items in the tent.

Note: You may have to limit how many can be in the tent at one time.

Optional: Put a full-length mirror in the tent.

What's Wrong, Doc?

To find a comic book store near you, call toll free 1-888-COMIC-BOOK. An automated system will ask you for your zip code that you can input with your telephone's keypad. They will then tell you about comic book stores in your area, including addresses and telephone numbers. Let the fun begin!

Supplies

Poster board (any color)

Colored markers

Carnival tickets (found at party stores)

Bandages (small and large sizes)

Craft sticks (for splints)

First-aid tape

Scissors

Cloth wraps

Small table and chairs

Doctor outfit

Nurse outfit

Age Adjustments: Glue, insurance forms (pretend) and pens

Directions

1. This carnival game lets children pay tickets for medical services while pretending to be their favorite cartoon characters.

2. Create a poster board sign with the name of the game and how many tickets it will cost to take care of injuries (pretend ones). Here are some ideas:

   Small bandage for small cut – 1 ticket   *Wrap a sprained ankle or wrist – 4 tickets*
   Large bandage for large cut – 2 tickets   *Wrap for a head injury – 7 tickets*
   Splint on sprained finger – 3 tickets   *Wrap a broken arm or leg – 10 tickets*

3. Stock the booth with medical supplies (be sure to have lots as the children get to leave with the ones they use!) and a table and chairs.

4. Have the children decide what cartoon character to be. Then tell them they can spend their tickets on one, two, or several injuries.

5. An adult or older child will need to be the doctor to take care of injuries. Another adult or older child can be the nurse.

6. When a child comes to the booth, the doctor or nurse asks them what character he is, what injury he has, and how he got hurt. (You're sure to hear some interesting answers!)

7. Then the doctor or nurse takes care of the child's injuries. If he has more than three injuries, he needs to go to the end of the line.

Tip: If the doctor and nurse can visualize how long a piece of tape or wrap they need, they should cut it before wrapping. This is also a safety measure.

Note: When making a finger splint, lay a craft stick under the finger and secure it with first-aid tape. Use the cloth wraps for sprained or broken arms and legs, or head injuries. For head wraps, start at the forehead and wrap toward the back of the head, then around a few times. Secure all wraps by tucking in the end pieces.

Age Adjustment: For **younger** children, draw pictures on the sign of the injuries and glue the number of tickets they cost next to them. You may prefer this regardless of age. Have **older** children fill out insurance forms (pretend) before treatment.

Orange, Apple, Banana Slot Machine

Supplies

Poster board (any color)

Colored markers

Carnival tickets
(found at party stores)

Three of the following:
blindfolds, chairs, paper
bags, oranges, apples,
and bananas

Whistle

You're hungry, it's late,
there's no food in sight.
Tell us your secret on
how you get a snack?

"I tiptoe out, get on
my bike, and ride to
McDonald's."

—Anonymous
Littleton, Colorado

Directions

1. Create a poster board sign with the name of the game and how many tickets it costs to play, which is 4 tickets per "pull." Also indicate how many tickets a child gets back if he makes a match, 8 tickets when all three fruits are the same.

2. To set up this game, blindfold three children and have them sit side-by-side in chairs. Give each child a paper bag containing one orange, one banana, and one apple. Instruct the children not to talk.

3. Have the third child on your right (facing you) hold up his right arm, elbow bent, like a slot machine handle. Also give him the whistle.

4. When a child pays his 4 tickets to play the slot machine, he pulls down on the arm of the third child, who blows the whistle. He and the other two blindfolded children quickly pull one piece of fruit from their bags, without peeking, and hold them up.

5. If all three pieces of fruit are the same, the player gets back 8 tickets. He has a choice to keep them or to play one or two more times. He then must move to another game or go to the end of the line.

Tip: To make the slot machine, use people other than guests—grandparents, neighbors, or siblings. If that's not possible, have the children take turns being the machine so everyone can play all the games.

Variation: To your sign, add different combinations of fruit that will win tickets back, such as two bananas and one orange wins 2 tickets.

The Twisted Slipper Mystery: A Cartoonival Adventure

It was a quiet day at the detective agency. The phone had not rung at all. I spent the time scraping gum off the bottom of my shoe. I had to do that every now and then.

I was just about to call it a day when I heard an unusual, scratchy sound coming from the hallway. I used my incredible power of reasoning to determine that someone or something was approaching my door, and that someone or something was dragging an object, a heavy object. I don't know how I know these things. It's just a gift.

Within seconds, the scratchy sound ceased. There was a tiny, timid knock on my door. I opened it but saw no one. When I felt a tug on the cuff of my trousers, I looked down. A good detective will check out every clue, after all.

Standing on the toe of my wing tip shoe was a mouse. I recognized him immediately. He was the cartoon mouse that was the super-hero mascot at the carnival every year. He looked exhausted. He held in his tiny fist a tail attached to a scuffed-up, wrung-out, no good, mean-tempered hyena. I knew the type, one of many cartoon characters that tried to spoil all the children's fun at the carnival every year.

The super-hero mouse was usually able to subdue these troublemakers. Watching him catch them, swing them over his head, and toss them into the rubbish bins was part of the carnival's charm. But today the mouse looked, to say the least, troubled.

I invited him in. He followed me into my office, dragging the hyena behind him. "This hyena," he said, "was involved in a dastardly plot. He and his smelly, moldy, flea-bitten, rats-nest friends were trying to topple the Twisted Slipper."

The Twisted Slipper is the favorite ride at the carnival, and evil cartoon characters were trying to shut it down. The mouse had obviously done all he could to stop them. "The rubbish bins are overflowing with cartoon bad guys," he continued. "That's why I dragged this one with me. There seems to be no end to them!"

I tossed the hyena into my own rubbish bin and offered the mouse a lemonade. He sipped it slowly, regaining his strength with every sip. I understood the situation. I knew what he wanted without him saying it. I pride myself at my mind-reading skills. He wanted me to get to the source of the Twisted Slipper gang.

I called the carnival office and told them to put out more rubbish bins. "There is going to be trouble," I said, "and you better be prepared." The mouse and I took the first train to the carnival. I paid my admission at the gate and looked around. There was an unusually large crowd of families buying cotton candy and popcorn, standing in line for the rides, and trying their luck at the games.

Everything looked perfectly normal to the untrained eye, but a good detective always checks out the shadows. And I saw many, many shadows that day. I knew in every shadow lurked an evil cartoon character. I watched as, one by one, they began their nasty work. The mouse fought them valiantly, but they just kept coming. They all seemed to have the same goal: to topple the Twisted Slipper.

A swarm of cartoon mosquitoes attacked the Twisted Slipper operator. The mouse swatted them with a 6-foot fly swatter. Three ugly cartoon buzzards began cutting down the Twisted Slipper with chain saws. The mouse grabbed them by their feathers, dipped them in popcorn butter, and sent them sliding down the rain gutters into the rubbish bins.

While the mouse worked, I slipped in and out of the shadows to find out where, oh where, had all the evil cartoon characters come from. I followed my instincts to the retired carnival ride warehouse. I jimmied the lock, opened the door quietly, and slipped inside. I saw faded carousel horses, broken Ferris wheel chairs, bent train tracks, and piles of mismatched nuts and bolts.

From a tiny office way in the back, a light was visible from under the door. I tiptoed along the wall, stopped by the door, and slowly turned the knob. Without making a sound, I sneaked inside, staying in my own shadow. There, hunched over a drawing board, was a crooked, cranky old man, with pens and paints all around him.

I watched him for awhile. He chuckled menacingly as he drew evil cartoon characters, one after the other, painting them with hideous colors. He worked faster than any cartoon artist I had ever seen. As soon as a terrible drawing was done, it came to life and slipped out the window to do its worst.

As you know, a good detective can go anywhere without being seen or heard. So I came up behind the old man, completely unnoticed, and tapped him on the shoulder. He jumped, falling off his stool, spilling his paints all over the floor.

He pulled himself up and we stood face to face. My blood ran cold as I looked right into the eyes of this creator of evil. "Why?" I asked. "Why are you out to topple the Twisted Slipper?"

"To many," he told me, "The Twisted Slipper is pure joy, but to me, it is pure terror." Just last year, he was a young boy, like any other boy enjoying the carnival. He loved the rides, and most of all, he loved The Twisted Slipper. He spent the whole day riding it. When one ride was over, he would pay again, over and over. He kept riding, and riding, and riding.

With each ride, his mind became more twisted, his hair turned grayer, his body got older. At the end of the day he was a crooked, cranky old man possessed with an evil desire for revenge.

He practiced drawing cartoons every day for the whole year, and by the time the carnival opened again, he was ready. He drew the worst creatures he could imagine, as fast as he could draw them. The drawings came to life and he sent them all out to destroy The Twisted Slipper.

After telling me his story, the old man sat down with his head in his hands. He looked up and his face seemed to soften. He looked over at the partly completed drawing on the board and shook his head sadly. "I realize now," he said, "that it was not The Twisted Slipper that was to blame, but my compulsion to ride it!"

He crumpled the last drawing and threw it into the rubbish bin. It was then I knew, although someone else might not have guessed, that the old man would never draw evil cartoon characters again.

Instead, he picked up his pen and began to draw super heroes. He drew heroes large and small, heroes that fly and heroes with amazing weapons. He sent them all out to save The Twisted Slipper.

The cartoon artist and I stood in the crowd with the families and watched as the new super heroes, along with the mouse, caught the evil cartoon characters, one by one, sometimes two by two, and flung them into the rubbish bins.

The crowd cheered and cheered! It was the most amazing day anyone can remember at the carnival.

After the last of the Twisted Slipper gang was safely put away, the mouse came over to me and the old man. He held up his tiny paw and the cartoon artist bent over and shook it with his finger.

My work was finished. I returned to my office to await my next mystery, but I carried in my pocket an incomplete sketch of a super hero. Someday, it might come in handy. Even a detective as good as me needs help now and then.

—Kathryn Totten, storyteller/author

Comic Book Creations

Supplies

11 x 17-inch white paper (four pieces per child)

Stapler

Scissors (lots of pairs)

Comic books (to cut up)

Newspaper comics (to cut up)

Glue sticks

Crayons

Markers (fine tip, one per child)

Directions

1. To make their books, have each child lay all four pieces of paper together, then fold them all in half width-wise and staple together at the fold, once at the top and once at the bottom.

2. Let the children cut out images from the comic books and the newspaper comics, and combine their different ones to create their own comic book fun.

3. Have them glue their comic creations into their books starting on the first page inside the front cover and ending on the last page before the back cover. Tell them they can make up one long story or have several short ones.

4. Instruct the children to write their story lines in conversation bubbles and/or in short sentences/phrases under their comic creations.

5. Finally, let them name their comic books and design and color the front and back covers, making sure to include their titles and names as the authors.

6. Have them swap their comic book creations with each other to read, making sure they get their own back to take home with them!

Midnight Snack Attack

Twizzlers® Twist-n-Fill candy or Cherry Twists

Bologna or cheese cut with cartoon cookie cutters

Popcorn

Cotton candy

Corn dogs

Cartoon fruit snacks

It's 2 a.m., you are exhausted, and there are still children awake—what drastic measures do you take?

"Turn on an educational TV show and tell the kids they have to watch because I'll ask questions at breakfast, and the one who answers the most might get a prize. No one ever makes it to the end of the show!"

—Karen Radeck
Germantown, Wisconsin

Video Recommendations

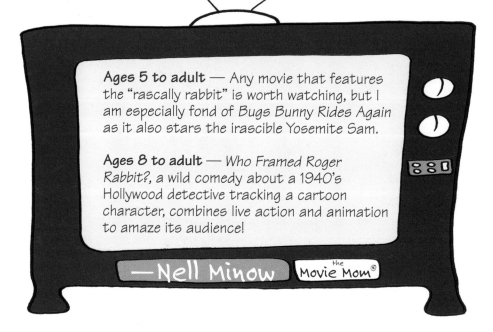

Ages 5 to adult — Any movie that features the "rascally rabbit" is worth watching, but I am especially fond of *Bugs Bunny Rides Again* as it also stars the irascible Yosemite Sam.

Ages 8 to adult — *Who Framed Roger Rabbit?*, a wild comedy about a 1940's Hollywood detective tracking a cartoon character, combines live action and animation to amaze its audience!

—Nell Minow the Movie Mom®

Create-a-Pancake

Ingredients and Supplies

Sausages

Frying pan

Pancake mix (plus any added ingredients)

Bowl and spoon

Pancake grill (oiled)

Butter

Whipped cream

Chocolate chips

Strawberries

Blueberries

Pancake syrup

Optional: Mickey Mouse waffle maker

Directions

1. Cook the sausages in the frying pan.

2. Make pancake batter and grill pancakes, starting with one per child. Serve with sausage.

3. Put all the other supplies on the table and let the children create their own cartoon characters.

Optional: If you have a Mickey Mouse waffle maker, substitute waffles for pancake. The kids can still decorate them.

Age Adjustment: For *younger* children, keep the pancakes small, but make them big enough to decorate. *Older* children will need larger pancakes and more of them.

Twenty Extra Fun Ideas

1. Rent inflatable carnival activities, such as a moonwalk, from a party rental company.

2. Have a carnival pie-eating contest. Be sure to have lots of wet rags to clean up the children's faces and your floor!

3. Use cartoon character plates, napkins, cups, even tablecloths. Get a variety!

4. Tell your guests to wear cartoon character pajamas, then take a group photo.

5. Ask your guests to bring new comic books for an exchange.

6. Trace each child's body onto butcher paper, then let him draw a cartoon face on it before hanging it up. Let him take it home.

7. Let the children be cartoon artists for a night, drawing their favorite characters or ones from "The Twisted Slipper Mystery: A Cartoonival Adventure" on page 38. Make sure they autograph their sketches—after all, one might be famous someday!

8. Make up and play a trivia game, for example, one question could be "Who is Fred Flinstone married to?"

9. Sing or hum as many cartoon theme songs as you can. An easy one is the Flinstones' theme song.

10. Have your guests act out favorite cartoon characters, not using sounds, while others guess who they are.

11. Suggest they imitate cartoon characters' laughs. Make this a guessing game, too.

12. Name cartoon characters and ask for any sayings or slogans associated with them, for example, Bugs Bunny says, "What's up, Doc?"

13. Lay a quarter in the bottom of a bucket of water. Give the children pennies to drop one at time, trying to cover up the quarter. This is a lot harder than it sounds!

14. Put plastic ducks (with a number written on the bottom) into a tub of water or wading pool. Let each child draw one duck to win a prize with that number on it.

15. Ask your guests what the best carnival ride is they've ever been on. Why?

16. Ask your guests if they've won anything playing a carnival game. What?

17. Set up lots of TVs and VCRs in the same room and show different cartoons at the same time.

18. Watch morning cartoons in the morning while eating breakfast. Let the children take turns wearing a popcorn hat. (See page 35.)

19. Play the game Topple™ after reading the "The Twisted Slipper Mystery: A Cartoonival Adventure" on page 38.

20. Play the game Twister™ after reading the "The Twisted Slipper Mystery: A Cartoonival Adventure" on page 38. *Caution:* Make sure the children are wearing non-skid footwear for this. Maybe provide slipper socks as favors!

You can't sleep because the kid next to you is giggling, snoring, or talking in their sleep—what do you do?

"I fall asleep before everyone else, but Mom says, RULES ARE LIGHTS OUT— GIGGLES OUT BY MIDNIGHT!"
—Theresa Ayers, age 10
Toledo, Ohio

Cartoonival Invitation

Twelve 4 x 5-inch blank
  notecards with envelopes
Black permanent marker
  (fine tip)
Copy paper
Scissors
Glue stick
Optional: Cartoon
  character sticker
  (one per envelope)

Cartoonival Puppet Show

Tube socks (one per child)
Lots of felt
  (assorted colors)
Lots of pom-poms
  (assorted colors)
Pipe cleaners
  (assorted colors)
Moving eyes (all sizes)
Assorted feathers
Fabric scraps
Scissors (several pair)
Fabric glue
  (several bottles)

Carnival Foot Longs and Carnival Corn

Sweet corn in husk
  (one per child)
Barbecue grill
Foot long hot dogs
  (one per child)
Large saucepan
Foot long buns
  (one per child)
Paper towels
Butter (melted)
Tall thin container
Ketchup
Mustard
Chopped onions
Pickles
Salt and pepper
Option #1: Regular
  hot dogs and buns.
Option #2: Frozen
  corn on the cob and
  wooden skewers.

Icy Slippery Drinks

Ice
Snow cone machine
  or ice shaver
Ice cream scoop
Paper cones
Flavored syrup
Spoon straws

Don't forget the
camera and film

Dress-Up Tent

Poster board (any color)
Colored markers
Carnival tickets
  (found at party stores)
Tent
Rope and hangers
Clothes and accessories
  (that make up
  cartoon characters)
Small tables and chairs
Optional: Full-length mirror

What's Wrong, Doc?

Poster board (any color)
Colored markers
Carnival tickets
  (found at party stores)
Bandages
  (small and large sizes)
Craft sticks (for splints)
First-aid tape
Scissors
Cloth wraps
Small table and chairs
Doctor outfit
Nurse outfit
Age Adjustments:
  Glue, insurance forms
  (pretend) and pens

Orange, Apple, Banana Slot Machine

Poster board (any color)
Colored markers
Carnival tickets
  (found at party stores)
Three of the following:
  blindfolds, chairs,
  paper bags, oranges,
  apples, and bananas
Whistle

Comic Book Creations

11 x 17-inch white paper
  (four pieces per child)
Stapler
Scissors (lots of pairs)
Comic books (to cut up)
Newspaper comics
  (to cut up)
Glue sticks
Crayons
Markers (fine tip,
  one per child)

Create-a-Pancake

Sausages
Frying pan
Pancake mix (plus any
  added ingredients)
Bowl and spoon
Pancake grill (oiled)
Butter
Whipped cream
Chocolate chips
Strawberries
Blueberries
Pancake syrup
Optional: Mickey Mouse
  waffle maker

Midnight Snack Attack

Twizzlers® Twist-n-Fill
  candy or Cherry Twists
Bologna or cheese cut
  with cartoon cookie
  cutters
Popcorn
Cotton candy
Corn dogs
Cartoon fruit snacks

CHAPTER FOUR

VACATION WITH ME

No postcards necessary for everyone to remember this vacation! Turn your house into an airport, your mini-van into an airplane, and take off to rent a large hotel room, connecting rooms, or even a suite! Or just have everyone meet you at the hotel. First fly your child's friends to "Hawaii" for a dip in the pool. Then decorate areas of your hotel room to whisk your guests off to "Italy" for dinner, "Las Vegas" for games, "Disneyland" for fun, and "Hollywood" for fame. After movie stars and popcorn, stories and sharing, let them sleep wherever their dreams may take them!

Order of Vacation With Me Party

Visit "Hawaii" (serve Hawaiian Poolside Drinks, swim, and take pictures of guests with heads through a life preserver)

Have dinner (Pizza Fun-Do) in "Italy" (hand out Candy Roses, see page 82, *Valentine School Parties… What Do I Do?®*)

Visit "Disneyland®" and make Mouse Ears

Create handprints and footprints in "Hollywood"

Get on pajamas and lay out sleeping bags

Read "The Postcard from a Paris Hotel"

Play Easy-Come, Easy-Go Card Game in "Las Vegas"

Watch videos with Midnight Snack Attack

Sleep (have the group make up a "location")

Have breakfast (French Toast a la Fun) in "France"

Brush teeth, get dressed, pack, call bellhop, return to "airport"

Claim luggage

Say good-bye!

The Vacation With Me Invitation

Supplies

Makes one

Pencil

9 x 12-inch orange construction paper

Scissors

9 x 12-inch green construction paper

Tape

Black permanent marker (fine tip)

School glue

Directions

1. Trace the pattern pieces on page 45, onto the orange construction paper and cut out: two tree trunks (pattern piece #1).

2. Trace the following pattern pieces onto the green construction paper and cut out: four palm leaves (pattern piece #2).

3. On one tree trunk, cut along the dotted line from the bottom to the circle. On the other, from the top to the circle.

4. Complete the tree trunk by sliding the two pieces together. Secure them with tape at the top and bottom, making sure you can open up the trunk to stand it up.

5. Using the black permanent marker, write the following vertically from the bottom on the tree trunk, one sentence per section: *Vacation with me! We will spend the night at a hotel. We will travel all over the world. This invitation is your airline ticket. Bring your swimsuit, sleeping bag, pillow, and pajamas. Please come!* (Two sections will be blank—you can always add more information!)

6. On the palm leaves, write the following: Party Given By (your name). Meet At (last name) Airport (your address or hotel). Day, Date, and Take-Off Time, and Day, Date, and Landing Time. Call Me To Reserve Your Seat (your phone number).

7. Glue one palm leaf to each section of the tree trunk, pointed ends out and information on top.

8. Hand deliver each invitation with the tree opened up. Who could resist?

Note: These also make great centerpieces for tables. Decorate them rather than write on them.

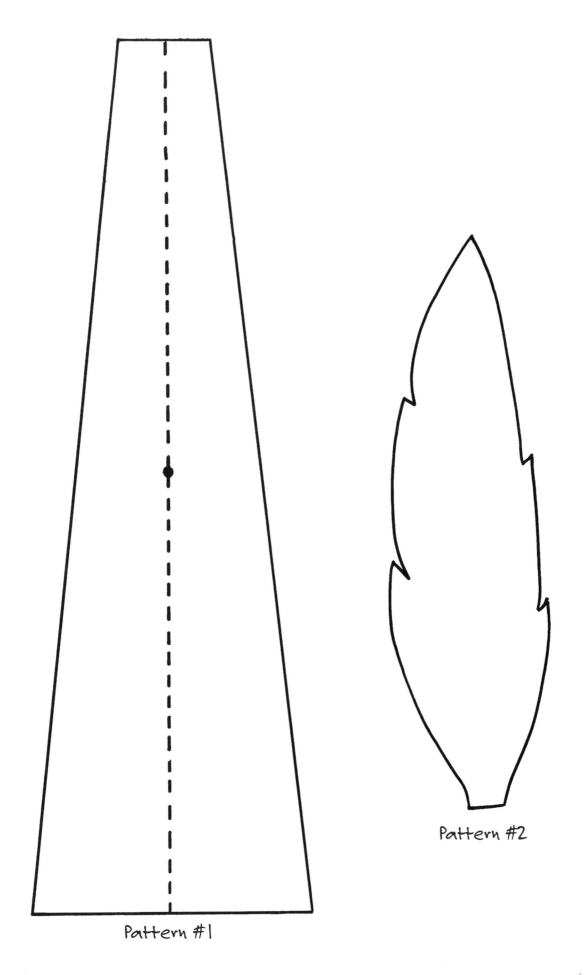

Pattern #1

Pattern #2

Hawaiian Poolside Drinks

Serve these in "Hawaii"

Ingredients and Supplies

Makes 5

Five Hawaiian leis

10-ounce can frozen strawberry daiquiri mix

Water

Ice

Blender

Five 8-ounce clear plastic cups

Knife

Five strawberries

Five large chunks pineapple

Five cocktail umbrellas

Five straws

Five cocktail napkins (Hawaiian theme)

Directions

1. Hang a lei around each child's neck as he enters the pool area.

2. Follow the directions on the daiquiri mix, substituting water for the rum.

3. Divide the daiquiris equally into the plastic cups.

4. Almost slice the strawberries in half and place one on each rim. Do the same with the pineapple chunks.

5. Complete with umbrellas and straws, then serve with cocktail napkins.

Tasty Pizza Fun-Do

Take your guests to "Italy"

Ingredients and Supplies

Makes 5

Red-checkered tablecloth

Box of breadsticks

Clear glass

15½-ounce jar pizza sauce

Fondue pot

1 cup shredded mozzarella cheese

1 teaspoon Italian seasoning

Spatula

One loaf French bread

Non-alcoholic wine

Five plastic wine goblets

Option 1: Crock-pot™

Option 2: Serving spoon and Italian-theme plates

Directions

1. Put the red-checkered tablecloth on a table or the floor to create "Italy."

2. Put the breadsticks in the glass and set on the tablecloth.

3. Pour pizza sauce into fondue pot and heat about 5 minutes.

4. Add cheese and Italian seasoning. Stir well with spatula, scraping the edges of the pot. Let the cheese melt slightly. This will only take a few minutes.

5. Rip the French bread into pieces. Tell the children to dip the bread into the pizza mixture and eat away.

6. Serve with non-alcoholic wine in plastic wine goblets.

Tip: If your group is large, borrow additional fondue pots.

Option 1: Use a Crock-pot™ in place of the fondue pot.

Option 2: If you prefer, scoop out sauce and put on plates with bread.

Throw Away Mouse Ears

Make these in "Disneyland®"

Supplies

Tape
Disney character pictures

Two black pipe cleaners
(per child)

Plastic headband (per child)

Directions

1. Hang Disney character pictures around the Disneyland® area of your hotel room.

2. Show the children how to twist their pipe cleaners around their headbands to form mouse ears.

3. Let them wear their Mouse Ears during their entire visit to "Disneyland®."

Note: Since these Mouse Ears aren't expensive you won't mind if the kids throw them away.

Movie stars have been immortalized at Mann's Chinese Theatre (Grauman's Chinese Theatre) since 1927. Over two million visitors tour every year. As of May, 2001, about 175 of the 200 cement blocks were filled with handprints and footprints. There is also a Hollywood Walk of Fame™, consisting of five acres of bronze stars with celebrities' names inscribed on them. There are other walks of fame, one in Canada, one in St. Louis, and a new one in Florida, the U.S. Space Walk of Fame. Search the Internet for "walk of fame"—you'll be amazed at how much you find.

Turn Into a Hollywood Star

Do this in "Hollywood"

Supplies

Tape
Chinese lanterns
  (found at import shops
  or craft stores)

Cut-out stars
  (found at party stores)

Colored markers

8½ x 11-inch card stock
  (two pieces per child)

Directions

1. Hang Chinese lanterns in area of your hotel room to represent Mann's Chinese Theater in Hollywood.

2. Write Welcome to Hollywood! on the stars and hang them up.

3. Have each child trace his handprint and footprint on separate pieces of card stock.

4. Let them add details, such as fingernails and toenails or borders.

5. Make sure they autograph their imprints—after all, they might be famous one day!

6. Hang up all the hand- and footprints for everyone to see.

The Postcard from a Paris Hotel

Ronnie couldn't believe his vacation was almost over. He had climbed up castles in Germany, lighthouses in Spain, and the Eiffel Tower right here in Paris, France. He and his parents were having dinner in the hotel tonight, and then tomorrow, going to the airport and flying home.

So his vacation was basically over. But he didn't want it to end. He wanted to make it last.

They were heading up to their room to dress for dinner. The elevator door opened and Ronnie's parents stepped in. "I want to buy just one more postcard," Ronnie said. "I'll be up in a few minutes, okay?"

Ronnie's father nodded. "Sure. Don't be too long." The elevator door closed.

Ronnie turned and walked toward the gift shop in the hotel lobby. It had just a few shelves stuffed with things like tooth-brushes and combs, maps and newspapers, and Eiffel Tower key rings. The postcards were on a revolving stand next to the cashier.

Ronnie carefully examined each one: the Mona Lisa he had seen at the Louvre, a gargoyle from atop the cathedral of Notre Dame, the Arc de Triomphe on the Champs Elysées. He already had post-cards similar to these. He was looking for something really different, something special, something he would keep forever and ever.

"Perhaps you would like this card, Monsieur," the gray-haired gentleman behind the register said, as he pulled a postcard out from under the counter. "It is, what do you say, unique." He handed it to Ronnie with a wink and a hint of a smile.

"Thanks," Ronnie said as he took the postcard. In an instant, he was entranced by the picture. It was shiny and sparkly, almost mirror-like. The scene looked familiar, but it wasn't in Paris. He started to turn the card over to read about it when suddenly the picture changed to someplace else, once again, not in Paris, but someplace he'd recently been. "This must be déjà vu, French-style," he thought.

Although Ronnie hadn't spoken out loud, the kindly cashier answered him: "No, Monsieur, déjà vu is just a feeling. The pictures on that card are real. They are of places you have been, and..."

The phone rang. "Oui, he is here. Oui, I will tell him you are waiting." The clerk hung up the phone. "That was your mother..."

"Wow!" Ronnie exclaimed. "There's the castle I climbed up last week in Germany. And the valley and mountains I saw from the castle! Look! Hey, it changed again! Now it's the lighthouse in Spain. It had over 100 steps, but I made it to the very top and saw a 100 miles away, yes, that far! See!"

But every time he tried to show the clerk the picture, it changed. Now it was of the Eiffel Tower, where he had just been. But it didn't look like any of the other pictures you see on TV or in movies. Instead, it was of the elevator, crowded with a group of French school children. Ronnie looked closer. They were talking. He could see their lips move! He could hear their high-pitched excited voices!

"This is no ordinary hologram, Mister!" Ronnie exclaimed.

"Excuse me, Monsieur," replied an unfamiliar voice, a female voice. "Who are you talking to?"

"Huh?" Ronnie looked up and saw a dark-haired girl in her twenties. "Where is the old man?"

"What old man? Are you alright? You seem confused," she asked. "Where are your parents?"

Then Ronnie remembered, his parents were waiting for him. He ran to the elevator, then ran back to pay for the postcard. "You couldn't have gotten that here," the pretty clerk told him. "You must have found it at another shop."

On his way back to the elevator, Ronnie bumped into a whole family of tourists without saying "I'm sorry," and then practically pushed over a potted plant, he was so captivated by the scenes on his postcard, all of the places he'd been, not just on this vacation, but of other trips.

There he was at Disneyland when he was just 7 years old. Then there he was in Las Vegas when he was 9. And Hawaii last Christmas! The elevator came and went several times. And all this time, Ronnie's parents were wondering what was taking him so long.

Finally, Ronnie "came" to just long enough to get on the elevator. The doors slowly closed, rattling and squeaking like they hadn't been oiled in eons. Ronnie pushed the button for his floor, then looked back down at his prize. But something had changed and it wasn't just the scene—this new scene did not look familiar. Hmmm, Ronnie thought, could this be a vacation my parents took before I was born?

Then he saw himself, only looking a little taller, a little older. He was helping his dad tie something down, a rope, attached to a sail. They were sailing their own yacht, out on the ocean! He was fascinated by the deep blue water that extended to the horizon. His dad yelled something to his mom even though she was standing only 10 feet away.

Lost in amazement, Ronnie didn't notice when the sky grew darker and the waves much higher. Lightning began flashing around them. The yacht started rocking back and forth, too much. Ronnie felt the hair on his neck rising.

And just as quickly as the storm had come up, there was a rugged beach, covered with pieces and parts of...their yacht! Ronnie

looked around, cold and shivering. Thank goodness, his parents were there, inflating a yellow rubber raft.

Ronnie closed his eyes for a second, just long enough to imagine a rescue. And sure enough, as they bobbed out on the water, a helicopter hovered overhead...

"Amazing, n'est pas?"

Ronnie looked up. Where had he come from? The old man from the gift shop. When had he gotten on the elevator? Ronnie hadn't remembered it stopping, or the doors opening and closing.

"You're dripping wet, Monsieur," the old man said. "Here, I have a towel. You have sand all over your face, and your hair, it is stiff from salt water. You need to clean up before your parents see you."

"What...How...Why...Who...Where..." Ronnie tried to form a question.

"Oh, I didn't get a chance to tell you. That postcard can take you everywhere you have been, and, more than that, everywhere you will one day be."

The elevator dinged and stopped. The doors slid open smoothly. Ronnie stepped out and turned to say "good-bye" to the mysterious gray-haired man, but he wasn't there.

Ronnie looked down to make sure his postcard hadn't disappeared, too. No, it was still there. He decided to put it under his T-shirt. It wasn't that he felt bad that he hadn't paid for it. He just knew he wouldn't be able to share it with his parents. It was so different, so special, so unique, it was just for him. Something he would keep forever and ever...

—*Kathryn Totten,* storyteller/author

The Easy-Come, Easy-Go Card Game

Play this in "Las Vegas"

Supplies

Tape
Large playing cards (found at party stores)

Two decks of playing cards
Assorted prizes (almost as many as number of children)

Directions

1. Hang large playing cards around an area of your hotel room to create "Las Vegas."

2. Seat everyone in a circle, then shuffle each deck of cards separately, like a pro.

3. Deal out one deck, one card at a time (kids can hold the cards or place them on the floor). Explain that it doesn't matter if one child has more cards than another, or if kids see one anothers cards, as it has no effect on the game .

4. Put the assorted prizes in the center of the circle, describing them and giving them each an easy-to-identify name.

5. Some kids are unfamiliar with the suits in a deck of cards, so using the second deck, "show and tell" the four suits—spades, clubs, hearts, diamonds. Then slip those cards back into the deck.

6. Begin playing by flipping over the first card in the deck, calling out what it is (number or face card, and suit), then showing it to everyone.

7. The child with the matching card gives it to the dealer, or passes it to the dealer through the other players. Explain that the child should not stand up because he will get to choose a prize and then hide it behind him. If he were to stand up later, everyone would see his prize. Tell the children it is important to pay attention to where each prize goes, especially the ones they want.

49

continued on next page

The Easy-Come, Easy-Go Card Game *continued*

8. Continue playing by flipping over another card, retrieving the matching card, and letting the bearer of that card choose a prize. Be sure that they name it, according to step #4, and have it passed to them unless they can reach it.

9. When there are no prizes left in the center of the circle (not everyone will have one), players have to "steal" them from those who are hiding them. But they must name or point to the child with the prize they want, and also name that prize correctly.

10. If they are right, they get that prize and hide it behind them. If they are wrong, they don't get anything.

11. When all the cards have been turned into the dealer, those with prizes behind their backs get to keep them.

Tip: Prizes that work well include: nail polish, make-up, and jewelry for girls. Boys like anything having to do with engines or sports.

Note: It is not unusual for some children to have several prizes and others to have none. So having lots of prizes gives more children a chance to win, and it makes the game more fun as it's harder to keep track of all the prizes and their specific names. There is always that one prize that all the children want, which makes them forget about where the other prizes are hidden and who has them.

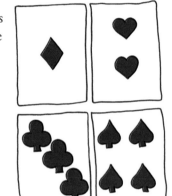

Age Adjustment: For *younger* children, have older children help with the cards or be prepared for this game to take an hour or more. For *older* children, speed up the game by calling out the cards quickly and not giving them much time to remember who has what prize.

Tell us about your favorite Slumber Party?

"It was at a hotel with six other boys. We swam, had pizza, hung out in the room, watched two videos, had breakfast in the hotel, and stayed up all night."

—Chris Hill, age 13
Canton, Ohio

Midnight Snack Attack

Junk from the vending machine

Room service (expensive, but kids love it)

Popcorn (from the lobby if available)

Individually wrapped cheese and crackers

Individually wrapped cookies

Peanuts

Video Recommendations

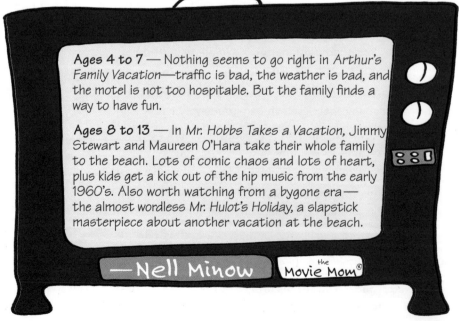

Ages 4 to 7 — Nothing seems to go right in Arthur's *Family Vacation*—traffic is bad, the weather is bad, and the motel is not too hospitable. But the family finds a way to have fun.

Ages 8 to 13 — In *Mr. Hobbs Takes a Vacation*, Jimmy Stewart and Maureen O'Hara take their whole family to the beach. Lots of comic chaos and lots of heart, plus kids get a kick out of the hip music from the early 1960's. Also worth watching from a bygone era — the almost wordless *Mr. Hulot's Holiday*, a slapstick masterpiece about another vacation at the beach.

—Nell Minow   *the* Movie Mom®

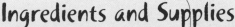rench Toast á la Fun

Treat your guests to "France" for breakfast

Ingredients and Supplies

French toast (served with complimentary breakfast)

Option 1: Frozen French toast, microwave or toaster, paper plates, plastic forks and knives, syrup, and butter

Option 2: Large croissants, paper plates, plastic knives, and butter

Although similar to the French version of a grilled cheese sandwich, croque monsieur, French toast is as American as apple pie. It was first served in 1724 in Albany, New York, and named after the owner of the restaurant, Joseph French. He didn't know his grammar very well and forgot to add the apostrophe "s" to "French," so rather than "French's toast," we still eat "French toast."

Directions

1. Be sure the hotel you're staying at has French toast on its complimentary breakfast menu.

Note: Be sure to tell your guests the true origination of French toast. (See sidebar.)

Option 1: Heat frozen French toast according to directions and serve on paper plates with syrup and butter.

Option 2: Buy large croissants at your grocer's bakery, and serve on paper plates with butter and knives.

Variation: Order French toast from room service.

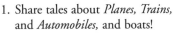wenty Extra Fun Ideas

1. Share tales about *Planes, Trains,* and *Automobiles,* and boats!

2. Sing the song "Fifty Nifty United States" by Ray Charles.

3. Play a matching game of food items with states. For example, cheese goes with Wisconsin.

4. Name football, basketball, hockey, and baseball teams and states they make their home base.

5. Talk about the different animals you've come across on vacation.

6. Ask your guests what their favorite vacation was? Why?

7. Ask your guests what their dream vacation would be? Why?

8. Tell funny stories about family trips.

9. Find out what other kinds of trips your guests have gone on besides family ones?

10. Pretend you're in preschool and play choo-choo train.

11. Share photos of different kinds of vacations.

12. Show home videos of vacations and serve popcorn.

13. Make a large black and white copy of a map of the United States. Have the children color the states they have gone to on vacation.

14. Put your finger on a spinning globe. After it stops, make up a vacation story there.

15. Start a vacation story with one sentence, pick someone else to continue, then go around the room until someone wants to end it.

16. Go around in a circle taking turns naming cities, states, or countries, starting with "A is for Alabama," then "B is for Buffalo," and so on. If someone misses, they are out.

17. Clip several ads from the travel section of a newspaper. Cut out the prices and mix everything up on the floor. Have your guests guess what prices go with what trips.

18. Go to the airport and watch planes take off and land.

19. Have your guests pretend to take a trip to the moon.

20. Put vacation clothes in a suitcase. Write the items on strips of paper and put in a hat. Have the children draw a strip, run to the suitcase, find the item, and put it on. Take a picture when they're all dressed in their new clothes.

The Vacation With Me Invitation

Pencil
9 x 12-inch orange
  construction paper
Scissors
9 x 12-inch green
  construction paper
Tape
Black permanent marker
  (fine tip)
School glue

Hawaiian Poolside Drinks

Five Hawaiian leis
10-ounce can frozen
  strawberry daiquiri mix
Water
Ice
Blender
Five 8-ounce clear
  plastic cups
Knife
Five strawberries
Five large chunks
  pineapple
Five cocktail umbrellas
Five straws
Five cocktail napkins
  (Hawaiian theme)

Tasty Pizza Fun-Do

Red-checkered tablecloth
Box of breadsticks
Clear glass
15½-ounce jar pizza sauce
Fondue pot
1 cup shredded
  mozzarella cheese
One teaspoon
  Italian seasoning
Spatula
One loaf French bread
Non-alcoholic wine
Five plastic wine goblets
Option 1: Crock-pot™
Option 2: Serving spoon
  and Italian-theme
  plates

Throw Away Mouse Ears

Tape
Disney character pictures
Two black pipe cleaners
  (per child)
Plastic headband
  (per child)

Don't forget the
camera and film

Turn Into a Hollywood Star

Tape
Chinese lanterns
  (found at import
  shops or craft stores)
Cut-out stars
  (found at party
  stores)
Colored markers
8½ x 11-inch card stock
  (two pieces per child)

The Easy-Come, Easy-Go Card Game

Tape
Large playing cards
  (found at party stores)
Two decks of playing cards
Assorted prizes
  (almost as many as
  number of children)

Midnight Snack Attack

Junk from the vending
  machine
Room service (expensive,
  but kids love it)
Popcorn (from the lobby
  if available)
Individually wrapped
  cheese and crackers
Individually wrapped
  cookies
Peanuts

French Toast á la Fun

French toast
  (served with
  complimentary
  breakfast)
Option 1: Frozen French
  toast, microwave or
  toaster, paper plates,
  plastic forks and
  knives, syrup, and
  butter
Option 2: Large
  croissants, paper
  plates, plastic knives,
  and butter

CHAPTER FIVE

Enchanted Castle

Take your guests back in time to a place of myths and legends, when men wore Knights'
Armor and Helmets, fought dragons, and jousted in tournaments to win their ladies' hearts.
When ladies wore Damsels' Hats, adorned with beads and flowing scarves, and waited for
their knights to come home from their dangerous quests. When kings and queens held feasts
full of song and jest, jugglers and magicians, tables laden with Turkey Legs, fruit, and the
finest of drinks. Only in your party kingdom, there is a Pillow Jousting Tournament rather
than one with lances. Your dinner guests are themselves the entertainment when they partake
in a Royal Court Parade around the neighborhood and shout out rhymes in "The Guests at
the Medieval Feast." Plus the damsel in the special story uses her brains, not her beauty, to
save her knight from the spell of "The Enchanted Castle." After you complete the evening
with a good old-fashioned movie or two, your guests' cups will overfloweth with fun, so much
so that they won't want to say their "farewells" come the morning dew!

Order of Enchanted Castle Party

Make Knights' Swords and Shields and Armor and Helmets, or Damsels' Hats, Glitter Stardust, and Feather Pens

Have the Royal Court Parade

Serve dinner (Medieval Turkey Legs with Fruit Daggers and Mugs of Root Beer) while reading "The Guests at the Medieval Feast"

Read "The Enchanted Castle Story"

Play the Pillow Jousting Tournament

Watch videos with Midnight Snack Attack

Sleep

Set the Royal Breakfast Table and eat

Brush teeth, get dressed, and pack

Say your farewells!

Sedan, the largest castle in the world, is located in France.

Enchanted Castle Invitation

Supplies
Makes one
Pencil

9 x 12-inch piece yellow construction paper

Scissors

Blue permanent marker

Tape

Directions

1. Trace the pattern pieces on page 55, onto the yellow construction paper and cut out: one castle (pattern piece #1) and one castle stand (pattern piece #2).

2. Write the following on the front of the castle (pattern piece #1):

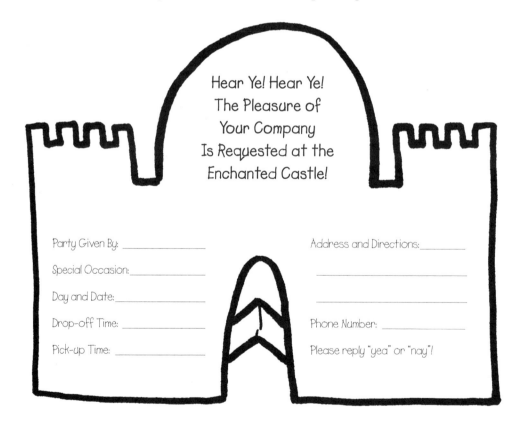

Hear Ye! Hear Ye!
The Pleasure of
Your Company
Is Requested at the
Enchanted Castle!

Party Given By: _____

Special Occasion: _____

Day and Date: _____

Drop-off Time: _____

Pick-up Time: _____

Address and Directions: _____

_____

_____

Phone Number: _____

Please reply "yea" or "nay"!

3. Fold the castle stand (pattern piece #2) on the dotted line. Tape each end to the back of the castle on the lines indicated on pattern piece #1, so the castle can stand up.

4. Ride your "trusty steed" to hand deliver the invitation.

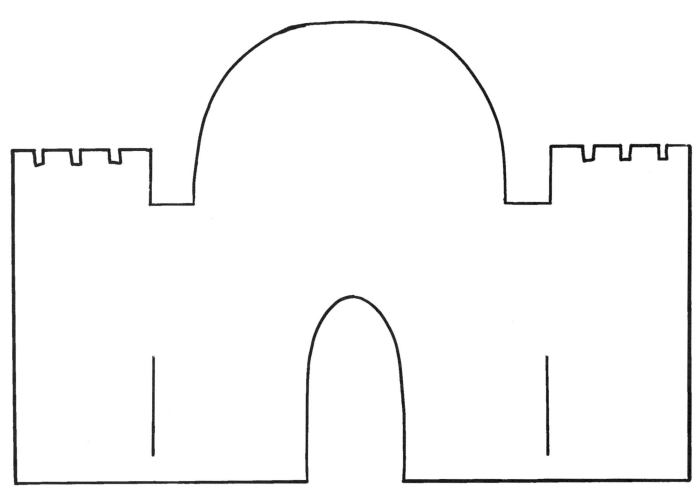

Pattern #1

Pattern #2

55

Knight's Sword and Shield

Supplies

Makes one

Handsaw
2½-foot piece of a 1 x 2
  (found at lumberyards)
Screwdriver
Two 1¼–inch #6 wood screws
9-inch piece of a 1 x 2
  (found at lumberyards)
Black electrical tape

Gold spray paint
Aluminum foil
Packaging tape (clear)
Pencil
Scissors
Large piece cardboard
Markers (assorted colors)
Option 1: Cording or ribbon
Option 2: Paint
  (assorted colors)

Directions

1. To make the sword, saw one end of the 2½-foot piece of wood to make a tip. *Caution:* Don't make it sharp. Just give it the illusion of a sword.

2. Screw the 9-inch piece of wood (crossbar) to the longer piece, leaving about 5 inches for a handle and 2 feet for the blade.

3. Wrap the handle with black electrical tape.

4. Spray paint the crossbar gold, and let dry.

5. Wrap aluminum foil around the blade, then cover the same area with the packaging tape, to both secure it and keep it from being too sharp.

6. To make the shield, draw and cut a shield-shape from the cardboard. (See illustration.)

7. For the shield's handle, cut a 2 x 12-inch strip of cardboard and securely tape down 2 inches to the top back of the shield and 2 inches to the bottom back of the shield.

8. Decorate the shield with colored markers, designing your own "coat of arms."

Option 1: Rather than using gold paint, wrap and tie cording or ribbon around the sword's crossbar to give it a fancier look.

Option 2: Rather than using markers, paint the shield, but allow time for it to dry.

Knight's Armor and Helmet

Supplies

Makes one
Pencil
X-acto® knife

Large piece cardboard
Duct tape
Silver spray paint

Clean plastic gallon
jug with handle at top
(from milk stores or
milk delivery service)

Pen

Historians are still
unsure if King Arthur of
"King Arthur and the
Knights of the Round
Table" was actually a
real person or just the
stuff of legend.

Directions

1. Using the illustration as a guide, draw and cut out a front (breastplate) and back (backplate) of armor from the cardboard. Also draw and cut out two shoulders.

2. Bend the shoulders on the dotted lines. Bring together sides A and B and tape to secure.

3. Tape the breastplate to the shoulders, then the shoulders to the backplate, as in the illustration. Put pieces of tape on the exposed sticky parts of tape.

4. Tape the breastplate to the backplate on one side near the waistline, and put a piece of tape on the sticky part.

5. To make the helmet, cut the top couple inches off the plastic jug.

6. As in the illustration, cut an M-shape in one side of the jug for the front of the helmet.

7. Put the helmet on the child's head and trace around the ears with the pen.

8. Take the helmet off and cut out the ear sections.

9. Spray paint all the pieces silver, and let dry.

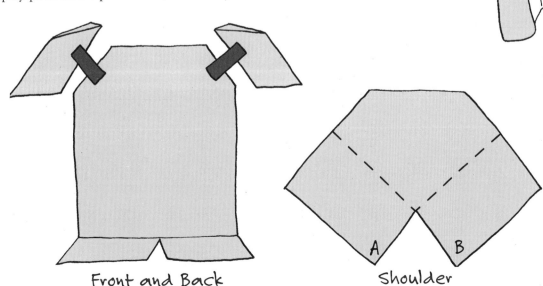

Front and Back

Shoulder

A   B

Damsel's Hat

Supplies

Makes one
Pencil
Scissors
White poster board

Sewing scissors
Satin fabric
(any color)
Iron

Glue gun
Glittery beads
Sheer fabric
(any color)

Directions

1. Draw and cut out a large circle from the poster board.

2. Draw and cut out a one-half "piece of the pie."

3. Using the sewing scissors, cut a piece of satin fabric a little larger than the circle. Iron if needed.

4. Pulling the fabric tightly and smoothing it as you go, glue it to the poster board. Then cut it to fit.

5. Overlapping the edges of the "piece of pie," form a cone-shaped hat. Glue it closed, fitting it to the child's head first if you like.

6. Glue glittery beads around the bottom and near the top, as in the illustration.

7. Cut a few strips of the sheer fabric and glue the ends to the top of the Damsel Hat.

Note: Choose coordinating colors of fabrics and beads.

Glitter Stardust

Supplies

Makes one
Star confetti
Fine white glitter

Small glass jar with lid
Glue gun
6-inch piece white
pipe cleaner

1½-inch pom-pom
(any color)

Directions

1. Put the confetti and the glitter into the jar, put on the lid, and shake to mix.

2. Glue the end of the pipe cleaner to pom-pom.

3. Use this "powder puff" to sprinkle Stardust Glitter in your hair.

Note: If you use a tall enough jar, you can store your powder puff in the jar with the lid on.

Damsel's Feather Pen

Supplies

Makes one

Scissors
Bic® pen (any color)
15-inch ostrich plume*
Glue gun
25 inches floral tape

25 inches satin ribbon
Charm (found at craft stores)
Option 1: Mason jar
Option 2: Assorted ribbons, bows, lace, or small feathers

Directions

1. Use the scissors to force or cut the cap off the pen. Don't cut into the ink barrel. *Caution:* Aim the pen away from yourself and others!

2. Insert the feather into the top of the pen. If you think it's too long, trim some of its "stem" before gluing it in place.

3. Keeping it taut, wrap the floral tape down the pen, starting at the bas of the feather and ending before the writing tip. Tear off excess tape.

4. Cover the pen with ribbon, winding it the same way as the floral tape, only gluing it at the top and bottom.

5. Glue the charm to the pen at the bottom of the feather.

Option 1: The pen stores nicely in a mason jar.

Option 2: Use your imagination to decorate your pen: with bows, dangling ribbons, lace, or small feathers.

* You can also use a turkey, pheasant, or peacock feather. To order, call Oakbrook Publishing House (toll-free) 1-888-738-1733 or go to www.whatdoidobooks.com.

Royal Court Parade

Supplies

None

Directions

1. Have the kids make their Knights' Swords and Shields and Armor and Helmets, or Damsels' Hats, Glitter Stardust, and Feather Pens.

2. Line them up and lead them through the neighborhood for a Royal Court Parade.

Note: If you can't have this parade during the daylight, you can always take the kids to an indoor mall.

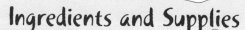

Medieval Turkey Leg with Fruit Dagger

Ingredients and Supplies

Makes one
Turkey leg
Loaf pan
½ cup cut-up fruit
Wooden skewer

Pastry brush
1 teaspoon melted butter
Paper plate
Age Adjustment: Chicken leg (drumstick)

Directions

1. Put the turkey leg into the loaf pan and bake for 1 to 1½ hours at 325°.

2. In the meantime, slide the cut-up fruit onto the wooden skewer to make the Fruit Dagger.

3. Before serving the Turkey Leg, brush with the melted butter.

4. Serve all on the paper plate.

Note: You may have to pre-order the turkey leg from your grocer's meat department.

Age Adjustment: For younger children, substitute a chicken leg (drumstick) or two for the turkey leg.

Mug of Root Beer

Ingredients and Supplies

Makes one   Root beer   Mug   *Optional:* Mason jar

Directions

1. Pour root beer into the mug.

2. Serve immediately while it still has a head (foam) on it.

Optional: Use a mason (canning) jar if you don't have a mug.

The Guests at the Medieval Feast

Supplies
None

Directions

1. While your guests are dining on their Medieval Turkey Legs with Fruit Daggers and Mugs of Root Beer, read them the poem below.

2. Explain to them that they need to participate and that it is quite proper to talk with their mouths full. After all, they are in medieval times!

The king's royal minstrel composed a poem in honor of a feast, but he didn't finish it. As the poem is read, can you supply the rhymes? **(The answers are in parentheses.)**

To prepare for the medieval feast
The queen required six maids
To wash and comb and twist her hair
Into long and beautiful _____ (braids).

The page brought the jewel-studded crown
On a pillow with a tassle
So the king would look his royal best
When his guests came to the _____ (castle).

The cooks roasted turkey and beef
And prepared the puddings and pies
And laid out platters of colorful fruits
A feast for their mouths and their _____ (eyes).

At last the castle was ready
Many guests in their coaches pulled in
And the king said to his royal followers
"Now, let the feast _____ (begin).

A lady of the royal court
Gave her favorite knight a glance
Hoping that when the music played
He would ask her for a _____ (dance).

The knights spoke of the tournament
And who would win the next day
The champion would get a kiss from the queen
And hear people shout _____ (hooray!)

While they watched the amazing tricks
Of the juggling jesters and fools
The ladies sat tall to keep their hats on
And showed off their rings and _____ (jewels).

When all the goblets and mugs were drained
And the platters were all picked clean
The guests came one-by-one to say
Goodnight to the king and _____ (queen).

—Poem by *Kathryn Totten,* storyteller/author

Note: You may want to have another adult or older child show off their juggling abilities or magic act tricks while your guests are eating, but not while you're reading this poem.

61

The Enchanted Castle Story

No! Unhand him, thou foul-smelling, mangy-winged creature!" Lady Arabella awoke from her dream with a terrible dread, her breathing laborious. In a moment, her two ladies-in-waiting were at her side.

"Calm yourself, my lady," whispered Jane as she mopped Lady Arabella's hot face with a cool cloth. May straightened the bed clothes which had become badly twisted. Lady Arabella sobbed.

"He is in danger—I know it," she repeated rapidly as she tried to shake off the fear from her dream. "Sir Frederick was sent on a quest by the king. There has been no word in a fortnight. Tomorrow, we must go after him. I shall place myself between my knight and any danger, if it will spare him."

Jane and May assured her they would prepare everything for the journey, then soothed her back to sleep. They did not know that at dawn the next day they would be in an ordeal that neither had even heard of before.

Jane brought breakfast to Lady Arabella at the usual hour and found her already out of bed, pacing the floor. The bread trencher, an edible plate, was laden with cheese, roast beef, and pomegranate seeds. May brought a cup of hot tea to complete the meal. They could scarcely get Lady Arabella to sit down to eat.

"We must discover where the king has sent Sir Frederick," she said. "Let us go by the backstairs to the knights' meeting chamber. They sit at the round table this morning. From behind the tapestry, we shall listen to all they say, and soon know where our journey will take us."

Through a maze of narrow staircases, dark halls, and hidden doors, Lady Arabella and her two attendants made their way to the heart of the castle where the king's knights gathered to discuss their comings and goings.

"Aye, it was dangerous," said Sir James. "That is why Sir Frederick was sent."

"It has been a long time since we last received word. Perhaps we should go after him," suggested Sir Baldwin.

"I know he is your friend, as he is to us all, but the king has need of us in other areas of the realm," said Sir Percival. "You must trust Sir Frederick to find his way to the Enchanted Castle, subdue the dragon, and return to tell us the tale."

"Oh!" squealed May from behind the tapestry. Lady Arabella silenced her with a glare, then the three of them made their escape unnoticed by the knights.

"You cannot mean to go to the Enchanted Castle, my lady," said the wide-eyed May as Jane wrapped Lady Arabella in her cloak.

"I mean to go at once," said Lady Arabella. "If you are afraid, you have my permission to stay."

May looked at Jane, who gave her an encouraging nod.

"I go where my lady goes," said May.

They traveled on foot, keeping to the dark woods, where they continued into the night. Lady Arabella's owl, a birthday gift from the king's wizard, acted as their guide. His eyes glowed to light their path. The first two nights were uneventful. They

walked as long as they could, then camped under a tree. They did not make a fire for fear of being found. They ate nuts and figs from their bags, and drank water from the stream.

On the third night, just before dawn, they saw the Enchanted Castle. "We will rest here awhile," instructed Lady Arabella. "We will need our strength once we get inside."

Jane and May looked frightened. Arabella was frightened, too, but she could not let them see it in her eyes, so she closed them for a time.

"The draw bridge is down, my lady," said May. "Shall we go in?"

"We cannot enter that way," answered Lady Arabella. "This is an Enchanted Castle. To enter by any ordinary means would mean certain danger."

She then instructed her owl to circle the castle. In what seemed like a moment, he had returned. He then led them to a crack in the castle wall.

"We will enter as the wind enters," said Lady Arabella.

"How can we possibly pass through that narrow way?" asked Jane.

Without explaining, Lady Arabella, with her owl on her forearm, walked toward the crack. She did not slow down as she approached it. Suddenly, she passed through it and disappeared. Jane and May stood with their mouths open, wondering what to do. Then the owl came back through the crack and flew to Jane.

"I will do as my lady did," she said to May. "If it works for me, you must do the same." Jane walked steadily forward with the owl until she passed through the wall. Moments later, breathless and flushed, May also entered the Enchanted Castle.

The wonders they encountered as they walked through the Enchanted Castle cannot fully be explained. The castle's furniture watched them, and talked to them, giving them misleading directions. A spoon in the kitchen tossed bits of potato at them. A pillow in the bed chamber jumped off the bed and hit Jane in the stomach with a candlestick. Lady Arabella grabbed the pillow and stuffed it into an armoire. "Quick, May," she said. "Lock it in with the key."

They made it back to the great hall, and exhausted, sat down on the cold floor. Lady Arabella stroked her owl as she tried to think. Suddenly, across the room, a door opened. They saw no one, but they heard footsteps coming toward them. Lady Arabella stood up, holding her owl, and bravely faced the invisible foe. Jane and May remained behind her, hugging each other for protection.

Lady Arabella spoke first. "We seek the knight who entered here a fortnight ago. We are willing to pay for his release."

A whisper was heard, or felt, from the direction of the footsteps. "The knight you seek, who seeks to slay the dragon, is bound by a chain deep in the castle, a chain that can only be broken with a riddle. I will tell you the riddle, but you must find the answer yourself."

"Then tell it, friend."

"What is more powerful than God, more wicked than the devil, rich men need it, poor men have it, and if you eat it, you will die?"

Lady Arabella turned to her ladies-in-waiting, searching their eyes for a clue to the riddle. They looked so tired. Perhaps she had brought them to this dangerous place for nothing...

And they looked hungry… "What have you eaten today?" She asked them.

"Nothing…" they both answered.

"Well, you must eat. If you continue to eat nothing, you will die."

"If it be God's will," said Jane. "His power is above all…"

"Just a moment, Jane," Lady Arabella said, "What is more powerful than God?"

"Nothing," said Jane, "not even the magic of this castle."

"May," asked Lady Arabella, "what is more wicked than the devil?"

"Why, nothing, my lady," said Jane.

"And poor men, what do they have?"

"Nothing…" said Jane... "and rich men need nothing!"

"That's it!" shouted May. "The answer to the riddle is nothing!"

The three of them hugged and danced in a circle. The owl flew around them hooting and flapping his wings. Suddenly, a rush of wind poured in from the doors and the floor beneath them began to crumble. They stepped from tile to tile, but the whole floor was breaking up. All three of them fell, deep into the castle.

The owl followed them and dusted them off with his feathers. Lady Arabella was the first to get to her feet. "Jane, May!" she shouted. "It is my knight. We have found him!"

Sir Frederick was breaking free from rusty chains. Lady Arabella ran to him, then suddenly stopped and curtsied respectfully. Sir Frederick's dimpled chin quivered slightly.

"My lady...how?" He did not wait for her answer. He took up his sword and shield and strode across the room to an iron gate, which he easily lifted with one hand. He had one thing in mind, to subdue the dragon. It was the quest he had accepted from the king.

The ladies followed him to the dragon's den. Lady Arabella gasped when she saw the creature—it was the one from her dream. He had ragged wings, patchy scales, and a sickly pale color. "That dragon is old and sick," she told Sir Frederick.

"Yes, my lady, but he still has much power," answered the knight. He moved close to the dragon, sword in hand. He held it high, ready to thrust it into the creature's chest.

The dragon gasped and breathed a puff of hot air, not fire. Sir Frederick lowered his sword. Everything in the castle is enchanted, he remembered. Do not follow an ordinary path. Do not subdue the dragon with a sword. Subdue him with a riddle.

"Dragon," he shouted, "you are more powerful than God, more wicked than the devil, rich men need you, poor men have you, and if someone eats you, they will die. You are…"

"NOTHING!" the ladies shouted, to the surprise of Sir Frederick.

At that moment, the dragon's wings and scales fell away, transforming him into a glistening white stallion. He stepped up to Sir Frederick and nuzzled him. Sir Frederick climbed on his back and rode over to Lady Arabella, lifting her up behind him. The owl flew to the stallion and perched on his head. Jane and May followed behind as they all made their way back to the king to report that the dragon was gone.

The night of their return, they attended the greatest feast ever held in the kingdom, and they presented the white stallion as a gift to the king. Jane and May would always have stories to tell about their journey, and Lady Arabella, from then on, had only good dreams.

— *Kathryn Totten,* author/storyteller

Video Recommendations

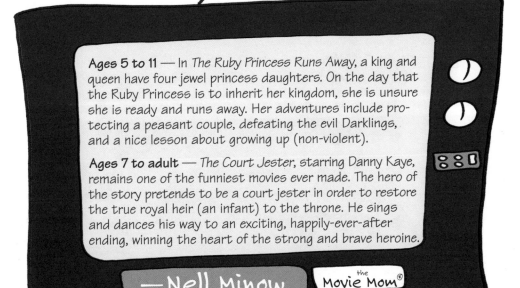

Ages 5 to 11 — In *The Ruby Princess Runs Away*, a king and queen have four jewel princess daughters. On the day that the Ruby Princess is to inherit her kingdom, she is unsure she is ready and runs away. Her adventures include protecting a peasant couple, defeating the evil Darklings, and a nice lesson about growing up (non-violent).

Ages 7 to adult — *The Court Jester*, starring Danny Kaye, remains one of the funniest movies ever made. The hero of the story pretends to be a court jester in order to restore the true royal heir (an infant) to the throne. He sings and dances his way to an exciting, happily-ever-after ending, winning the heart of the strong and brave heroine.

— Nell Minow the Movie Mom®

Midnight Snack Attack

Pickles on a stick

Jousting marshmallows (on both ends of skewers)

Popovers (don't bake well at high altitudes)

Soft salted pretzels

Gold chocolate coins

Steak on a stick

Pillow Jousting Tournament

It's 2:00 am, you are exhausted, and there are still children awake, what drastic measures do you take?

"Divide and conquer! If need be, I move the kids to separate rooms to sleep. By themselves in a room, they usually fall asleep very quickly. I've also threatened that they'll have to sleep on the floor in my room!"

—Teri Bavley
Prairie Village, Kansas

Supplies

Black permanent marker
Poster board

Two blankets
Two pillows
Crown

Optional: Poster board, two blankets, two pillows, and a smaller crown

Directions

1. Set up and draw a tournament with brackets on the poster board as in the illustration. Select pairs of two to joust each other as in step #3 and write their names in the brackets.

2. Fold each blanket into a 2-foot square. Lay both on the floor in an open area about a foot apart. Give pillows to the first pair of children

3. On "Go," they will start to joust (pillow fight) each other. *Caution:* No head shots allowed. This game is meant to be fun, not dangerous.

4. First one to step off the blanket is out. The winners move to the next *bracket*.

5. The next pair jousts and so on until all the pairs have played.

6. The winners joust each other until only two remain.

7. They have a Pillow Joust-off to crown the Pillow Jousting King or Queen.

Tip: Have an adult present to stop the jousters if they get out of control. They can continue only if they can control themselves.

Note: You can make a crown as in Royal Breakfast Table, page 65.

Optional: Turn this into a double-elimination tournament with a second piece of poster board, two more blankets and pillows, and a smaller crown. The "losers" will then have a second chance at winning and being crowned the Prince or Princess.

Variation: If the game goes well and time allows, the King or Queen and the Prince or Princess may be asked to defend their titles by playing another round.

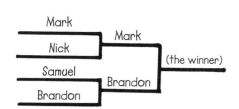

Royal Breakfast Table

Ingredients and Supplies

Scissors
4 x 24-inch strip gold poster
  board (one per child)
Glue gun
Flat beads (assorted)
Stapler

Bowls (one per child)
Spoons (one per child)
Cereal (assorted)
Milk
Optional: Knife and bananas

Queen Wilhelmina of The Netherlands defended that country's neutral position during WWI. After the German's invaded in WWII, she set up a court-in-exile in England, where she stayed in touch with The Netherlands via radio, becoming a symbol of Dutch resistance.

Directions

1. Before the party, cut crown points in the long edges of the poster board strips.

2. Glue beads onto the crowns, making each crown a little different.

3. Staple the ends of the strips together to form the crowns.

4. Set the Royal Breakfast Table with the crowns over the bowls, and spoons, cereal, and milk.

5. Let your guests choose and wear the crown they like, and pour their own cereal and milk. If needed, readjust their crowns to fit heir heads and restaple.

Optional: Cut up bananas and serve with the cereal.

Twenty Extra Fun Ideas

1. Boys come dressed as knights, princes, or kings. Girls come as damsels, princesses, or queens. (Let them braid each other's hair before taking a picture of the royal court.)

2. Put signs on the bathroom doors: Damsels (for girls) and Knights (for boys).

3. Practice doing calligraphy on parchment paper.

4. Talk like they did in the days of yore, for example, "Hold thy tongue."

5. Hire a magician and ask him to come dressed as a wizard.

6. Rent a how-to-juggle video to teach your guests the fundamentals of juggling.

7. Have a "best jester" contest. See who tells the best joke to the group.

8. Play King or Queen for the Day, granting the winners with certain powers for an hour.

9. Sing "I'm Henry the VIII, I Am," by Herman's Hermits.

10. Have a Nerf® Double Crossbow tournament.

11. Play Capture the Flag. (Search the Internet for the rules.)

12. Play cannonball toss by stacking up tin cans, then knocking them down with black plastic balls from a bowling set (or plastic balls spray painted black).

13. Have a Dungeons & Dragons video game tournament.

14. Design a maze using patio furniture, cardboard boxes, and assorted items from the garage. Boys can also build catapults for added fun.

15. Play dice on barrels turned upside-down.

16. Have a sandcastle-building contest.

17. Build castles using decks of cards.

18. Make an edible castle using ice cream cones, cookies, candy, and frosting to "glue" it all together.

19. Show your guests how to make homemade root beer.

20. Let them make-up toasts and then raise their mugs to each other's health.

Enchanted Castle Invitation

Pencil
9 x 12-inch piece yellow
 construction paper
Scissors
Blue permanent marker
Tape

Knight's Sword and Shield

Handsaw
2½-foot piece of a 1 x 2
 (found at lumberyards)
Screwdriver
Two 1¼–inch #6 wood
 screws
9-inch piece of a 1 x 2
 (found at lumberyards)
Black electrical tape
Gold spray paint
Aluminum foil
Packaging tape (clear)
Pencil
Scissors
Large piece cardboard
Markers (assorted colors)
Option 1: Cording or ribbon
Option 2: Paint (assorted
 colors)

Knight's Armor and Helmet

Pencil
X-acto® knife
Large piece cardboard
Duct tape
Silver spray paint
Clean plastic gallon
 jug with handle at top
 (from milk stores or milk
 delivery service)
Pen

Damsel's Hat

Pencil
Scissors
White poster board
Sewing scissors
Satin fabric (any color)
Iron
Glue gun
Glittery beads
Sheer fabric (any color)

Glitter Stadust

Star confetti
Fine white glitter
Small glass jar with lid
Glue gun
6-inch piece white pipe
 cleaner
1½-inch pom-pom
 (any color)

Don't forget the
camera and film

Damsel's Feather Pen

Scissors
Bic® pen (any color)
15-inch ostrich plume*
Glue gun
25 inches floral tape
25 inches satin ribbon
Charm (found at craft
 stores)
Option 1: Mason jar
Option 2: Assorted
 ribbons, bows, lace,
 or small feathers

Royal Court Parade

None

Medieval Turkey Leg with Fruit Dagger

Turkey leg
Loaf pan
½ cup cut-up fruit
Wooden skewer
Pastry brush
1 teaspoon
 melted butter
Paper plate
Age Adjustment: Chicken
 leg (drumstick)

Mug of Rootbeer

Root beer
Mug
Optional: Mason jar

The Guests at the Medieval Feast

None

Midnight Snack Attack

Pickles on a stick
Jousting marshmallows
 (on both ends of skewers)
Popovers (don't bake
 well at high altitudes)
Soft salted pretzels
Gold chocolate coins
Steak on a stick

Pillow Jousting Tournament

Black permanent marker
Poster board
Two blankets
Two pillows
Crown
Optional: Poster board,
 two blankets, two pillows,
 and a smaller crown

Royal Breakfast Table

Scissors
4 x 24-inch strip gold
 poster board (one per
 child)
Glue gun
Flat beads (assorted)
Stapler
Bowls (one per child)
Spoons (one per child)
Cereal (assorted)
Milk
Optional: Knife and bananas

CHAPTER SIX

Sports You've Never Heard Of

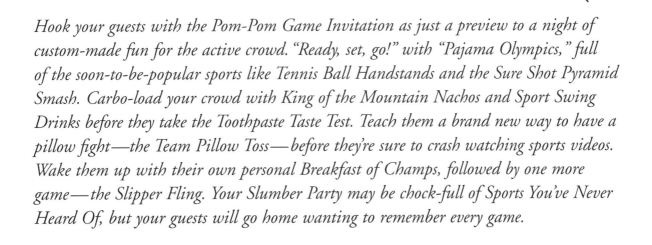

FINISH LINE

Hook your guests with the Pom-Pom Game Invitation as just a preview to a night of custom-made fun for the active crowd. "Ready, set, go!" with "Pajama Olympics," full of the soon-to-be-popular sports like Tennis Ball Handstands and the Sure Shot Pyramid Smash. Carbo-load your crowd with King of the Mountain Nachos and Sport Swing Drinks before they take the Toothpaste Taste Test. Teach them a brand new way to have a pillow fight—the Team Pillow Toss—before they're sure to crash watching sports videos. Wake them up with their own personal Breakfast of Champs, followed by one more game—the Slipper Fling. Your Slumber Party may be chock-full of Sports You've Never Heard Of, but your guests will go home wanting to remember every game.

Order of Sports You've Never Heard Of Party

Make the Hanger Hammock

Read "Pajama Olympics"

Do Tennis Ball Handstands

Play Toothbrush Balance

Play Sure Shot Pyramid Smash

Eat dinner (King of the Mountain Nachos with Sport Swing Drink)

Get on pajamas and lay out sleeping bags

Take Toothpaste Taste Test

Play Team Pillow Toss

Watch videos with Midnight Snack Attack

Sleep

Eat Breakfast of Champs

Do the Slipper Flings

Brush teeth, get dressed, and pack

Say good-bye!

Sports You've Never Heard Of Pom-Pom Game Invitation

Supplies

Makes 12

Glue gun

12 inches yarn (per invitation)

Twelve toilet paper tubes

Twelve 1½-inch pom-poms

Copy paper

Pen

Scissors

Glue stick

Directions

1. For each invitation, use the glue gun to attach one end of yarn to the inside of a toilet paper tube near the edge.

2. Glue the other end of yarn to a pom-pom.

3. Make copies of the invitation.

4. Fill in the details, cut out, and glue around the tubes with the glue stick.

5. Hand deliver these and show your friends how to play: Hold the tube upright and swing the pom-pom around, trying to get it into the tube.

Please come to my Slumber Party— this Pom-Pom Game is just a preview of all the Sports You Never Heard Of that you will get to play!

Party Given By: _____

Special Occasion: _____

Day and Date: _____

Drop-off Time: _____

Pick-up Time: _____

Address and Directions: _____

_____

_____

Phone number: _____

Please call and tell me if you can come!

Hanger Hammock

Supplies

Makes one

Wire hanger

Wire cutters

Pliers

Scissors

24 inches curling ribbon

Net bag (from vegetables or fruit)

Three tennis balls

Glue gun

Two 15 mm moving eyes

Doll hair (found at craft stores)

Pen

½ x 3-inch strip paper

Tennis racquet swizzle stick (found at liquor or kitchen stores)

How many children should you invite to a Slumber Party?

"Around fifteen, because it's fun to play games at night with that many."

—Emily Appleby, age 9
Littleton, Colorado

Directions

1. Holding the hook in one hand and the middle of the bottom in the other, pull the hanger straight, then bend the two ends up to make a hammock stand, as in the illustration.

2. Use the wire cutters to snip off the hanger hook.

3. Use the pliers to pinch the other end into a point to hold the ribbon (see step #5).

4. Cut the ribbon in half.

5. Spread the net bag open for the hammock and tie it to the ends of the stand with the ribbon halves. Tie it high enough to keep it from dragging on the "ground."

6. Curl the ribbon halves, starting from the hammock ends and going out.

7. Lay the three tennis balls inside the hammock.

8. Glue the moving eyes and hair to the first tennis ball for a head.

9. Personalize by writing your name on the strip of paper and gluing it onto the hair for a visor.

10. Lay the tennis racket swizzle stick inside the hammock.

Tip: Ask tennis-playing friends or a tennis club for their old balls—they always have some.

Pajama Olympics

About a month ago, I was just about to climb into bed when I heard the doorbell ring. My dad opened the door and I caught only a few words of the muffled conversation he had with the stranger. Dad called up to me: "There is someone I want you to meet."

"I'm in bed," I said, because I practically was and didn't feel like meeting anyone, especially an adult.

"We're coming up," I heard my father say, and I heard both sets of footsteps tromping up the stairs and then coming toward my room. I jumped into bed and pulled the covers over my head, but I had forgotten to turn out the light.

"I'm in bed," I called out, this time telling the whole truth.

"Can we come in?" Dad asked as he knocked on my door.

"I'm almost asleep," I said, because I wished I was.

"With the light on?"

I didn't have an answer for that one.

"Open the door," Dad said calmly, "or you'll be sorry."

Was I in trouble? What had I done? I couldn't think of a thing. But Dad didn't really sound mad, so I got up and let him and the stranger in.

Dad was smiling, no, he was grinning. He pointed to the man standing next to him and said, "This is Coach Jasper from the Pajama Olympics. He is here to give you a try-out."

"What?" I asked, thinking this had to be a dream, especially since Mr. Jasper looked more like a mad scientist than an athlete. His white hair stuck out from his head in tufts. His small black eyes had crinkled corners, as if he had spent his entire life smiling. Plus he was wearing striped flannel pajamas and his feet were bare.

"Coach Jasper wants you to try-out for his team for the Pajama Olympics," Dad repeated.

"I'm going back to bed," I said, convinced I was dreaming.

"Bed? Why, you can go to bed any night!" said Dad. "Right now, you have the opportunity of a lifetime, and I won't let you pass it up."

"Okay," I mumbled, "let the try-out begin."

Coach Jasper spoke with a foreign accent. It was pretty hard for me to understand him. "Yoo muss shtand on het," he demanded. I figured out that he wanted me to stand on my head. Well, this was something I was good at, so I stood on my head with my feet against the wall. I could see how proud my dad was of me.

Then Coach Jasper put a tennis ball on my left foot. He showed me how to toss it up, and catch it with my right foot. It took a little practice, but soon I could do it without help. He smiled for the first time and I started to like him.

"Theees shyld ees natooral! (This child is a natural!)," exclaimed Coach Jasper. "Leds dry one more think. (Let's try one more thing.)" I stood up and he told me to stand against the wall, with my feet shoulder-width apart. He put a pillow in my hands, stepped back, and called, "Toss!" It was the first thing he said that I understood right away. I threw the pillow to him with all I had, without moving away from the wall. It landed with a firm thud in Jasper's hands. "Perfect!" cheered Jasper.

The next event I tried out for was the toothbrush balance. With my left hand behind my back, Coach Jasper extended my right hand in front of me. He told me to make a fist and hold out my index finger. He balanced my toothbrush across it and told me to stand on one leg. Then he timed me as I balanced.

"Sreee secund! Amazink! (Three seconds. Amazing!)" He was very impressed and said that, with training, I could balance for 5 seconds, which would put me in the national finals.

Next, Coach Jasper stacked some Dixie® cups on the dresser like a pyramid. He handed me a pile of rubber bands, which I shot at the pyramid. I knocked the whole thing down with two tries. He was overcome with emotion, actually hugging my dad, who had been standing there beaming as if I were a star football player.

As quickly as it has started, my try-out for the Pajama Olympics was over. Coach Jasper said I was really good, the best he had seen in years. He offered me a chance to represent my country and train at the Pajama Olympics Training Center. He said I would live there and go to school there, too, that this would open up a whole new world of possibilities to me.

My Dad put his arm around my shoulder and said, "I will miss you, but your country needs you. You can leave tomorrow."

So the next day, I got on a plane and flew to the Pajama Olympics Training Center in Featherbed, South Dakota. I have been here for a month now. I have met a lot of new friends who are training just like me, and we work out every night for four hours. We are training for Sports You Never Heard Of, but Coach Jasper says the whole world will know about them before long. The best part is I have a whole drawer full of new pajamas, and they look just like Coach Jasper's!

— *Kathryn Toten,* storyteller/author

Tennis Ball Handstands

Supplies

Three tennis balls

Directions

1. Have three kids at the same time do a handstand against a wall. Be sure all breakables are out of the way.

2. Place tennis balls on their left feet and see who can balance the longest, before the balls bounce!

Note: Take pictures of each group doing its handstands and make copies for each kid to surprise him later.

Age Adjustment: After putting the tennis balls on older kids' left feet, tell them to juggle their balls into the air, trying to catch them with their right feet.

Toothbrush Balance

Supplies

New toothbrushes (one per child)

Directions

1. Tell the children to make a fist with one hand, extend their index fingers, and balance their toothbrushes on them.

2. Have them put their other hands behind their backs and stand on one leg to see how long they can balance their toothbrushes.

Sure Shot Pyramid Smash

Supplies

Fifteen 5-ounce Dixie® cups
Masking tape
Twelve rubber bands

Optional: Set of cups and rubber bands in a plastic zipper bag

Directions

1. Stack the cups at the edge of a table, tops down, into a pyramid with five cups on the bottom row, then four, then three, two, and one on top.

2. With the masking tape, mark a starting line on the floor about 10 feet away from the pyramid.

3. Stand the kids behind the starting line and give each child three rubber bands to aim and shoot at the pyramid. *Caution:* Before shooting, be sure there is no one standing by the cups. Redo the pyramid between shots.

4. Give each child a turn, but be prepared to go through this game more than once.

Note: You need a dozen rubber bands because some will get shot "out of sight."

Optional: Give the kids a point for every cup that falls off the table. Highest score wins his own set of cups and rubber bands in a plastic zipper bag!

Age Adjustment: For *younger,* less-experienced rubber band shooters, move the line up about 5 feet. For *older,* more-experienced shooters, move the line back 5 feet.

King of the Mountain Nachos

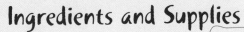

Ingredients and Supplies

Tortilla chips
Large microwavable plate
Grated cheddar cheese
Chunky salsa

Optional: Small paper plates, refried beans, cooked ground beef, sliced black olives, guacamole, and sour cream

Directions

1. Lay out the tortilla chips on the large microwavable plate, stacking them high.

2. Generously sprinkle the grated cheddar cheese over the chips.

3. Pour the chunky salsa over the top.

4. Microwave your King of the Mountain Nachos 1 to 2 minutes to melt the cheese.

Optional: Let the kids make up individual plates of nachos with their choice of ingredients. Microwave each plate 30 seconds to 1 minute.

Sport Swing Drink

Ingredients and Supplies

Makes one

24 inches yarn
20-ounce sport drink
with screw cap

Glue gun
1-inch pom-pom

Directions

1. Wind one end of the yarn around the neck of the bottle. Glue to secure.

2. Glue the other end of the yarn to the pom-pom.

3. When the drink is empty, have the child try to swing the pom-pom into the bottle.

Toothpaste Taste Test

Supplies

Aluminum foil

Five different kinds toothpaste

Crayons (one per child, plus one extra)

8½-inch square piece plain paper (one per child, plus one extra)

Directions

1. Wrap foil around each tube of toothpaste so no one can see any of the writing or colors on the tubes. You'll need to take the caps off.

2. Give each child a crayon and piece of paper, and have them trace their non-writing hand, palm side up, onto the paper. Trace your own hand the same way with the extra crayon and piece of paper.

3. Have everyone number the fingers on their drawings starting with the pinkie as #1, the ring finger as #2, and so on, ending with the thumb as #5. Number your drawing the same way.

4. Squirt a glob out of the first tube of toothpaste onto the children's real pinkie fingers. Then peek under the foil and write the name of the toothpaste onto your drawing (#1 - pinkie), without letting the children see the name.

5. Have the kids taste the toothpaste on their pinkies, then write what kind they think it is on their drawings (#1 - pinkies).

8. Do the same with each toothpaste until you've gone through all five kinds.

7. The one with the most right wins. Put the tubes in the bathroom for the kids to use later.

Age Adjustment: Have older kids write down the name of the toothpaste and any slogan or jingle that goes along with it.

Team Pillow Toss

Supplies

Three blankets
Three pillows without cases
Black permanent marker

Poster board
Masking tape

Directions

1. Fold each blanket to the exact size of the pillows.

2. Divide the kids into teams of no more than five per team, then number the teams.

3. Draw one column per team on the poster board, numbering the columns to correspond to the team numbers.

4. Place a starting line on the floor with masking tape. Set the blankets 5 feet from the tape.

5. Give one child from Team #1 a pillow to toss. Tell him the object is to land it directly onto any of the blankets. Give him two more shots with the two other pillows.

6. Write down his score for his team as follows:

   10 points for landing a pillow completely on top of a blanket with no part overhanging

   1 point for each corner of a pillow on the blanket

7. Have one child from Team #2 play, then one from Team #3, and back to Team #1 and so on until all the children have played.

8. Add up the scores. The winning team members get first choice at where they want to sleep when it's time to lay out sleeping bags.

Age Adjustment: Older kids may need the line moved farther back.

Video Recommendations

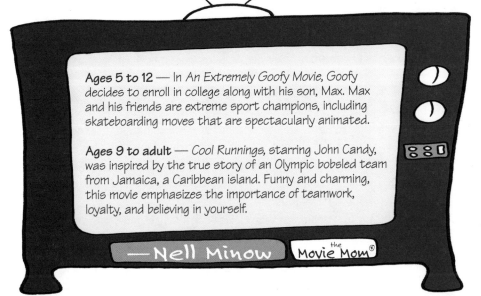

Ages 5 to 12 — In *An Extremely Goofy Movie*, Goofy decides to enroll in college along with his son, Max. Max and his friends are extreme sport champions, including skateboarding moves that are spectacularly animated.

Ages 9 to adult — *Cool Runnings*, starring John Candy, was inspired by the true story of an Olympic bobsled team from Jamaica, a Caribbean island. Funny and charming, this movie emphasizes the importance of teamwork, loyalty, and believing in yourself.

—Nell Minow the Movie Mom®

Midnight Snack Attack

Trail mix

Granola bars

Apple and orange slices

String cheese

Slim Jim brand meat sticks

Gu® (found at sports stores)

75

Breakfast of Champs

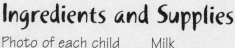

Ingredients and Supplies

Photo of each child

Glue stick

Individual boxes of
cereal (one per
child, plus extra)

Milk

Bowls (one per child)

Spoons (one per child)

Knife

Bananas (one per
every two children)

Plate

Option 1: Polaroid
camera

Option 2: Large
boxes of cereal

Directions

1. Before the party, secretly collect photos of your party guests from their parents. Make sure they don't want them back. (A "trading card" from a sport would be perfect.) Glue the photos onto the individual cereal boxes.

2. When it is time to eat, stack the cereal boxes in a pyramid shape so the photos are all facing out.

3. Set up milk, bowls, and spoons nearby.

4. Slice the bananas in half (without peeling them) and place them on a plate.

5. Let the kids open their personal Breakfast of Champs boxes carefully, so they can save the boxes, then dump the contents into their bowls. Some kids may not like their kind of cereal so let them choose from the extra boxes.

6. If need be, help them slice up their bananas onto their bowls of cereal before pouring on the milk and digging in!

Note: Some kids will want to cut the dotted lines on their boxes to use them as bowls, so explain to them that doing so might ruin their pictures.

Option 1: Take a Polaroid picture of each child as he arrives at the party.

Option 2: Have large boxes of cereal for the extras.

Slipper Flings

Supplies

Pillowcase

Soft slippers
(three or more
pairs)

Pen
Paper

New pair of
slippers

Directions

1. Have two adults stand in an area without any breakables and hold open the pillowcase. Line up the slippers 10 feet away from the pillowcase.

2. Have a child put on all the pairs of slippers, one pair at a time, and try to fling them, one foot at a time, into the pillowcase. Write down his name and score, 1 point per slipper in the pillowcase.

3. Line up the slippers again and have a second child go and so on until all the children have had a turn.

4. The one with the highest score wins. If there is a tie, have a "fling-off" until there is a winner who gets the new pair of slippers.

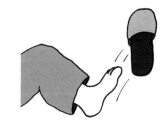

Twenty Extra Fun Ideas

1. Play soccer using a balloon instead of a ball, and laundry baskets for the goals.

2. CAREFULLY go floor skiing, sliding with slippery socks across a wooden floor.

3. Toss rubber bands, trying to ring them around a broom handle.

4. Play Frisbee with heavy paper plates.

5. Take a trip through Coney Island by riding bikes around orange construction cones.

6. Push hardboiled eggs across the floor with your nose.

7. Play Cotton Bowl football by blowing cotton balls with a straw across a table.

8. Bowl by lining up paper cups in bowling pin formations, then bowling them down with oranges.

9. Create, name, and play a new sports game using a broom, a hula-hoop, and a beach ball.

10. See how well you can juggle odd-shaped items such as toothbrushes.

11. Toss playing cards into a bucket.

12. See how many jump ropes you can tie together and twirl, and how many kids can jump at once.

13. Play mini-league baseball using a miniature bat and a ping-pong ball.

14. Play musical sleeping bags by walking around the bags and jumping into them when the music is turned off. The kid without a bag is out.

15. Play lava jump by setting up a lava flow with furniture in your house. The object is to jump from one piece of furniture to another without falling into the river of lava.

16. Have fun playing Slumber Party dodge ball by hiding behind pillows, blankets, and sleeping bags and then hitting others with tennis balls.

17. Mark a long line on the floor with masking tape, then do somersaults and cartwheels staying on the line.

18. Draw a circle with chalk outside and do the "circle squeeze," seeing how many kids can fit into the circle.

19. Play popcorn basketball by tossing popcorn into paper cups with holes cut out of them.

20. If your dog is super friendly, play tag and make him "it"!

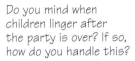

Do you mind when children linger after the party is over? If so, how do you handle this?

"Yes! I offer to drop those children off at home. My husband, on the other hand, will entertain those kids with a game of touch football."

—Laura H. Siegel
Englewood, Colorado

Sports You've Never Heard Of Pom-Pom Game Invitation

Glue gun
12 inches yarn
(per invitation)
Twelve toilet paper tubes
Twelve 1½-inch pom-poms
Copy paper
Pen
Scissors
Glue stick

Hanger Hammock

Wire hanger
Wire cutters
Pliers
Scissors
24 inches curling ribbon
Net bag (from vegetables or fruit)
Three tennis balls
Glue gun
Two 14 mm moving eyes
Doll hair (found at craft stores)
Pen
½ x 3-inch strip paper
Tennis racquet swizzle stick (found at liquor or kitchen stores)

Tennis Ball Handstands

Three tennis balls

Toothbrush Balance

New toothbrushes (one per child)

Sure Shoot Pyramid Smash

Fifteen 5-ounce Dixie® cups
Masking tape
Twelve rubber bands
Optional: Set of cups and rubber bands in a plastic zipper bag

King of the Mountain Nachos

Tortilla chips
Large microwavable plate
Grated cheddar cheese
Chunky salsa
Optional: Small paper plates, refried beans, cooked ground beef, sliced black olives, guacamole, and sour cream

Sport Swing Drink

24 inches yarn
20-ounce sport drink with screw cap
Glue gun
1-inch pom-pom

Toothpaste Taste Test

Aluminum foil
Five different kinds toothpaste
Crayons (one per child, plus one extra)
8½-inch square piece plain paper (one per child, plus one extra)

Team Pillow Toss

Three blankets
Three pillows without cases
Black permanent marker
Poster board
Masking tape

Midnight Snack Attack

Trail mix
Granola bars
Apple and orange slices
String cheese
Slim Jim brand meat sticks
Gu® (found at sport stores)

Breakfast of Champs

Photo of each child
Glue stick
Individual boxes of cereal (one per child, plus extra)
Milk
Bowls (one per child)
Spoons (one per child)
Knife
Bananas (one per every two children)
Plate
Option 1: Polaroid camera
Option 2: Large boxes of cereal

Slipper Flings

Pillowcase
Soft slippers (three or more pairs)
Pen
Paper
New pair of slippers

Don't forget the camera and film

CHAPTER SEVEN

The Hunt

What do scavenger hunters, rebus busters, and riddleologists all have in common? Fun at your party where they will hunt out everything from triplets to bagels. You'll start their brain juices flowing by giving them their very own Tip Books for Riddleologists. Keep them pumped by taking them to an indoor mall to play Shop-Til-You-Drop Scavenger Hunt. After spending time "shopping," they'll need to go Riddling for Gold. And what else will get them to settle down to watch a video or two but the promise of chocolate in Name That Candy Bar? Even the morning routine is filled with a Fun Breakfast Hunt that will make them always want to come back to your parties for more!

The Hunt Invitation

Supplies

Makes 12

Twelve paper lunch bags
Copy paper (any color)

Stapler
Pen

Directions

1. Make twelve copies of the pattern pieces on this page and page 81, and cut out: the rebus card (pattern #1) and the clue cards (patterns #2 to #7).

2. Staple each rebus card (secret message) onto the front of a lunch bag. The rebus says, *I hope you can come.*

3. On the back of the smiley face clue card (pattern #2), write *Party Given By* (your name) *for* (speccial occassion).

4. On the back of the sleeping bag (pattern #3), write *The Hunt Slumber Party.*

5. On the back of the sun (pattern #4) write *Day* (day) and *Date* (date) of your party.

6. On the watch (#5), write *Drop-off Time* (time) and *Pick-up Time* (time).

7. On the house (#6), write *Address* and *Directions* (fill in). Include a small map if needed.

8. On the telephone (#7), write *RSVP* (your phone number).

9. Put all six clue cards in the lunch bag.

10. Repeat steps #2 to #9 for each invitation.

11. Hunt down your friends to hand deliver your invitations.

Variation: You may want to write all the information on the clue cards behind the rebus card just in case one of the clue cards gets lost.

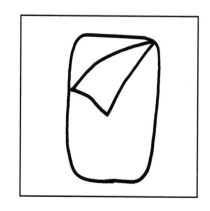

Pattern #2

Pattern #3

Pattern #4

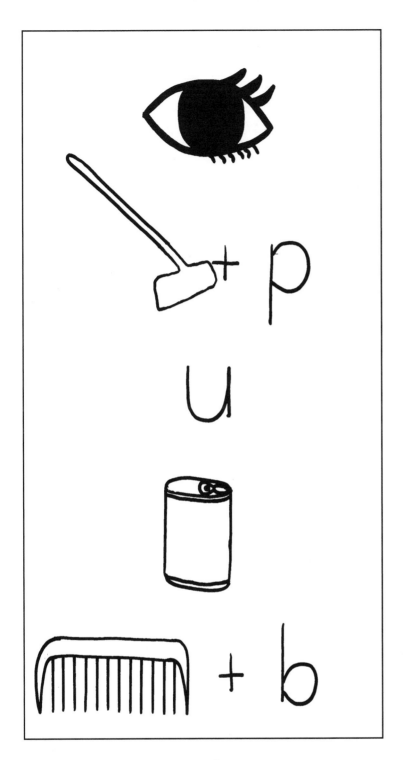

Pattern #1

Pattern #5

Pattern #6

Pattern #7

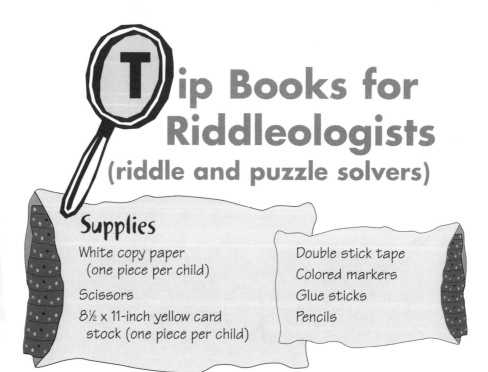

Tip Books for Riddleologists
(riddle and puzzle solvers)

Supplies

White copy paper
(one piece per child)

Scissors

8½ x 11-inch yellow card
stock (one piece per child)

Double stick tape

Colored markers

Glue sticks

Pencils

Directions

1. Make copies of the Tips and the License on page 83, one per child,
   and cut out separately.

2. Fold the card stock in half widthwise, press firmly on the crease, then open
   up the card stock.

3. Lay a piece of double stick tape along the crease line, on the right side,
   from the top to the bottom.

4. Lay the left edge of the License on the tape at the bottom, then lay another
   strip of tape on the left edge of the License.

5. Close the Tip Book and press firmly along the entire crease to seal the tape.

6. Open the book without breaking the seal, bend the front cover back to where
   the seal starts, and crease it to create a "binding."

7. Then bend the License back toward the front cover and crease at the binding.

8. Glue the Tips from step #1 onto the right inside of the book, lifting the
   License out of the way if needed.

9. Choose a marker to draw a picture of yourself on the Riddleologist License,
   then use a pencil to fill in the details. Be sure to sign in to make it official.

10. Choose a marker and write on the front cover: Tip Book for Riddleologists.

11. On the left inside of the book, draw a light pencil line widthwise to divide
    the page in half. Choose a marker and draw the top half of your body above
    the pencil line.

12. Choose another marker and draw the bottom of your body below
    the pencil line, except with your other hand. This will be hard, but
    drawing with the hand you don't normally write with will help you
    use both sides of your brain, which is what Riddleologists do!

13. Autograph your picture with either hand.

Age Adjustment: You may need to help younger children with the
double stick tape.

(10) Tips for Riddleologists

1. Always read the riddle twice.
2. Look for clues in the riddle itself.
3. Give lots of answers before choosing one.
4. Give answers you know aren't right. This will clear your head to find the right answer.
5. Think like a Riddleologist, logically at first, then creatively.
6. Think of the letter "X." This makes your brain cross over from the left side (the logical part) to the right side (the creative part).
7. Laugh and have fun. You won't get stressed-out and you'll think better.
8. Eat brain food, such as fish, and drink lots of water.
9. Believe in yourself and trust your intuition.
10. Stick with it. YOU CAN DO IT!

Follow these tips and you earn your Riddleologist License.

Riddleologist License

Expires when you don't use the tips!

Name _____

Address _____

City, State, Zip Code _____

Phone Number _____

Height and Weight_____

Signature _____

Date Issued _____

Mall Hunt

Ray wanted to find the perfect birthday gift for his mother. Amy, his cousin, was a much better shopper than he, so he asked her to go to the mall with him to help. They looked at the usual things: scented candles, hand lotion, and bubble bath. But this time, Ray wanted to give his mother something really unusual.

They stopped for a snack. Ray slurped his root beer float while Amy dipped each of her fries in ketchup, licking the ketchup off before eating them. She always did this when she was deep in thought.

Ray was getting discouraged. "Maybe I should just buy my mom a giant cookie and get it over with," he said.

"Shhh!" said Amy. She was listening to the radio station that was broadcasting from the mall that day. "I just heard something!" She grabbed her cousin by the sleeve and said, "Come on!"

Gator Radio, WGTR, was giving away a giant stuffed alligator to the first team to finish a scavenger hunt. "Now that's an unusual birthday gift," Amy said as they ran toward the center court of the mall.

"You're right, and my mom loves Gator Radio. She'd love to have a giant stuffed alligator!" Ray and Amy got a copy of the scavenger hunt, along with about twenty other teams. The DJ counted down… 10, 9, 8… 3, 2, 1, and the teams were off.

Ray was in charge of reading their list. "We have to find a coin from one of our birth years, a candy wrapper, a comb with a missing tooth, a broken shoelace, a dead battery, and then someone wearing the same item of clothing as one of us. Wow, Amy, this is going to be tough."

"Of course it is, but we can do it. Let's get going."

Ray and Amy stopped everyone at the bottom of the escalator. A lady found a gum wrapper in her purse, but not a candy wrapper, and she had a brush, not a comb. No one they asked had coins from their birth years. They decided to ask a store clerk to check for that.

After two different clerks told Ray and Amy they were too busy to help them, and no one seemed to have candy wrappers or be eating candy at the moment, Ray realized they could buy a candy bar and ask the store clerk to check the coins. It worked! They got a candy wrapper and a coin back that matched his birth year!

Now they just needed a comb with a missing tooth, a broken shoelace, a dead battery, and someone wearing the same item of clothing as one of them, but they'd used up so much precious time already.

Then Amy saw a line of people at the movie theater. "A captive audience," she told Ray. An older boy from Ray's school heard them asking for broken combs and shoelaces. "Hey, kid, you need this?" he asked.

Amy poked Ray in the ribs with her elbow. "Go see what he has," she said.

Ray had never talked to him before, but he decided to get over it since he really wanted the giant stuffed alligator for his mom. "Do you have a broken comb or shoelace?" he gulped. "We're on a scavenger hunt."

"Just look down, kid."

Ray couldn't believe it! The older boy had a broken shoelace! "Can I have it?" he asked. "I can buy you some new shoelaces."

"Just go stand in that line over there and get me a small Coke," the older boy said, "and the shoelace is yours."

"Thanks," said Ray. "I'll be right back." He ran by Amy to tell her the good news and since she was almost done with the people in line, she decided to try a different tactic.

"I'll be over at that watch kiosk," she told Ray. She remembered her dad needing a new watch battery once and getting one at a shop.

"Hi," she said to the clerk. "You wouldn't happen to have any dead watch batteries, would you? We're doing this scavenger hunt…"

"Say no more," the clerk said. "I was wondering when someone would ask me!" As he handed Amy a dead battery, he explained that he had heard the announcement from Gator Radio and wished he could have joined in the fun.

Ray found Amy, showed each other their prizes, but wasted no time getting the last items on their list. They still needed a broken comb and someone wearing the same item of clothing as one of them. These would be hard.

"Well," Ray said, remembering the candy bar, "we could always buy a new comb and break it." Just then a nice old gentleman on his daily walk around the mall tapped him on the shoulder.

"I hear you need a broken comb, young man," he said.

"Yes, sir," replied Ray. "Do you have one?"

"No, but I can make you one!" He pulled out his comb from his back pocket, broke off a tooth, and said, "I don't have that much hair left anyway to comb."

"Thank you, sir, thanks a lot!" The man smiled and went on his way.

"Wow, that was nice," Ray said, but noticed that Amy wasn't even listening to him.

"How much money do you have left, Ray?"

"Twenty dollars. Why?"

"I remember seeing a T-shirt just like yours down that way. Buy it for me, and the stuffed gator is yours!"

"That's a great idea, Amy!" The two of them raced to the store, bought the shirt, and ran to the radio station. Amy was pulling her new shirt over her head and bumping into people along the way, so Ray ran ahead. He was the first one back to the DJ.

Ray showed the DJ the coin and his school ID with his birthday on it. He showed him the the candy wrapper, the broken shoelace, and the watch battery. The DJ had a battery tester, and sure enough, it had no zing whatsoever.

"Looks like you almost have it, kid," the DJ said. "Where is someone wearing the same item of clothing as you?"

"I'm right here!" Amy came running up, grinning from ear to ear.

"Congratulations!" the DJ said. "The gator is yours. What are you going to do with it?"

"Am I on the air?" Ray asked. "Cuz it's a surprise."

"Okay, then I'll cover the mic and you can whisper it."

"It's a birthday gift for my mom. She loves Gator Radio," beamed Ray.

"Well, I guess that is a surprise. We'll keep your name and what you're doing with it a secret, then." Then the DJ covered the mic again and said to Ray, "and I'll just have to play your mom a song on her special day."

"Wow," said Ray. "Thanks a lot."

As Ray and Amy struggled to the escalator with the giant stuffed alligator, they wondered where Ray could hide it from his mom.

"At least I got her the perfect gift this year. Thanks for all your help, Amy. You're almost as good at scavenger hunts as you are at shopping!"

—Kathryn Totten, *storyteller/author*

The makers of Fritos® Corn Chips, Frito Lay, sell their products all over the world, yet most of their farmers are in Illinois and Nebraska.

Chili-in-a-Bag

Ingredients and Supplies

Makes one

Individual size bag Fritos® Corn Chips

½ cup chili (homemade or store-bought)

Serving spoon

3 tablespoons shredded cheddar cheese

1 tablespoon chopped onion

Spoon

Directions

1. Carefully open the top of the Fritos® bag, without ripping it.

2. Cook or warm the chili then spoon into the bag, on top of the Fritos®.

3. Sprinkle the shredded cheese on top of the chili.

4. Sprinkle chopped onions over the cheese. Be sure to ask the child if he wants onions.

5. Serve the Chili in a Bag with a spoon, telling the child to hunt for the surprise (chips) inside.

Mint Milkshake Hunt

Ingredients and Supplies

Makes one

1 cup vanilla ice cream

¼ cup milk

½ teaspoon mint extract

Blender

One Oreo® chocolate sandwich cookie

12-ounce cup

Spoon

Straw

Directions

1. Put the ice cream, milk, and mint extract into a blender. Mix until thick and creamy.

2. Put the Oreo® cookie in the bottom of the cup, pour the milkshake on top, and serve with the spoon and straw.

3. Let each child "hunt" for an edible surprise in the bottom of his cup.

Shop-Til-You-Drop Scavenger Hunt

Play this game in an indoor mall

Supplies

Computer
Printer paper

Watch (one per team)
Pens (one per team)

Directions

1. Type the Scavenger Hunt Items below on the computer and print one per team.

2. Take the kids to an indoor mall with adults for chaperons, and divide them into teams of three to five. A good place to start and end is in the center court.

3. Give one person on each team a watch and synchronize the times. Give another person on each team a copy of the list and a pen.

4. Explain that they have one hour to get as many points as they can by having the items (which are people) sign their lists. The point values are after each item. The team with the highest points wins.

5. The bonus points only count if they have found all the other items, but they can get the bonus items signed when they find them.

6. Tell the kids the following rules and any others you think apply. Be firm: If the rules are not followed, everyone will go home before finishing the game.

RULE 1: Do not be rude to anyone.

RULE 2: Do not interrupt business, anyone buying or selling.

RULE 3: Do not go near any exits or doors leading outside or to other parts of the mall, such as ones that read "Employees Only."

RULE 4: Do not run.

RULE 5: Do not be overly loud.

RULE 6: Report any strange problems to me or the nearest mall employee.

RULE 7: No cheating. You are on the honor system.

Note: Be sure parents know you will be taking their kids to a mall.

Variation: Send someone from another team with each team to prevent cheating.

Age Adjustment: For *younger* children, have an adult go with each team similar to adults going with children door-to-door selling items to supervise.

> Tell us about your favorite Slumber Party?
>
> "We had a scavenger hunt and then made things out of the stuff we had gotten. We designed an outfit out of toilet paper and played a bunch of games. One of my favorite games was when Mom hid something in a paper bag. Everyone knew what was in the bag except the person that was 'selling it.' They had to try to sell it with a commercial and everyone got to ask them questions. It was fun."
>
> —Kristi Lackey, age 12 Normandy Park, Washinton

Scavenger Hunt Items

Have the person you find sign next to each item

Someone with red hair - 2

Someone pushing a baby in a stroller - 3

Someone wearing a (your sports team) anything - 3

Someone wearing boots - 4

Someone carrying a (store at the mall) bag - 2

Someone with a beard - 1 (Not Santa!)

Someone wearing glasses - 2

Someone wearing anything (the closest holiday) - 3

Person sitting on a bench - 1

Someone throwing a coin into a fountain - 3 (Omit if no fountain.)

Someone using an elevator - 3 (Omit if no elevator.)

Someone eating or drinking something - 1

Someone chewing gum - 2

A couple holding hands - 4

A lady with pink nail polish - 3

Bonus Scavenger Hunt Items

Santa's or the Easter Bunny's autograph - 12

Twins - 8

Triplets or more - 16

Someone taking a picture - 10

Someone with a pet - 6

Riddling for Gold, Blindfold

Supplies

Black permanent marker

Strips of paper

Masking tape

Pots of chocolate gold coins
(one per team)

Tip Books for Riddleologists
(see page 82)

Blindfolds
(one per team)

Directions

1. Before the party, decide how many teams you want moving around your house and choose names for them from the following: Beam Team, Cream Team, Dream Team, Gleam Team, Scheme Team, Steam Team, and Theme Team.

2. Decide how many of the riddles (see page 89) to use per team. Use the same amount but different ones as they may hear them getting solved. Write the riddles on separate strips of paper, without the answers *(in blue)*.

3. Fold them in half and label each team's riddles with their name and a number. For example: Steam Team #1, Steam Team #2, and so on. Keep in mind that riddle #1 leads to the answer for #2 and so on.

4. Tape the riddles, except riddle #1's, around the house in the correct places *(the answers)*. Don't put them in the main party room or let the kids see you. Perhaps ask another parent or an older child to do this during one of the previous activities. Place the pots of chocolate gold coins at the end of each riddle trail.

5. To begin, ask the kids to bring their Tip Books for Riddleologists to the main party room. Divide them into teams and tell them their names. Tell them to use their Tip Books to solve the riddle you will give them, which in turn will lead them to their #2 riddle and so on until they will find a big surprise.

6. Tell the team members they have to stay close together, to work as a team and help each other. Then blindfold one member on each team to make sure they stay together and don't run too fast around the house.

7. Give the teams their #1 riddles, telling them to not open them yet. Remind them that they can only read their own riddles and in the correct order. You can always send an adult or older child with each team to make sure they follow this rule.

8. Let the Riddling for Gold, Blindfold begin!

Note: Be sure to have lots of chocolate gold coins in the pots so each child can have several.

Variation 1: You can play this game with no blindfolds, but kids will be hurrying around the house and some may get left out or hurt.

Variation 2: If you have a small house, you may double up where you put the riddles, but each team will need their own riddles to solve.

Age Adjustment: For older children, choose more riddles to solve or blindfold everyone except the "readers of the riddles."

Riddles

1. I'm big, flat, and you sleep with me. Soft pillows, blankets, and sheets stay with me. ***Mattress***

2. You sit at me daily. I hide your knees. Say excuse me to leave if you please. ***Kitchen Table***

3. You turn me on and warm me up. Cold food I am not. ***Oven***

4. I clean you up day and night. I have a mirror for such a beautiful sight. ***Bathroom***

5. I welcome you and all your guests. I have a bell that visitors press. ***Front Door***

6. I open in the morning, close by night. On sunny days, I let in light. ***Window*** (Add a clarifier here to identify what room you want them in, such as: P.S. You sleep by me, or P.S. You wash dishes by me.)

7. I hide most anything and lots of junk, clothing mostly, and they hang a lot. ***Closet***

8. Rub-a-dub-dub, you're soaking in me. Please don't fall, I'm slippery. ***Bathtub***

9. I'm typically full after dinner, just like you. After washing and drying I'll be empty, too. ***Kitchen Sink***

10. You brush at me daily morn, noon, and night, along with soaping your hands for a healthy life. ***Bathroom Sink***

11. I am so cool, you use me a lot, for milk and eggs, veggies, and pop. ***Refrigerator***

12. I cover you when you're indoors. You must look up and not at the floor. ***Ceiling***

13. You watch movies on me and lots of cartoons, and everyday the evening news. ***TV***

14. I'm always downstairs, never up. Sometimes I'm finished, sometimes not. ***Basement***

15. I'm never inside. I can be cold, wet, or hot. Sometimes the wind blows, sometimes not. ***Outside***

16. I'm in most every house but have my own mouse. Sometimes fish are seen to protect my screen. ***Computer***

17. I'm at all family dinners, I have chairs galore, and when the holidays are here, I can seat even more. ***Dining Room Table***

18. I'm soft and pillowy. Several people can sit on me. I can be in any room but you can find me in the living room. ***Sofa***

19. You can take me up or you can take me down, but I never move around. ***Stairs*** P.S. Some say I "stare" a lot.

20. You can lean on me and slide on me. And often you see through me. ***Handrail*** P.S. You'll never "stare" without me.

21. I'm outside your front door and I rhyme with torch. ***Front Porch***

22. I am a place with many doors and in this place your cars are stored. ***Garage***

23. I'm attached to the house, outside the door. I'm not just a build-on, I am also grilled on. ***Deck***

24. We're usually white sitting side-by-side. We wash and we dry and we love that Tide®. ***Washer and Dryer***

25. I'm found in the kitchen and I heat real fast, with buttons and timers and see-through glass. ***Microwave***

Scavenger hunts used to be all fun and games. But teachers now hold Internet scavenger hunts for their students because it's easy and fun for them to find knowledge facts online.

Name That Candy Bar

Ingredients and Supplies

Assorted candy bars
(one per two children)

Aluminum foil
Pen

Sticky notes
Small bowl

Sharp knife

Directions

1. Before the party, unwrap all the candy bars, cut each into four smaller candy bars, and rewrap them with aluminum foil. Write the name of the candy bars on sticky notes and attach to the smaller bars underneath, as explained in step #3.

2. When it's time to play, use the toothpick to poke five holes into the top of the foil of each bar, so you can smell the candy. DO NOT do this sooner as the aroma will be lost.

3. Have the kids sit in a long line and line up the candy bars on the floor in front of them, sticky notes underneath. Hand the first child in line a candy bar, without the sticky note. Give him one guess, without feeling, squeezing, or unwrapping it, to Name That Candy Bar by its smell. If he gets it, he gets the candy bar and can eat it then or save it for later.

4. If he doesn't guess the candy bar, he hands it to the next child in line who tries to win it and so on until the candy bar is won. If the candy bar can't be guessed, put it in the bowl for any child that doesn't win as in step #6.

5. Hand a second candy bar to the second child in line, without the sticky note, and play until that candy bar is won. If needed, pass it to the first child in line, but stop it where it started.

6. Continue playing until all the candy bars have gone through the line-up. Let the children who didn't win one, choose one from the bowl.

Midnight Snack Attack

Cracker Jacks®
(hunt for the prize)

Tootsie Roll® Pops
(hunt for the soft center)

Hostess® Twinkies®
(hunt for the creamy center)

Cheese hotdogs
(hunt for the cheese)

General Mills Lucky Charms®
(hunt for the marshmallow shapes)

Jelly donuts
(hunt for the jelly)

Video Recommendations

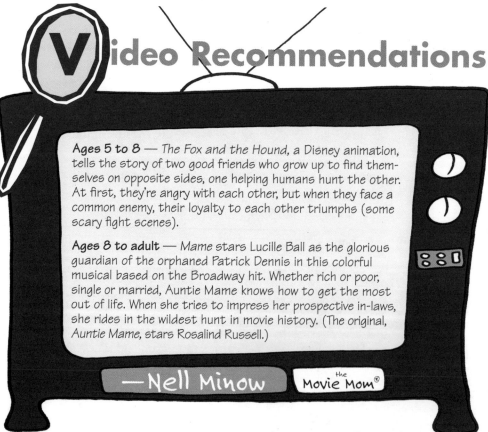

Ages 5 to 8 — *The Fox and the Hound*, a Disney animation, tells the story of two good friends who grow up to find themselves on opposite sides, one helping humans hunt the other. At first, they're angry with each other, but when they face a common enemy, their loyalty to each other triumphs (some scary fight scenes).

Ages 8 to adult — *Mame* stars Lucille Ball as the glorious guardian of the orphaned Patrick Dennis in this colorful musical based on the Broadway hit. Whether rich or poor, single or married, Auntie Mame knows how to get the most out of life. When she tries to impress her prospective in-laws, she rides in the wildest hunt in movie history. (The original, *Auntie Mame*, stars Rosalind Russell.)

—Nell Minow the Movie Mom®

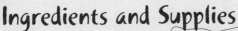un Breakfast Hunt

Ingredients and Supplies

Breakfast foods such as bacon and eggs, pancake mix and syrup, cereal and milk, bread and bagels, cereal bars, and juice

Cooking supplies such as pots and pans, whips and spatulas, toaster or toaster oven, plates and bowls, silverware and glasses

Directions

1. Before the kids wake up, hide all the breakfast ingredients and "supplies in different places so your child will also have to hunt as in step #2. *Caution:* Don't hide things up high if you're worried about kids climbing.

2. Let the children go on their Fun Breakfast Hunt, choosing what they want and preparing their items themselves.

Note: Be nearby to assist, especially for safety reasons.

Age Adjustment: Younger children will need help preparing most of their breakfast, but will have fun going on their hunt.

1. bathrobe
2. brush
3. breakfast
4. camera
5. campout
6. candy
7. comb
8. dark
9. dream
10. early bird
11. flashlight
12. food
13. fortunes
14. friends
15. fun
16. games
17. giggles
18. goodnight
19. late
20. memories
21. midnight snack attack
22. morning
23. movies
24. music
25. noise
26. night light
27. night owl
28. pajamas
29. party
30. pillow fight
31. popcorn
32. psst
33. quiet
34. rise 'n' shine
35. scary stories
36. sleeping bags
37. sleepover
38. slippers
39. slumber
40. snorer
41. stars
42. stuffed animal
43. tag
44. time to wake up
45. tired
46. toothbrush
47. toothpaste
48. tv
49. videos
50. whisper

Slumber Party Word Hunt

Supplies

Copies of word hunt
(one per child)

Pencils (one per child)

Directions

1. Give a copy of the word hunt and a pencil to each child.

2. Explain that the 50 words are hidden in the puzzle. They might be spelled forward, backward, up, down, or diagonally.

3. The object is to find as many as they can and circle them. If they don't find them all, they can always finish at home!

B	A	S	E	L	G	G	I	G	C	N	O	I	S	E
R	R	Z	G	I	O	L	E	O	A	M	A	E	R	D
E	E	S	R	A	T	S	M	O	V	T	G	R	B	B
A	M	S	L	U	M	B	E	R	S	U	P	A	R	A
K	A	L	A	V	U	B	D	S	G	T	O	M	U	T
F	C	E	T	I	S	S	U	A	A	H	P	I	S	H
A	N	E	S	D	I	A	M	M	B	G	C	D	H	R
S	I	P	D	E	C	E	V	A	G	I	O	N	C	O
T	G	O	N	O	S	E	J	J	N	F	R	I	A	B
G	H	V	E	S	F	P	V	A	I	W	N	G	M	E
O	T	E	I	E	R	T	P	P	P	O	R	H	P	R
O	O	R	R	I	Q	I	A	T	E	L	I	T	O	T
D	W	U	F	V	G	R	R	Y	E	L	S	U	I	M
N	L	P	A	O	E	E	T	A	L	I	E	N	T	T
I	T	A	S	M	O	D	Y	S	S	P	N	A	H	E
G	H	R	D	S	W	D	A	R	K	K	S	C	S	T
H	G	T	O	O	T	H	B	R	U	S	H	K	H	O
T	I	S	E	I	R	O	M	E	M	R	I	A	E	W
F	L	E	A	R	L	Y	B	I	R	D	N	T	T	A
O	H	R	U	J	Y	D	N	A	C	H	E	T	S	K
R	S	T	H	G	I	L	T	H	G	I	N	A	A	E
T	A	S	T	S	N	O	R	E	R	U	G	C	P	U
U	L	W	H	I	S	P	E	R	F	Q	F	K	H	P
N	F	S	T	G	N	I	N	R	O	M	S	O	T	P
E	S	C	A	R	Y	S	T	O	R	I	E	S	O	L
S	L	I	P	P	E	R	S	Q	U	I	E	T	O	L
S	T	L	A	M	I	N	A	D	E	F	F	U	T	S

Twenty Extra Fun Ideas

1. Have a scavenger hunt around the neighborhood.

2. Hunt for anthills.

3. Turn off the lights. Have one guest be "it" and all the others switch places. "It" has to feel their heads and faces to guess who they are.

4. Hunt for pennies in a pile of sand.

5. Hunt for the most colorful item in the house.

6. Hunt through old photographs and tell a story about your favorite one.

7. Hunt through magazines for your favorite person.

8. Go to a thrift store and have the kids hunt for the best toy they can find for $1.00 or less.

9. Put six hardboiled eggs and six uncooked eggs (all in the shell) in a bowl. Hunt for the hard boiled eggs by seeing how they spin differently.

10. If this is a birthday party, have the guests hide their presents so your child will have to hunt them down.

11. Send the birthday child on a treasure hunt for his cake.

12. Hide everyone's shoes, or slippers, the right in a different place than the left, and send the kids to hunt for them. First one back with both his shoes wins.

13. Play hide 'n' go seek.

14. Hide some uncooked strands of spaghetti (needles) in a pile of cooked spaghetti (haystack), and let the kids go hunting.

15. Ask everyone to bring a riddle and solve them using their Tip Books for Riddleologists. (See page 82.)

16. Purchase a hidden picture book and give every child a page to do.

17. Play the alphabet game by giving each child a sheet of paper and a pencil. Let them go around the house finding objects that start with A, B, C, and so on. First one finished win.

18. If you have a large group, play Heads-Up, 7-Up. Choose seven players from the group. All the others get in their sleeping bags, put their heads down so their eyes are hidden, and put their right hands out in a fist with their thumbs up. When you call out "heads down, thumbs up." The seven players go around and push one thumb down. Then all seven say, "Heads-Up, 7-Up." Those with their thumbs down stand up and try to guess who pushed their thumbs down. If they guess right, they get to switch places.

19. Play charades.

20. Play Where's Your Partner? (See page 36, *Valentine School Parties…What Do I Do?*®)

The term "rebus" for a puzzle of pictures, or parts of words, may have come from the Latin phrase, non erbis sed rebus, which means "not by words but by things."

The Hunt Invitation

Twelve paper lunch bags
Copy paper (any color)
Stapler
Pen

Tip Books for Riddelologosts

White copy paper
  (one piece per child)
Scissors
8½ x 11-inch yellow
  card stock (one piece
  per child)
Double stick tape
Colored markers
Glue sticks
Pencils

Chili-in-a-Bag

Individual size bag
  Fritos® Corn Chips
½ cup chili (homemade or
  store-bought)
Serving spoon
3 tablespoons shredded
  cheddar cheese
1 tablespoon chopped onion
Spoon

Shop-Til-You-Drop Scavenger Hunt

Computer
Printer paper
Watch (one per team)
Pens (one per team)

Riddling For Gold, Blindfold

Black permanent marker
Strips of paper
Masking tape
Pots of chocolate gold
  coins (one per team)
Tip Books for Riddleologists
  (see page 82)
Blindfolds (one per team)

Don't forget the camera and film

Name That Candy Bar

Assorted candy bars
  (one per two children)
Sharp knife
Aluminum foil
Pen
Sticky notes
Small bowl

Midnight Snack Attack

Cracker Jacks®
  (hunt for the prize)
Tootsie Roll® Pops
  (hunt for the soft
  center)
Hostess® Twinkies®
  (hunt for the creamy
  center)
Cheese hotdogs
  (hunt for the cheese)
General Mills Lucky
  Charms® (hunt for the
  marshmallow shapes)
Jelly donuts (hunt for
  the jelly)

Fun Breakfast Hunt

Breakfast foods such
  as bacon and eggs,
  pancake mix and syrup,
  cereal and milk, bread
  and bagels, cereal bars,
  and juice
Cooking supplies such as
  pots and pans, whips
  and spatulas, toaster
  or toaster oven, plates
  and bowls, silverware
  and glasses

Slumber Party Word Hunt

Copies of word hunt
  (one per child)
Pencils (one per child)

CHAPTER EIGHT

Wedding Glamour

Invite your closest friends to spend the night as you get glamorous, dream about finding the perfect man, and trade beauty secrets for your special day. Pick up your guests in a limousine, take them to get their hair and nails done, or treat them to a "reception" at the local buffet restaurant. Play Wedding Designers, Something Old, Something New, Something Borrowed, Something Blue, and Kiss-the-Groom (using a poster of your favorite teen star). Learn how to make jewelry you can eat and paper flowers. Put them together for a bridal bouquet and toss it to see who gets to throw the next Slumber Party!

Wedding Glamour Pop-Up Invitation

Order of Wedding Glamour Party

Make Your Own Wedding Flowers

Eat dinner (Dress-the-Bride Dinner with Maid of Honor's Toast)

Read "A Perfect Life" (serve everyone an apple and a can of pop to take tab off like in story—put tab on a yarn necklace)

Become Wedding Designers (use your Wedding Flowers)

Play Kiss-the-Groom Game

Play Something Old, Something New, Something Borrowed, Something Blue

Get on pajamas and lay out sleeping bags

Watch videos with Midnight Snack Attack.

Sleep

Create Breakfast Jewelry

Brush teeth, get dressed, and pack

Throw birdseed as your guests leave

Supplies

Makes 12

Pencil

Twenty-four 3 x 5-inch unlined index cards

Scissors

Twelve 14-inch pieces ½" white lace

Glue gun

Tape

Twelve 4 x 5½-inch blank notecards with envelopes

White copy paper

Glue stick

Pen

Optional: Twelve stamped postcards

Directions

outside

1. For each invitation, trace and cut pattern pieces on page 97, onto two unlined index cards: wedding cake (pattern piece #1) onto one card, cake topper/bride and groom (pattern piece #2) and pop-up stand (pattern piece #3) onto the second card.

2. Cut a piece of white lace into four pieces to fit the four tiers of the wedding cake, then glue in place.

3. Tape the cake topper/bride and groom on top of the wedding cake (facing forward, same side as lace).

inside

4. Fold the pop-up stand along the fold lines, and tape the edges together, to form a cube. Tape side A of the pop-up stand to the back of the wedding cake (not the lace side) in the middle of the bottom edge.

5. Tape sides B and C to the inside fold of a blank notecard so the wedding cake pops up when the card is opened. Repeat steps #1 to #5 for each invitation.

6. Make twelve copies of the wedding banner (pattern piece #4) and the invitation, and cut all out. Use the glue stick to glue the banner to the front of each notecard and the invitation inside the cards below the wedding cake.

7. With the pen, fill in the details and deliver to your wedding guests.

Optional: If you'd like to include a reply card, insert self-addressed stamped postcards with the invitations. Have lines for "name," "can come," and "can't come."

Wedding Glamour Party!

Please come to my Slumber Party.

Party Given By: _____

Special Occasion: _____

Day and Date: _____

Drop-off Time: _____

Pick-up Time: _____

Address and Directions: _____

Phone Number: _____

Please call and tell me if you can come.

So why does a wedding cake almost always consist of tiers? Traditionally, the top tier is the bride and groom as newlyweds. The bottom tier stands for the family they will eventually have, and each tier in the middle represents one of their future children.

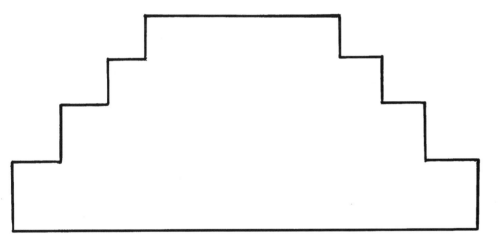

Pattern #1

Pattern #2

Pattern #3

A
B
C

Pattern #4

Wedding Glamour Party

Make Your Own Wedding Flowers

Supplies

Makes one

Eight 5 x 8-inch pieces white tissue paper

White pipe cleaner

Optional: White facial tissue

Pattern #1

Directions

1. Stack all eight sheets tissue paper directly on top of each other.

2. Fold the entire stack of tissue accordion-style.

3. Wind the pipe cleaner around the center of the folded tissue, leaving a "stem" to hold your flower.

4. Carefully unfold and fluff the tissue on both sides of the pipe cleaner until you have made a wedding flower.

Note: Make several flowers and twist the stems together for a bouquet. Create a colorful bouquet for bridesmaids by using different colors of tissue paper.

Optional: Use white facial tissue instead of tissue paper.

Pattern #2

Pattern #3

Maid of Honor's Toast

Serve this with dinner

So why do we call it a "toast" when we raise our glasses in honor of the bride and groom? In the sixteenth century, a small crust of bread would be put in a goblet of wine and passed around until it got to the person "of the moment," who would finish off the wine and eat the bread.

Ingredients and Supplies

Non-alcoholic champagne

Plastic champagne glasses (found at party stores)

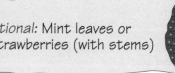

Optional: Mint leaves or strawberries (with stems)

Directions

1. Serve non-alcoholic champagne in plastic champagne glasses.

2. Have each girl take a turn making a toast as if she were the Maid of Honor.

Optional: Add mint leaves or strawberries (with stems) for an extra special drink.

Variation: Let each girl take a turn being the bride, too.

Dress-the-Bride Dinner

Ingredients and Supplies

Makes one
Knife
2 x 2½ x ½-inch chunk
   cheddar cheese

Two ½-inch slices
   salami (with skin)

Paper plate
Three pretzel sticks
Two black olives
   (pitted)
Butter knife

Thin slice mozzarella
cheese
Optional: Crackers
and mustard

Directions

1. Prepare one "bride" per girl before the party, leaving step #7 until it's time to eat.

2. Cut the cheddar cheese chunk into a bride's body as in the illustration. "Peel" one salami slice and cut it into two feet for the bride. Set aside the body and feet, and discard or eat any leftovers.

3. Slit the skin of the other salami slice (bride's head), then peel the skin back and partway up each side of the slice, for the bride's hair (a flip). Set the slice on the paper plate.

4. Carefully break one pretzel stick into three pieces. Insert one piece into the bottom of the head for the bride's neck. (Set the other pieces aside.) Insert the neck into the bride's body from step #2.

5. Insert the two remaining pretzel sticks (not pieces) into the sides of the body for the bride's arms. Slide the olives onto the ends of the arms for the bride's hands.

6. Insert the two remaining pretzel pieces from step #4 into the bottom of the bride's body for her legs. Insert the legs into the salami pieces from step #2 (bride's feet).

7. Let each girl use a butter knife to cut a slice of mozzarella cheese into a wedding dress that she places over the body (and as much of the neck, arms, and legs as she chooses) to Dress-the-Bride. Let the girls show off their brides before they eat them!

Tip: If the salami skin doesn't "flip" well in step #3, roll it up on a pencil.

Optional: Serve crackers and mustard on the side.

A Perfect Life

Cynthia turned the stem of her apple, one turn for each letter of the alphabet. "One...A...two...B...three...C..." Finally, after seven turns, the stem broke off. "G! My future husband's name will start with the letter G." She took a big bite of her apple and chewed it thoughtfully. "G" names ran through her head. "Gregory, no, that sounds too stuffy. George, no, that's too old fashioned. Gavin, Gus, Gabriel, Gray. Yes! That's it!" Cynthia smiled. In her perfect life, her husband's name would be Gray.

Monica sat down beside her and opened her can of juice. "What's up?" she asked. "You're smiling."

"I was just thinking about my future perfect life," she admitted. She put the apple stem in her skirt pocket. She planned to keep it, to show it to Gray after they were married.

"I want to live by the ocean," said Monica. "My house will be a little white cottage with a stone fence around it. My husband will be a fisherman and while he is out at sea, I will knit him thick sweaters. One day, he comes home with a single, perfect pearl. We can tell it is very valuable, but we don't want to sell it. Instead, we put it away in a little box and once a year, we have a special candlelight dinner. My husband takes out the pearl, gazes into my eyes, and tells me that even the pearl cannot compare to my beauty!"

Cynthia sighed, "That sounds soooo romantic!"

Amy sat down across from the dreaming girls and took a sandwich out of her brown paper bag. Taking a bite, she looked from Monica to Cynthia. "What?" she asked, with her mouth full.

"You would think it's stupid," said Monica. "You're not interested in romance."

"I'll tell you about romance," whispered Amy, bending forward so they could hear her.

"You?" asked Cynthia, raising her eyebrows. "I thought you just dreamed about horses."

"I do want to have lots of beautiful horses," continued Amy, "But...I will live on a ranch in Montana. One day, I see this rider. He's tan and has long wavy hair and a mustache. His horse sees a snake and throws him. I quickly ride over. I can see he's not too hurt, so I go after his horse. I manage to get the reins and gentle him, then I bring him back to this guy.

"He has dark brown eyes and I can't stop staring at him. He needs first aid, so I take him back to the ranch with me. After that, he rides over every day to bring me little gifts, help out with the horses, anything to be near me. We fall in love and get married. He sells his ranch for a fortune and together we build up my ranch until we have hundreds of horses, with barns and stables fit for a king and queen!"

"Why, Amy! I didn't know you had it in you!" said Cynthia.

"So tell us about your perfect life, Cynthia," said Monica, elbowing her. "By any chance, does it have something to do with that apple of yours? Where's the stem?"

Amy giggled.

Cynthia took one last bite of her apple. She fingered the stem in her skirt pocket. "My perfect life starts with a fabulously handsome man named Gray."

Both of her friends leaned in to hear.

"I will have a little boy and a little girl. We will live in a small house, in a small town, where we walk to town to do the shopping, and all the people mow their lawns at the same time on Saturdays. But one summer, Gray takes us on vacation to Scotland. He takes us to see beautiful old castles that are mostly crumbling ruins.

"Then we come to a castle that is still perfect. It has tapestries on the walls, huge fireplaces, servants to cook and clean, riding stables, and everything! He tells us we are going to stay the night. We dress up special for dinner. The children and I are sitting at this 10-foot long table with crystal and china. The servants are ready to serve us something that smells heavenly. Then Gray walks in wearing a kilt. He looks more handsome than ever!

"The butler pulls out the chair at the head of the table and calls Gray, 'My Lord.'

"Gray winks at me as he sits down. 'Do you like it here?' he asks.

"I smile and say, 'Yes, and the children love it, too.'

"'Good,' he says. 'This is my castle!'

"We stay forever and have everything we could ever want. Gray is totally rich!"

"Wow!" said Monica slowly. "You got all that from twisting the stem off your apple?"

"Uh-huh," nodded Cynthia, but she knew it was just her perfect imagination.

The bell rang for class and as they walked through the door, Cynthia tossed her apple core into the trash can, making sure the stem was still in her pocket.

—*Kathryn Totten*, storyteller/author

After reading "A Perfect Life," give the girls apples with stems, or cans of pop, and tell them to twist the stems off their apples, or the tabs off their cans of pop, while going through the alphabet. Let the girls make up stories about their future lives and share them with each other. (If you use cans of pop instead of apples, have strands of yarn ready for the girls to slip their tabs onto for necklaces.)

Wedding Designers

Supplies

Each team needs:

Three rolls white toilet paper

Ten white pipe cleaners

Lace (assorted sizes and types)

Paper

Pen

Optional: Father or older male

Directions

1. Divide the girls into teams of three or four. Choose one girl from each team to be a bride. The others will be the Wedding Designers.

2. Give each team a set of supplies.

3. Tell the designers to design and dress their bride in a wedding gown and veil or headdress. Tell them the following:

   • There will be a fashion show in one hour.

   • Consider the bride's feelings, but no idea is too wild.

   • They may only use the supplies you give them and anything already on the bride or themselves, but nothing else.

   • The wedding gown can be any length they choose.

   • They may make any kind of veil or headdress, but they must make something.

   • They have to write a description of the wedding gown and veil or headdress to be read during the fashion show.

4. Every 15 minutes, announce how much time is left. When you announce the last 15 minutes, be sure to remind the girls to write out their descriptions if they haven't done so.

5. At the end of the hour, hold a fashion show with each bride carrying the Wedding Flowers (see page 98) she and her designers made before dinner. As each bride walks "down the aisle," read the description of the gown and veil and headdress.

6. At the end, have the girls vote for their favorite design.

Optional: If a father or older male is at the party, have him walk the brides down the aisle.

Variation: If you have a staircase and enough room for the guests to watch from the bottom, have the brides come down it while playing or humming "The Wedding March," then read the description while they pose at the bottom of the stairs.

Kiss-the-Groom Game

Supplies

Pushpins
Poster of a "cute" guy (facing forward)

Lipstick (assorted colors)
Mirror

Blindfold
Facial tissue
Pen

Directions

1. Use pushpins to hang up the poster so it is eye level with the girls.

2. Let a girl choose a lipstick, then use the mirror to apply it.

3. Blindfold her, spin her around three times, direct her towards the poster, and let her kiss the "cute" guy where she thinks his lips are.

4. Un-blindfold her and give her a pen to write her name next to her lips. Give her a tissue to wipe off her lips.

5. Let each girl take a turn choosing a lipstick and kissing the poster.

6. The girl whose lips are closest to the guy's lips gets to keep the poster.

Note: If you're concerned about the girls sharing lipstick, purchase one lipstick per girl and let them keep the one they use.

What could a parent do to make a wedding theme party more realistic?

"Create a "cyber mall" and give each girl a set amount of "cyber money." In the cyber mall, include as many things as you can pertaining to weddings —wedding dresses (with a wide range of prices), jewelry, flowers, cakes, caterers, reception halls, and honeymoon destinations (with varying lengths of stay and locations). Don't forget things like hotels for out-of-town guests and travel expenses. Have the girls pick their wedding dates and then plan everything they want to do. Don't give them enough money to buy everything, but do give them enough to have a nice wedding by using problem-solving and compromising skills. For example, 'Well, I really want to go to Hawaii for my honeymoon, so I will get the dress that is slightly less expensive, or I will get a different cake topper.'"

—Veronica Chavez,
Wedding Planner,
Aurora, Colorado

Something Old, Something New, Something Borrowed, Something Blue.

Supplies

Boot box with lid
Hair net (for "old")
Baby bonnet
(for "new")

Wedding veil
(for "borrowed")
Blue Ring Pop®
(for "blue")

Wedding music
Pennies with
current year
(one per player)

Directions

1. Have the girls sit in a circle. Show everyone the items, except the wedding music and pennies, and place them in the boot box, being sure to mention you borrowed the wedding veil from someone. (Just pretend if you really didn't.) Mention that lots of old people wear hairnets. Don't say much more about the other items.

2. Put the lid on the boot box and pass it around while playing wedding music.

3. Randomly stop the music. Whoever has the box, opens it up and takes out any item to wear.

4. Continue playing the music and passing the box around until all the items are gone.

5. Stop the music and say the following wedding phrase as you point to the girl wearing the item:

> Something old (hairnet),
> Something new (baby bonnet),
> Something borrowed (wedding veil),
> Something blue (candy ring),
> A lucky six pence for your shoe.

6. As you say the last line, hand each girl a penny. Then give pennies to the rest of the girls.

"Something old, something new, something borrowed, something blue..." We have all heard this phrase referring to items the bride wears. But what does it mean? "Something old" reminds the bride of her connection to family, so she sometimes wears a piece of jewelry of her mother's or grandmother's. "Something new" stands for good luck, often represented by the bridal gown. "Something borrowed" symbolizes the bride's friends or family members and their loyalty to her. She does need to return the item, however. "Something blue" represents faithfulness in a marriage. Typically, the bride will wear a blue garter.

The tradition of the bride sticking a silver sixpence or coin in her shoe symbolizes her desire for good fortune.

Midnight Snack Attack

Wedding cake

Fortune cookies

Ring Pop® (candy ring) with candy necklaces

Jordan almonds

Hors d'oeuvres (with cellophane frills toothpicks)

Petits fours

Jordan almonds are served as wedding favors in different amounts to symbolize different things: Three almonds represent the bride, the groom, and a future child. Five almonds represent wealth, health, fertility, longevity, and joy. Most often, the almonds are wrapped in netting tied with a ribbon to match the bride's colors.

Video Recommendations

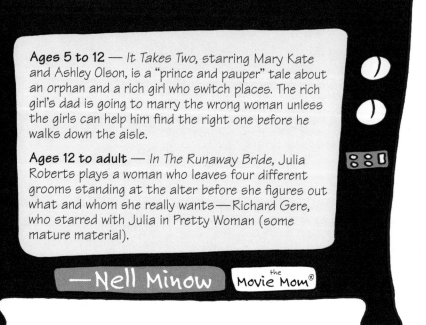

Ages 5 to 12 — *It Takes Two*, starring Mary Kate and Ashley Olson, is a "prince and pauper" tale about an orphan and a rich girl who switch places. The rich girl's dad is going to marry the wrong woman unless the girls can help him find the right one before he walks down the aisle.

Ages 12 to adult — In *The Runaway Bride*, Julia Roberts plays a woman who leaves four different grooms standing at the alter before she figures out what and whom she really wants—Richard Gere, who starred with Julia in *Pretty Woman* (some mature material).

—Nell Minow   the Movie Mom®

Breakfast Jewerly

Ingredients and Supplies

General Mills Cheerios®
Kellogg's® Froot Loops®
Several bowls

Red shoestring licorice (two strands per girl)

Optional: Any cereal with center hole

Directions

1. Dump the cereals into several bowls.

2. Give each girl two strands of licorice, one for a necklace (short or long) and the other for bracelets. Have the girls break one strand into two pieces for two bracelets. They'll need to "size" their bracelets around their wrists, but make sure they keep all the strands/pieces long enough to "tie the knots" in step #3.

3. Have the girls tie loose knots in one end of each of their three licorice strands/pieces.

4. Starting at the other ends, the girls will then thread pieces of cereal onto their strands in any kind of pattern they wish.

5. When the licorice strands are almost full, they should carefully undo their first knots and have someone help them tie their Breakfast Jewelry around their necks and wrists with new knots.

6. Tell them they can eat their Breakfast Jewelry as soon as they have packed their bags to leave.

Tip: Most girls will be nibbling on the cereal while creating their jewelry, so be sure to have lots.

Optional: Use any cereal that has a center hole.

Twenty Extra Fun Ideas

1. Rent a limousine to pick up all your guests.

2. Treat them to a "reception" at a restaurant.

3. Make and decorate a wedding cake.

4. Have them sign a wedding guest book.

5. Take them to a beauty school (it's cheaper than a salon) to get their hair and nails done.

6. Pair off your guests to let them do each other's makeup. For extra fun, blindfold the girls who are applying the makeup.

7. Set up three areas—one with makeup, one with hair supplies, and one with wedding clothes. Rotate groups of girls through the stations to get glamorous for a fashion show.

8. Take photos of the girls posing in a wedding gown.

9. Show the girls how to sew wedding ring pillows, then play a relay race with rings on the pillows.

10. Use a glass or car marker (sold at party stores) to decorate a car, with the owner's permission, of course! *Caution:* Do not use shoe polish. It can hurt the paint.

11. Make "Just Married" signs. Have a contest to see whose is the best.

12. Give everyone a champagne party popper (found at party stores) or Just Married Bubbles®.

13. Play Ring-the-Bride by tossing a hula-hoop over a "bride."

14. Play Who's Got the Ring? (like Button, Button, Who's Got the Button?)

15. Play musical chairs to "Chapel of Love" or another popular wedding song.

16. Let the girls write their own wedding vows and tuck them away for that special day.

17. Have them design and draw the perfect wedding gown.

18. Make paper fortune tellers with a wedding theme. (See page 83, *Valentine School Parties... What Do I Do?®*)

19. Help the girls get into shape for the wedding day by leading an exercise routine in the morning (or use an exercise video).

20. Toss a bouquet to see who gets to throw the next Slumber Party!

Wedding Glamour Pop-Up Invitation

Pencil
Twenty-four 3 x 5-inch
  unlined index cards
Scissors
Twelve 14-inch pieces
  ½-inch white lace
Glue gun
Tape
Twelve 4 x 5½-inch
  blank notecards
  with envelopes
White copy paper
Glue stick
Pen
Optional: Twelve
  stamped postcards

Make Your Own Wedding Flowers

Eight 5 x 8-inch pieces
  white tissue paper
White pipe cleaner
Optional: White facial
  tissue

Maid of Honor's Toast

Non-alcoholic champagne
Plastic champagne glasses
  (found at party stores)
Optional: Mint leaves
  or strawberries (with
  stems)

Dress-the-Bride Dinner

Knife
2 x 2½ x ½-inch chunk
  cheddar cheese
Two ½-inch slices salami
  (with skin)
Paper plate
Three pretzel sticks
Two black olives (pitted)
Butter knife
Thin slice mozzarella cheese
Optional: Crackers
  and mustard

Wedding Designers

Three rolls white
  toilet paper
Ten white pipe cleaners
Lace (assorted sizes
  and types)
Paper
Pen
Optional: Father
  or older male

Kiss-the-Groom Game

Pushpins
Poster of a "cute"
  guy (facing forward)
Lipstick
  (assorted colors)
Mirror
Blindfold
Facial tissue
Pen

Something Old, Something New, Something Borrowed, Something Blue

Boot box with lid
Hair net (for "old")
Baby bonnet
  (for "new")
Wedding veil
  (for "borrowed")
Blue Ring Pop®
  (for "blue")
Wedding music
Pennies with current
  year (one per player)

Breakfast Jewelry

General Mills Cheerios®
Kellogg's® Froot Loops®
Several bowls
Red shoestring licorice
  (two strands per girl)
Optional: Any cereal
  with center hole

Midnight Snack Attack

Wedding cake
Fortune cookies
Ring Pop® (candy ring)
  with candy
  necklaces
Jordan almonds
Hors d'oeuvres
  (with cellophane
  frills toothpicks)
Petits fours

Don't forget the camera and film

CHAPTER NINE

WISH UPON 'A' STAR

Start this spectacular party off with the children wishing for good weather. Then nothing will keep them from sleeping out under the stars on a trampoline, unless they've always dreamed of camping in a tent. If you don't own a big one, borrow or rent one, or better yet, let the kids make their own out of their sleeping bags hung over ropes. This activity alone will take them 'til dark, when you give them their Overnight Survival Kits, complete with flashlights to make Secret Wishes and play Flashlight Bingo (with glow-in-the-dark balls and pens, of course!). Let them bid to wear each other's pajamas, then after a good night's sleep in the great outdoors, treat your super stars special with made-to-order Shooting Star Omelets before wishing them farewell.

Wish Upon A Star Invitation

Supplies

Makes one

8½ x 10-inch (not 11-inch) piece plain white paper

Scissors

12-inch piece yarn (any color)

9 x 12-inch piece construction paper (any color)

Pencil

Permanent blue marker

Glue

Optional: Large envelope and star stickers

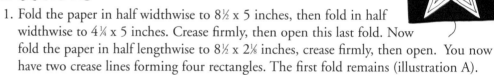

Directions

1. Fold the paper in half widthwise to 8½ x 5 inches, then fold in half widthwise to 4¼ x 5 inches. Crease firmly, then open this last fold. Now fold the paper in half lengthwise to 8½ x 2⅛ inches, crease firmly, then open. You now have two crease lines forming four rectangles. The first fold remains (illustration A).

2. With the fold away from you, bring the upper left corner down to the horizontal crease line about 1 inch from the right edge. Make sure the new fold starts at the top of the vertical line before creasing it (illustration B).

3. Take the same corner as in step #2 (was upper left) back to the left edge, and crease (illustration C).

4. Now bring the right edge of the folded paper from step #1 all the way over the triangular shape fold formed in steps #2 to #3, and crease (illustration D).

5. Take the far left point to the right edge, line it up, and crease (illustration E).

6. You now have a triangular shape with uneven edges on the bottom. Cut at an angle on the dotted line as in illustration E. Discard the bottom part and open up the top part to see your five-point star.

7. Fold the star back up. As in illustration F, cut on the dotted lines almost to the edge WITHOUT cutting all the way through, first from the right, then from the left, and so on for six cuts.

8. Carefully open up your expandable five-point star. Poke a small hole in the center. Thread the yarn through it knot for the "pull string" (illustration G). Your guests will pull up on this to read the details of the invitation (see step #9).

9. Lay the star on the construction paper, lightly trace with the pencil, and remove. In the center of the star shape, with the permanent marker, write: *Come Sleep Under the Stars!*

10. On the five points of the star, write:
    - *Party Given By:* and *Special Occasion:*
    - *Drop-off Time:* and *Pick-up Time:*
    - *Phone Number:* and *Please Tell Me If You Can Come!*
    - *Day and Date:*
    - *Address and Directions:*

    Then fill in the details.

11. With the glue, "draw" a thin line just inside the pencil line of the star shape. Be careful not to cover up your words with glue. Lay the expandable star on top of the star shape, knot side down, and carefully press down the edges. Let dry before delivering your invitation.

Optional: Put your invitation in a large envelope decorated with star stickers.

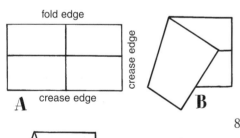

A — fold edge / crease edge / crease edge

B

C

D

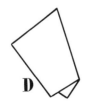

E — cut on dotted line

F — cut on dotted line

G

108

Pillowcase Wishes

Decorate your own pillowcase, then make a wish!

Supplies

White pillowcases
(one per child)

Black permanent marker

Fabric paint (assorted colors)

Large envelopes
(for folded pillowcases)

Pens
Option 1: Sequins
Option 2: Permanent markers
(assorted colors)

Directions

1. Wash and dry the white pillowcases before the party.

2. With the black permanent marker, draw two stars on one side of each pillowcase, a small one to write a wish and a large one to write the reason for the wish.

3. Have each child think of a wish, why he wants it to come true, and who he thinks could grant him his wish.

4. Then with the fabric paint, let the children write their wishes in the small stars on their pillowcases, and the reasons for their wishes in the big stars.

5. Have them decorate their pillowcases around the stars with the paint.

6. Since the pillowcases will need to dry overnight, the children should only decorate the one side.

7. In the morning, give each child a large envelope for his pillowcase, and tell him he can mail or hand deliver his wish to the person he thinks can grant it. Have him write his name in the return address area to identify his envelope for when it is time to leave.

In 2001, the Make-A-Wish Foundation® celebrated twenty years, granting wish number 80,000 to a seriously ill child. Making their dreams come true doesn't heal these children, but it does help them and their families during a difficult time. Disneyland® is one of the foundation's best supporters, as well as the most wished-for places to visit.

Option 1: Let those that want sequins, stick them in the paint on the pillowcases. Explain that they can fall off in the wash and may be uncomfortable for sleeping.

Option 2: Decorate the pillowcases with permanent markers instead of paint so you can do both sides.

Variation: Let the children autograph each other's pillowcases on the non-decorated sides instead of delivering the pillowcases to their own special make-a-wish people.

Cloud-Filled Dinner Star

Ingredients and Supplies

Makes one

Two knives

1 tablespoon peanut butter

Two slices bread

2 tablespoons marshmallow creme

3½-inch star cookie cutter

Directions

1. With one knife, spread peanut butter on one slice of bread and set aside.

2. With the other knife, spread marshmallow creme on the other slice of bread.

3. Put the slices together with the peanut butter and marshmallow creme on the inside.

4. Cut a Cloud-Filled Dinner Star from the sandwich with the star cookie cutter.

Note: The kids might enjoy making these themselves.

Milky Way Galaxy Shakes

Strawberry swirl ice cream makes these extra dreamy

The Japanese celebrate Tanabata (or Star Festival) on July 7th. They write wishes on small pieces of colored paper and hang them from bamboo trees along with lots of paper decorations. This tradition came from a Chinese story about a prince and princess who lived in the sky but were kept apart by the King. The Milky Way separated them, and they were only allowed to see each other one day a year, on July 7th.

Ingredients and Supplies

Makes 4

Two 2.05-ounce Milky Way® candy bars

Blender

4 cups (1 quart) ice cream

Banana

Four glasses

Spatula

Optional: Food processor

Directions

1. Break up the candy bars in small pieces and put in the blender with the ice cream and banana.

2. Mix until blended, scoop out into the glasses with the spatula, and serve immediately. Be prepared to make more!

Note: If your blender isn't big enough, make half of the recipe at a time.

Optional: If you don't have a blender, use a food processor.

The Swan in the Stars

This story is based on mythology

A long time ago, in Ancient Greece, there were two boys who were best friends. Phaethon (FAY thin) was good looking and athletic, with long wavy hair. He was also very proud and got angry quickly. His best friend was Cygnus (SIG ness). He was quiet and gentle, and very loyal to Phaethon.

One day Phaethon and Cygnus went hunting with some other boys. They had to climb over tall boulders and swim across a swift river. Everyone had a hard time keeping up with Phaethon because he could climb and swim better than anyone.

Some of the boys began to yell at him, "Who do you think you are, Phaethon, one of the gods?"

Phaethon stood tall and grinned at them all. "Yes," he said, "as a matter of fact, my father is Helios, the sun god. He drives the fiery chariot across the sky each day!"

The boys laughed at him. "Oh, a son of the gods! Why don't you prove it?"

Phaethon's face turned red with anger. He stormed away, promising that he would prove to all of them that he was the son of Helios.

Cygnus followed. "Don't worry about them, Phaethon," he said. "They are just embarrassed because they cannot keep up with you."

Phaethon loved his friend, but even Cygnus could not calm him down this time. "I am going to ask my father to let me drive the chariot. Then everyone will believe me."

Cygnus begged his friend not to do it. It was too dangerous. "It does not not matter what the other boys say," he said. "I believe you are the son of Helios."

But Phaethon was determined. He said good-bye to his friend and started on his journey.

After many days of travel and many dangers, he arrived at the golden palace of the sun. He knelt before his father and asked for a favor. "Yes, my son," promised Helios, "you may have anything you want."

Phaethon looked into the face of his father and said, "Let me drive the chariot, just once. If I drive the chariot, everyone will believe I am your son."

Helios was horrified. This was not possible. Phaethon would certainly be killed. "Please, my son," Helios begged, "release me from my promise to grant you anything."

But Phaethon was determined. Unable to do otherwise, Helios sighed and agreed.

In the morning, the heavens were opened by the goddess Eos. Helios brought Phaethon to the sun chariot. He pointed out the track that Phaethon must follow through the sky. "You must stay in the middle between the North and South Poles," he warned. "Do not go too high or two low in the sky, or disaster will follow!"

Phaethon was impatient and not really listening. He snapped the whip and the horses flew off. Now the horses could tell that the chariot was not as heavy as usual, and that the reins weren't as tight. They began to rear up, flying wildly across the sky. They flew past dangerous creatures—the serpent, the bears, the lion, and the scorpion.

Phaethon was frightened, more than he'd ever been! The horses crashed against stars, then swooped downward. As they came near the earth, the fiery chariot made the mountains smoke and the rivers boil. The crops were scorched and the animals cried from the heat.

The smoke became so thick that Phaethon fainted. Then his long hair caught on fire and he fell headfirst toward the earth. As his hair burned, a flash of light streaked across the heavens, appearing like a comet. He landed in a river and the fire was, at last, put out. The horses flew away with the sun chariot, in the correct path across the sky.

Cygnus watched the terrible chariot ride of his best friend, Phaethon. "Oh, Phaethon, why did you do it? Now you are gone."

He wanted to honor his friend, so he dove into the water many times to collect all of his bones and had them buried in a solemn ceremony. The most powerful of the Greek gods, Zeus, then honored Cygnus for his loyalty and patience with a constellation.

Because Cygnus means swan, Zeus placed the sign of "The Swan in the Stars." It is a constant reminder of true friendship. It dips into the water below the horizon and then rises again, over and over, just as Cygnus did for his best friend.

—Retold by Kathryn Totten, storyteller/author

Overnight Survival Kit

Package up one of these for each party guest

Scientists can tell time based on the position of The Big Dipper (or any star) in relation to Polaris, the North Star, which is in The Little Dipper.

Supplies

Makes one

Permanent markers (assorted colors)

Gift bag with handles

Star stickers

Map of house

Plastic snack bag

Teddy Grahams®

Flashlight

Notepad

Toothbrush

Travel-size toothpaste

Word Search (found on page 92)

Glow-in-the-dark pen

Glow-in-the-dark necklace

Directions

1. Using a permanent marker, personalize the gift bag with the child's name. Then decorate with star stickers.

2. Draw a map of your house to make it easier for the child to find his way to the bathroom, for example, in the middle of the night

3. Fill the plastic snack bag with Teddy Grahams® (to help the child sleep).

4. With a permanent marker, personalize the flashlight, notepad, and toothbrush with the child's name.

5. Put all the above items in the gift bag, along with the toothpaste, Word Search (in case of insomnia), pen, and necklace.

6. Hand out before playing any of the games that use a flashlight.

Note: Glow-in-the-dark items can be purchased at most party stores.

Secret Wish Upon A Star

Save this game for after dark

Tell us about your favorite Slumber Party game?

"Flashlight Tag. My mom, step-dad, and friends go outside and get on teams of two and hide, except for the team that's 'it.' They have a flashlight and shine the light on somebody whose team is then automatically 'it.'"

—Ashley Williams, Age 11 Ankeny, Iowa

Supplies

Flashlights (one per child from Overnight Survival Kits, above)

Directions

1. Have the children get their flashlights and sit in a circle, either outside on a blanket or inside on the floor in a dark room.

2. Ask one of the children (or an adult or older child) to read "Flash Your Lights" (see page 113) aloud. He will need to use his flashlight to read, and pause ever so slightly when he comes to the words in **bold** (see step #3).

3. Tell the other children to keep their flashlights off to start, but to listen for the words **FLASH** and **LIGHT**. As soon as they hear **FLASH** or **LIGHT**, they should turn on their flashlights.

continued next page

4. The reader should then call out the name of the child who turns on his flashlight first, asking him to make a Secret Wish. (Make a wish of your own that every child will get a chance to make a wish!)

5. At the end of the story, go around in the circle so every child can tell what he wished for. If a child wants to keep his wish a secret, he just says "Secret Wish" when his turn comes.

Note: In case of a tie (two children turning on their flashlights at once), have them each make a Secret Wish.

Flash Your Lights

Brad and Janice were excited about the family camping trip. They had been packing their backpacks. Brad's pack was already heavy, but his sister had only a few things in hers. It was still **LIGHT.**

"What do you have in there, Brad?" Janice asked. "Are you taking everything you own on this camping trip?"

Brad sighed, "I know I'm going to need all this stuff."

"Well, let's look at it again. Maybe you can leave something out," suggested Janice.

Brad began to pull out the contents of his backpack. He pulled out an extra pair of dry socks, a light blue sweatshirt, a fishing pole, and a book of ghost stories.

"You will need all of those," Janice said.

Brad pulled out his camera, but he accidentally touched the button. **FLASH!** "I guess I just took a picture of all of my camping stuff," he said.

"I'll put it in the scrapbook," Janice said.

Next, Brad pulled out a pair of in-line skates.

"Brad, you can't use those on a mountain trail!" laughed Janice.

"I thought they would make the hike go faster...but I guess not. I'll leave them here." Brad tried his backpack on again, and it felt lighter. "I bet I have room for this now," he said. From under his bed, Brad pulled out a big bag of candy.

Janice laughed and reached into her backpack. "It will go great with this!" she said, as she pulled a bag of corn nuts. "Trail food. This family really knows what to take on a camping trip."

The car ride to the mountains seemed really long. Brad and Janice tried to make the time go faster by playing games. They looked for each letter of the alphabet on license plates and road signs.

When they got stuck at the letter "Q," they switched to another game called "**LIGHTS.**" If a car drove by with its headlights on, they tried to be the first to call out. The time went by in a **FLASH.**

When they got to the trailhead, the pine trees smelled fresh. A gentle breeze tickled the back of their necks as they hiked up the trail. When they got hungry, they munched on Brad's candy and Janice's corn nuts.

There were big rocks and tree roots in the trail, and once Janice tripped, but Brad reached out in a **FLASH** and kept her from falling. "Do you still think you could have used your in-line skates on this trail?" Janice asked.

"No," said Brad, "because I would have been way ahead of you, and then who would keep you from falling?"

Pretty soon, the family stopped hiking to fish for a while. Janice held onto her fishing pole tightly, dangling a shiny lure into a pool in the stream. She felt a light tug, and she pulled back quickly on her fishing pole. She had a nice trout on the line.

Brad ran over and helped her get it into the net. The shiny scales **FLASHED** in the sunlight. Pretty soon they had a string full of fish. It was time to make camp and build a fire so they could cook them.

While their parents pitched the tents, Brad and Janice collected firewood. Janice found a beautiful **LIGHT** blue flower. "It's a Mountain Columbine," she told her brother proudly.

With their arms full of sticks, they returned to the camp. Brad built the fire by stacking little twigs against each other in a teepee shape. Around these, he stacked some thicker sticks.

He struck a match, and in a **FLASH,** they saw a flicker of fire and heard the crackle of burning wood. They took turns adding larger pieces, and soon they had a good fire going.

It was getting dark when they sat down to eat their fish dinner. Then they roasted marshmallows to a beautiful **LIGHT** tan color. It was getting cool, so they pulled their sweatshirts out of their backpacks.

Brad looked up and saw a **FLASH** of **LIGHT** streak across the sky. "It's a shooting star! Make a wish," he said. The whole family sat quietly looking up at the sky, hoping to see another shooting star.

"What did you wish for?" asked Janice.

"Not telling. Secret Wish," Brad whispered back as they curled into their sleeping bags.

"I'll tell you my wish," said Janice. "I wished for another day just like this tomorrow."

In a **FLASH,** they were both asleep.

—*Kathryn Totten,* storyteller/author

Flashlight Bingo

Supplies

Copy paper
Scissors
Black permanent marker
Seventy-five glow-in-the-dark bouncing balls (found at party stores)
Pillowcase

Flashlights (one per child, from Overnight Survival Kits)
Glow-in-the-dark pens (one per child, found at party stores)
Option 1: Mini marshmallows
Option 2: Really cool flashlights for prizes

Directions

1. Before the party, make copies of the Flashlight Bingo cards on pages 115 to 118, one per child per game you plan on playing. Cut out the cards.

2. Use the black permanent marker to write the following letters and numbers on the seventy-five bouncing balls: B-1 to B-15, I-16 to I-30, N-31 to N-45, G-46 to G-60, and O-61 to O-75. Write as large and as legibly as you can.

3. Put the balls in the pillowcase for the "bingo call" balls.

4. Have the children get their flashlights and then choose a "bingo caller," perhaps an adult or older child.

5. Give each child a glow-in-the-dark pen and a Flashlight Bingo card. Explain the game as follows:

- *The "bingo caller" will choose a ball from the pillowcase and hold it up for everyone to see.*
- *They should use their flashlights to read the ball.*
- *Then they use their flashlights to see their cards, and their glow-in-the-dark pens to cross off the number if they have it.*
- *The caller continues to choose balls until someone has marked off a row, either vertical or horizontal, and yells "Flashlight!" (not "Bingo!").*

6. Play as many games as you like, but give each child a new card each time.

7. When you're finished playing, throw all the balls into the yard and let the children search for them with their flashlights, returning the balls to you for the next Slumber Party!

Caution: Tell them to walk slowly and aim their flashlights on the ground so they won't slip and fall on the balls.

Option 1: Give all the players a small plastic bag of mini marshmallows (clouds) for card markers instead of using glow-in-the-dark pens. You will not have to hand out new cards for each game.

Option 2: Give cool new flashlights to every winner. In case of more than one winner, have them draw bouncing balls from the pillowcase—lowest number wins.

Age Adjustment: For *younger* children, call out the letter and number on each ball while they're reading them with their flashlights.

B	I	N	G	O
1-15	16-30	31-45	46-60	61-75
8	16	31	47	61
4	30	33	60	75
2	19	40	58	66
15	21	39	50	73
6	25	45	59	74

B 1-15	I 16-30	N 31-45	G 46-60	O 61-75
6	17	32	46	62
1	20	35	51	72
3	22	42	57	63
14	24	37	48	64
12	30	38	49	65

B	I	N	G	O
1-15	16-30	31-45	46-60	61-75
5	18	34	52	67
7	23	36	54	69
9	26	41	53	68
10	27	43	60	70
11	30	44	55	71

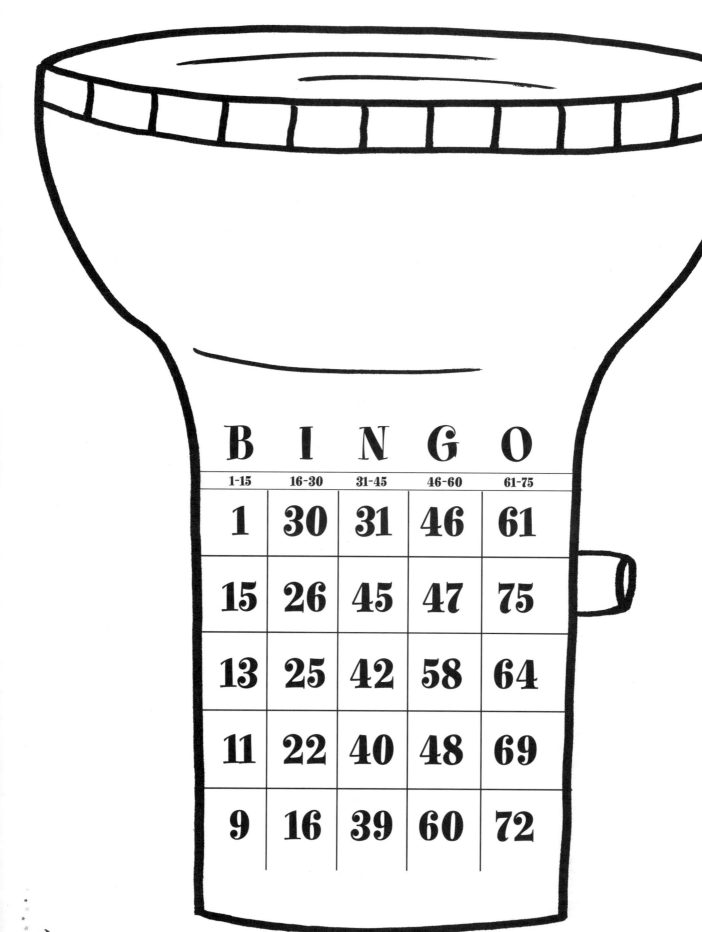

B	I	N	G	O
1-15	16-30	31-45	46-60	61-75
1	30	31	46	61
15	26	45	47	75
13	25	42	58	64
11	22	40	48	69
9	16	39	60	72

Wish to Bid Pajama Auction

Supplies

Pen

5-inch cut-out stars (as many as children)

Clothesline (2 feet per child)

Clothespins (two per child)

Play money (lots)

Optional: Straight pins

Tell us about your favorite Slumber Party?

"When we slept in a tent outside."

—Megan Bradford
age 9
Watkins, Colorado

Directions

1. On the invitations, ask the children to each bring two pair of pajamas, or whatever they plan to sleep in.

2. Write a number on each cut-out star, starting with number "1" and going up to the number of children.

3. Hang the clothesline near the front door or possibly outside where all the neighbors will see it. (Let them be curious!)

4. As your guests arrive, have them hang one pair of pajamas each on the clothesline with clothespins. Limit each child to only 2 feet of line and two clothespins.

5. When you're ready to play the game, give everyone a numbered star, an assortment of play money, and explain that you will be auctioning off the hanging pajamas for them to wear for that night only. (If any child doesn't want to wear the pair they "buy" during the auction, he can wear the other pair he brought.)

6. Choose an auctioneer, perhaps an adult or older child, and explain to the children that to bid, they should hold up their numbered stars to make their bids official. The auctioneer will see their numbers and their bids will be acknowledged.

7. Then take the first pair of pajamas off the line. Ask someone to start the bidding by holding up his numbered star and saying how much he will "pay." If no one opens the bid, the auctioneer can start it or go to the next pair of pajamas, but emphasize that every pair needs to be "sold."

8. When all the pajamas have been sold, tell the children to take very good care of their new pajamas and return them to the clothesline in the morning, where the real owners can get them to take home.

Optional: Pin any second piece of a pair of pajamas to the top piece using straight pins. This will allow for better viewing.

Midnight Snack Attack

S'mores made in microwave

Star fruit (sliced)

Milky Way® candy bars

Roasted hot dogs (over BBQ grill)

Roasted marshmallows (over BBQ grill)

Star-shaped cookies

Video Recommendations

Ages 7 to adult — Disney's finest animated feature, *Pinnochio*, is simply sensational. The music, including "When You Wish Upon A Star," and the story, about learning to tell the truth, work hard, and love others, are both timeless.

Ages 9 to adult — *Galaxy Quest* is a wildly funny outer space adventure. Stars of a cheesy sci-fi TV show discover that aliens thought their show was real and created a spaceship just like the one on the show. They want the actors to help them fight a mean alien who looks like a lizard. Top talent, great special effects, and fresh and funny plot twists make it exciting and just plain fun.

—Nell Minow   the Movie Mom®

Shooting Star Omelets

Ingredients and Supplies

Eggs (two per child)

Salt and pepper

Bowl

Wire whip

Butter (1 tablespoon per child)

Frying pan

Diced tomato, green pepper, and onion

Spatula

Diced ham and crumbled bacon (cooked)

Grated cheese

Plates and forks (one each per child)

Decorating Décors candy stars

Directions

1. Take every child's omelet order according to the above ingredients.

2. Break all the eggs into the bowl with salt and pepper, and whip until blended.

3. Melt 1 tablespoon of butter in frying pan on medium-high heat. Toss in the first child's vegetable order and sauté for 1 to 2 minutes.

4. Then add his meat order and spread out evenly in the pan. Pour two eggs of the blended eggs over the vegetables and meat. If needed, rock the pan back and forth to spread the eggs evenly over the pan. Do not stir.

5. After 1 to 2 minutes more, sprinkle the child's cheese order over the cooking eggs.

6. Then tilt the pan, lift the edge of the eggs up with the spatula, and let the uncooked egg flow underneath. Almost immediately, fold the lifted edge over the opposite edge. You should now have a semi-circle.

7. Cook the omelet until barely brown on both sides.

8. Slide it onto a plate and sprinkle Decorating Décors candy stars on and around it.

Twenty Extra Fun Ideas

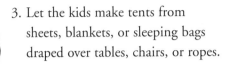

1. Let the kids sleep outside on a trampoline.

2. Try to name all the constellations.

3. Let the kids make tents from sheets, blankets, or sleeping bags draped over tables, chairs, or ropes.

4. Call your local weather station to see if it's a good night to watch for shooting stars.

5. Tell the children to find a special star and make-a-wish.

6. Have them take turns using telescopes and binoculars. Ask them what they see?

7. Teach them to set up your family-size tent.

8. Find the Big Dipper and the Little Dipper.

9. Point out the North Star and ask where it got its name. (Have the answer.)

10. Play volleyball with a glow-in-the-dark beach ball.

11. Sing songs around a campfire (or a barbecue grill or "pretend" fire).

12. Tell ghost stories while sitting around a fire.

13. Have the kids name as many movie stars as they can in 20 seconds.

14. Ask them to name their favorite super sport stars. Then rock stars.

15. Set up an extra tent and call it a chit-chat tent for those who aren't tired and want to keep talking.

16. Pretend a large bucket is a wishing well and toss pennies into it while making wishes.

17. Fold star confetti into napkins and when your guests use them, tell them to make a wish so their star wishes will fly.

18. Sing "Twinkle, Twinkle, Little Star."

19. Visit a planetarium.

20. Record everyone's wish on a video (privately) and play the video at breakfast.

Tell us about your favorite Slumber Party?

"We set up tents indoors and the girls brought Beanie Babies®. Each girl got a canteen (favors). We made s'mores, sang campfire songs, and made sleeping bags for the Beanies."

—Nicole LaDuca, age 12
W. Islip, New York

Wish Upon A Star Party Invitations

8 ½ x 10-inch piece plain white paper
Scissors
Yarn
9 x 12-inch construction paper (any color)
Pencil
Glue
Optional: Large envelope

Pillowcase Wishes

White pillowcases (one per child)
Black permanent marker
Fabric paint (assorted colors)
Large envelopes (for folded pillowcases)
Pens
Option 1: Sequins
Option 2: Permanent markers (assorted colors)

Cloud-Filled Dinner Star

Two knives
1 tablespoon peanut butter
Two slices bread
2 tablespoons marshmallow creme
3 ½-inch star cookie cutter

Milky Way Galaxy Shakes

Two 2.05-ounce Milky Way® candy bars
Blender
4 cups (1 quart) ice cream
Banana
Four glasses
Spatula
Optional: Food processor

Overnight Survival Kit

Permanent markers (assorted colors)
Gift bag with handles
Star stickers
Map of house
Plastic snack bag
Teddy Grahams®
Flashlight
Notepad
Toothbrush
Travel-size toothpaste
Word Search (found on page 92)
Glow-in-the-dark pen
Glow-in-the-dark necklace

Secret Wish Upon A Star

Flashlights (one per child from Overnight Survival Kits, above)

Flashlight Bingo

Copy paper
Scissors
Black permanent marker
Seventy-five glow-in-the-dark bouncing balls*
Pillowcase
Flashlights (one per child, from Overnight Survival Kits)
Glow-in-the-dark pens (one per child)
Option 1: Mini marshmallows
Option 2: Really cool flashlights for prizes

Wish to Bid Pajama Auction

Pen
5-inch cut-out stars (as many as children)
Clothesline (2 feet per child)
Clothespins (two per child)
Play money (lots)
Optional: Straight pins

Don't forget the camera and film

Shooting Star Omelets

Eggs (two per child)
Salt and pepper
Bowl
Wire whip
Butter (1 tablespoon per child)
Frying pan
Diced tomato, green pepper, and onion
Spatula
Diced ham and crumbled bacon (cooked)
Grated cheese
Plates and forks (one each per child)
Decorating Décors candy stars

Midnight Snack Attack

S'mores made in microwave
Star fruit (sliced)
Milky Way® candy bars
Roasted hot dogs (over BBQ grill)
Roasted marshmallows (over BBQ grill)
Star-shaped cookies

CHAPTER TEN

Full Speed Ahead

Full of energy-zapping activities, the boys will actually beg you to let them sleep! All night long, they get to do what boys do best—pretending to be racecars and squealing their brakes, chasing and hitting each other with pillows, listening to a ghost story about a motorcycle rider, complete with a snake tattoo. You'll make Candy Motorcycles for the boys to take home as favors, to savor a long time before eating them. When the boys are on empty, Fill 'em Up with drinks out of a gas can and Pilot-Tested Airplane Food, after the pilot takes them on a Wacky Airplane Ride. And for breakfast, they get eggs, toast, and bacon with a "twist" they can't get anywhere else!

Airplane Invitation

Supplies

Makes 7

Rubber cement
Seven pieces of each:
- 6 x 11-inch green construction paper,
- 6 x 11-inch cardboard,
- 3 x 11-inch black construction paper, and
- 3½ x 6-inch green construction paper

White-out
Pen
Seven heavy books
Roll of Lifesavers® (14 candies)

Seven of each:
   small rubberbands,
   sticks of gum (still wrapped),
   Smarties® and
   peppermint candies
   (with twisted wrappers)

Order of Full Speed Ahead Party

Run Outdoor Car Races (serve Fill 'em Up Drink)

Serve dinner (Pilot-Tested Airplane Food) and tell Wacky Airplane Ride

Play Capture the Socks

Get on pajamas and lay out sleeping bags

Read "Ghost Rider"

Make Candy Motorcyles

Watch videos with Midnight Snack Attack

Sleep

Have breakfast (Helicopter Eggs, Toast, and Bacon)

Brush teeth, get dressed, and pack

Take-off!

Directions

1. For each invitation, glue one large piece green paper (grass) on one piece cardboard.

2. Glue one piece black paper (runway) down center of grass.

3. Glue one small piece green paper across grass and runway, at one end of invitation.

4. With white-out, make a dotted line down middle of runway.

5. With the pen, copy the invitation below and fill in the details.

6. Put a heavy book on top of all while the glue dries.

7. For each airplane, unwrap Lifesavers® and thread a rubber band through two candies (wheels). Hook ends of rubber band over ends of a stick of gum (wings).

8. Insert Smarties® (body) under wings, between wheels and over middle of rubber band, pushing it through one-third the way.

9. Glue one peppermint candy (propellers) to short end of body.

10. Remove book and position airplane at end of runway (opposite end from invitation) with propellers at the top. Glue down tail of airplane.

11. Fly your invitations directly to your party guests!

Full Speed Ahead Slumber Party

Get ready for a flight
Come spend the night
Pack your pillow and bed
For Full Speed Ahead!

Party Given By: _____

Pick-up Time: _____

Special Occasion: _____

Address and Directions: _____

Day and Date: _____

_____

Drop-off Time: _____

Phone Number: _____

Race to the phone and tell me you can come!

Outdoor Car Races

Supplies

Pillow (only one)
Sleeping bags (one per boy)
Whistle
Optional: Checkered flag

Directions

1. Play this game outside on the lawn.

2. Choose one boy to be "it." Give him the pillow.

3. Have all the other boys lay their sleeping bags on the grass, half to the left and half to the right, tops facing each other, about 10 to 20 feet apart (the farther apart the better).

4. Put the boy who is "it" in the very middle. Tell the other boys to stand in front of any sleeping bag. It doesn't matter.

5. Blow the whistle to start each race. The boys will run across to another sleeping bag, making car noises (like "Vroom! Vroom!") while the boy in the middle tries to hit them with the pillow. He can't touch them after they squeal their brakes (saying "Screech!") and slip into any sleeping bag (as long as it's on the opposite side).

6. If a boy does get "hit," he is out and he takes a sleeping bag with him, sitting on it on the sidelines while cheering on his fellow "drivers."

7. The last driver wins the car race. Run another race with a new "it."

Tip: Serve the Fill 'em Up Drink between races.

Optional: Have a parent (official) wave the checkered flag if the boys get out of control.

Rollerblade, Inc. created the first in-line skates, but didn't include brake pads on the heels and toes until 1993!

Fill 'em Up Drink

A real "gas" with the Outdoor Car Races

Ingredients and Supplies

Ginger ale
New plastic gas can
Clear plastic cups

Directions

1. Pour ginger ale into a new gas can.

2. Let the boys take their cups and Fill 'em Up!

Pilot-Tested Airplane Food

A big dinner production that really takes off!

Do you have "kitchen rules" during Slumber Parties?

"The kitchen lights are out after dinner, but I do make several snacks (no refrigeration needed) and have them out on the table so the kids can eat whenever they are hungry. Also, everyone gets a cup with his name on it so he can get water if he wants."

—Velvet Shogren
Wichita, Kansas

Ingredients and Supplies

Scissors

Plain paper

Pen

Chairs (one per boy)

Sticky notes

TV dinners (one per boy)

Soda pop (assorted)

Plastic cups

Ice

Bags of peanuts (one per boy)

Cocktail napkins

Plastic silverware

Option 1: TV set

Option 2: TV trays

Directions

1. Before the party, cut strips of paper to make a boarding pass for each boy, writing on the strips their names, their seat assignments (1A, 1B, 2A, 2B, and so on), and the name of "your airlines."

2. Hand them out to the boys as they get to the party, telling them to be very careful not to lose them. They are their tickets to dinner.

3. Set up chairs to represent airplane seating. Put a sticky note on each seat with the seat number on it (1A, 1B, 2A, 2B, and so on).

4. Call the boys to "board the airplane," collecting their tickets, and telling them to find their seats according to their seat assignments.

5. Introduce yourself as the head flight attendant and go through the typical airplane announcements and procedures, such as demonstrating a seatbelt and an oxygen mask. Have a second flight attendant (a parent) in the kitchen heating the TV dinners, some in the oven and some in the microwave.

6. Then tell the "Wacky Airplane Ride" found on page 127.

7. Serve "your passengers" soda pop in plastic cups with ice, along with the bags of peanuts. Don't forget the cocktail napkins. Announce that you'll be coming through with dinner soon.

8. Serve the TV dinners with plastic silverware, and refresh everyone's drinks.

Tip: Some neighbors may let you heat TV dinners in their ovens.

Note: Why not call your airlines Wacky Airlines, and get a dad (pilot) to tell the "Wacky Airplane Ride"!

Option 1: Set up the chairs in front of a TV set, but only turn it on for a half-hour show while the boys are eating. You could also start a video, but finish it after "landing."

Option 2: Set up TV trays in front of the chairs.

Wacky Airplane Ride

Tell this after the boys "board the plane" for dinner

Supplies
None

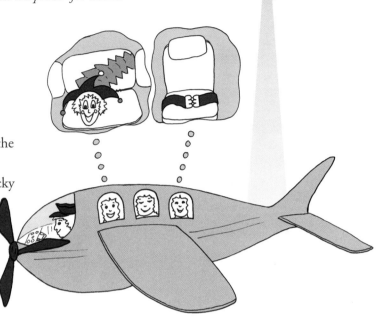

Directions

1. Be sure to read the story below before the party, even practicing the motions (in parentheses), so you can make it as wacky as possible.

2. Explain to "your passengers" that as you tell them the story, you will make motions and they should copy you while staying in their seats as much as possible.

Hi! My name is Zane (point to self)

I'm a pilot on a plane (spread arms out like wings)

Not an ordinary plane (shake head)

This plane is plain insane (point to head, making a circular motion)

Come along if you dare (raise eyebrows)

Up into the air (point up)

On a Wacky Airplane Ride! (make a crazy face)

The seat belt buckles (pretend to fasten seat belt)

Are shaped like knuckles (point to knuckle)

On this Wacky Airplane Ride! (make a crazy face)

The bathroom spins around (turn around)

Like a merry-go-round (turn around again)

The seat belt buckles (pretend to fasten seat belt)

Are shaped like knuckles (point to knuckle)

On this Wacky Airplane Ride! (make a crazy face)

Lean back in your chair (lean back)

And the dentist will be there (pretend to pull a tooth)

The bathroom spins around (turn around)

Like a merry-go-round (turn around again)

The seat belt buckles (pretend to fasten seat belt)

Are shaped like knuckles (point to knuckle)

On this Wacky Airplane Ride! (make a crazy face)

The window shades rattle (move fingers around)

Like a herd of running cattle (run in place)

Lean back in your chair (lean back)

And the dentist will be there (pretend to pull a tooth)

The bathroom spins around (turn around)

Like a merry-go-round (turn around again)

The seat belt buckles (pretend to fasten seat belt)

Are shaped like knuckles (point to knuckle)

On this Wacky Airplane Ride! (make a crazy face)

The overhead pops (jump up)

Like a Jack-in-the-box (nod your head)

The window shades rattle (move fingers around)

Like a herd of running cattle (run in place)

Lean back in your chair (lean back)

And the dentist will be there (pretend to pull a tooth)

The bathroom spins around (turn around)

Like a merry-go-round. (turn around again)

The seat belt buckles (pretend to fasten seat belt)

Are shaped like knuckles (point to knuckle)

On this Wacky Airplane Ride! (make a crazy face)

Tip: Have a dad (pilot) tell this story.

—Kathryn Totten, *storyteller/author*

Capture the Socks

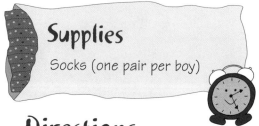

Supplies

Socks (one pair per boy)

Directions

1. Include on the invitation for each boy to bring or wear a pair of socks.

2. In a large area, have all the boys get on their hands and knees with their socks on.

3. Tell them to try to pull each other's socks off while keeping their own on.

4. The winner is the one who captures the most socks or who doesn't lose his socks. Or there could be two winners!

The anemometer is an instrument invented in 1450 that measures wind speed.

Ghost Rider

One summer night, two boys were walking down a dirt road, shooting pebbles at the signs with slingshots. There were no streetlights, of course, but the moon was full, giving the night an eery glow. It was getting close to midnight. The boys' parents didn't know they were out looking for trouble. One set of parents thought his son was spending the night at the other boy's house, and the other set thought the same thing. The oldest trick in the book, but maybe not the smartest.

This wasn't the first time the boys had been sneaking around around midnight. They'd been getting away with it almost all summer. They had laughed silently, their eyes dancing up and down, when their parents talked at dinner about the neighbors complaining. Somebody had turned on lawn sprinklers and left them running all night. Somebody had taken shirts off a clothesline and drug them in the mud. And somebody had cut open half a dozen watermelons in a field and left them to rot in the morning sun.

But so far, nobody suspected the boys, and they were proud of themselves. So far.

But tonight, with the full moon beckoning them on, they were bored, having done all the tame pranks they could think of. They wanted to do something more exciting, like drive a car, or a truck, or a motorcycle! Yeah, that's it! Anyone can drive a car, but we want to ride a motorcycle. And they knew just where they could borrow one.

Ghost Rider *(continued)*

A mile down the road stood an old house and barn. It had been empty for years, but now there was someone living there. They had seen him ride by on a motorcycle a month ago and turn into the dirt drive, disappearing into the night. He wore torn jeans and a sleeveless shirt. He had a tattoo of a snake on his right arm. They could see it clearly in the moonlight. His thin, brown hair was pulled back into a ponytail. He hadn't noticed them as he blew by. They hadn't ventured up the drive then, but the house looked dark. They thought they heard the sound of glass breaking.

As they approached the dirt drive on this night, one month later, they stopped walking. They stopped talking to listen. They put their slingshots into their hip pockets. They rolled up the sleeves on their T-shirts, so they would look tough. When they couldn't hear anything or see anything, they slowly and quietly, one step at a time, went up the drive.

The trees lining the drive were so old and so untended that they formed a canopy, blocking out most of the light from the moon. The boys could hardly see in front of them. They had to be oh-so-careful not to trip on rocks, or on tree roots, or in dried-up mudholes. The drive seemed so much longer than they had remembered.

At last, they came out into the moon's light. They saw the house. They noticed a few new broken windowpanes, which was strange if someone was living there. But it was quiet and still. Nothing stirred. They slowly walked past the house to the barn. Suddenly, an owl hooted at them from a lone tree in the yard. Then nothing but silence. Even the breeze had stopped.

The boys gulped, and with eyes wide open, went up to the barn. Its door of rotting wood planks was closed. As they reached for the handles, one on each side, they saw a flickering light through the gaps in the boards. They strained their eyes to see where the light was coming from, and knew, if they wanted to find out, they'd have to go in.

They opened the door, oh-so-slowly, trying their best to keep it from squeaking on its rusty hinges. They meant to keep it open, but when they saw the motorcycle right in front of them, they were so excited that they let it go, and somehow it slammed shut—all on its own.

They stepped closer to the motorcycle. Its chrome gleamed in the moonlight coming through what roof remained on the barn. The boys had to reach out and touch the machine before them. Ouch! It was hot! As if it had just been ridden. But they hadn't heard it or seen it, and they'd been on that road for a few hours now.

A bat swooped down at them, so close they felt the air move above their heads. They jumped a little, but one little bat didn't scare them. They saw the flickering light again. It moved toward them. They stepped back, away from the motorcycle.

Then the light was gone. Only a tiny red dot remained. Out of the darkness, into the moonlight, stepped the man they had seen only once before. A cigarette hung from his snarled lips. He towered above the boys, but didn't seem to see them, just like before. By the light of the moon and the glow of his cigarette, the boys could see the stubble of beard on his face, his hollow cheeks, his cold black eyes. He didn't say a word.

He got on the motorcycle and revved it up. It coughed and exploded a few times, but as quickly as he had come out of the shadows, the rider roared past the boys, the snake tattoo hissing at them. He raced toward the barn door. The boys gasped, knowing it was closed. But the motorcycle rider road right through it without breaking a board, without leaving a trace that he'd been there. No dust. No tire tracks.

The boys ran to the door and swung it open just in time to see the rider go past the house, down the drive, and under the trees. They could hear him for a long, long time. When they couldn't anymore, they turned back to close the barn doors. At their feet was an old, yellowed newspaper.

One of the boys picked it up and barely made out the date. The paper was 10 years old. "Lemme see that," the other boy said, grabbing the paper. He read the headline aloud: *Motorcycle Accident Takes Life of Unidentified Man with Snake Tattoo.*

He dropped the paper and looked at the other boy. Suddenly, it wasn't important to close the barn door. It wasn't important to "take a ride." It wasn't important to stay out late. The boys ran all the way home, each to his own house and bed and covers, which they pulled over their heads.

After that, they never sneaked out again to play pranks on the neighbors or look for excitement in all the wrong places. Instead, they spent their summers dribbling basketballs in their driveways or playing kick-the-can with the neighbor kids.

But every so often, when the moon was full, they could hear in the distance a rumble. They'd look at each other and nod, then decide it was time to go in.

—Kathryn Totten, *storyteller/author*

Candy Motorcycle

Sure to give the boys more than a "sugar high"!

You can't sleep because the kid next to you is giggling, snoring, or talking in his sleep—what do you do?

"I take a bowl of pop-corn, dump it on his head, then get everyone else to attack him with pillows."

—John Detweiler, age 11
Littleton, Colorado

"I throw my pillow at him."

—Mitch Schupanitz, age 7
Littleton, Colorado

Ingredients and Supplies

Makes one

Two Bubble Tape® bubble gums (any flavor)

Glue gun

Two 1.8-ounce rolls SweetTARTS® (any flavor)

Three 0.8-ounce boxes RED HOTS®

Three boxes NERDS® (snack size, any flavor)

1.84-ounce box Junior® Mints

Three 0.29-ounce PEZ® fruit candies

Small pack sport (trading) cards

Two packs gum (five-stick, any flavor)

Three 0.8-ounce boxes Lemon-Head® candies

Knife

Two 1.14-ounce rolls LIFESAVERS® (any flavor)

Two sticks gum (any flavor)

Directions

1. Make these favors ahead or let the boys assemble them.

2. Lay the Bubble Tape® bubble gums flat, 3¼ inches apart, for the wheels. Glue one roll SweetTARTS® to the Bubble Tape® gums, to their centers, two-thirds the way down, for one tailpipe. Turn all over and glue the other roll SweetTARTS® to the wheels for the other tailpipe. *Caution:* Watch for dripping glue.

3. Glue the three boxes Red Hots® together, large sides together, so you can read RED HOTS on both sides of the "bigger" box you've made. Glue one box of Nerds® sideways, in front of and even with the bottom edge of the "big" Red Hots® box.

4. Lay flat and glue the Junior® Mints box on top the RED HOTS®, even with the Nerds®. Then glue this group of candy to the SweetTARTS® (tailpipes) between the Bubble Tape® gums (wheels), with the RED HOTS® on the SweetTARTS®, for the engine.

5. Glue two PEZ® candies together, large sides together. Then glue to the top of the Bubble Tape® gum in front of the NERDS®, so they're touching the Junior® Mints.

6. Glue the other two boxes of NERDS® together so they look like a little seat (not the motorcycle seat) for the front end of the motorcycle. Set this on top of the PEZ® candies ("seatback" toward center of motorcycle) and slide the sport cards, upright, picture facing forward, between the NERDS® (front end) and the Junior® Mints, for the windshield. Glue all down.

7. Glue the two packs of gum together, large sides together. Then glue to the top of the Junior® Mints, so you can read the large sides, front ends close to the sport cards, for the gas tank.

Candy Motorcycle *(continued)*

8. Glue two boxes Lemon-Head® candies together, large sides together. Then lay flat and glue the shorter sides to the backends of the gum packs, on top of the Junior® Mints, so they hang out over the Junior® Mints. Glue the third box of Lemon-Head® candies to the backend of the first two Lemon-Head® boxes, for the backrest of the motorcycle seat.

9. Glue the third PEZ® candies to the center of the RED HOTS®, on the side of the motorcycle that is "leaning" the most, for a kickstand.

10. Slice both rolls LIFESAVERS® in half. (You'll only need three halves.) Set and glue one half, foil end toward front, into the NERDS® "seat" (front end), for the headlight. Set and glue two LIFESAVERS® halves at an angle, foil ends toward back, to either side of the gum packs, right behind sport cards, for the handlebars.

11. Bend and glue the two sticks of gum to the tops of the Bubble Tape® gums (wheels), one "under" the PEZ® candies and the other under the Junior® Mints, for the front and back fenders. Race off to Candy Land!

Tip: You may have to go to several stores to find all the candy needed. Check at grocery, drug, discount, and party stores. Other candy may be substituted as long as it is of similar size and shape.

Note: When gluing, be sure the boys can read all the labels. Eventually, they will want to eat the candy!

Age Adjustment: For **younger** boys, have an adult help with the glue gun.

What's a good tip for a parent planning a Slumber Party?

"Don't do the same thing year after year for the same kids."

—Nick Ripple, age 12 Littleton, Colorado

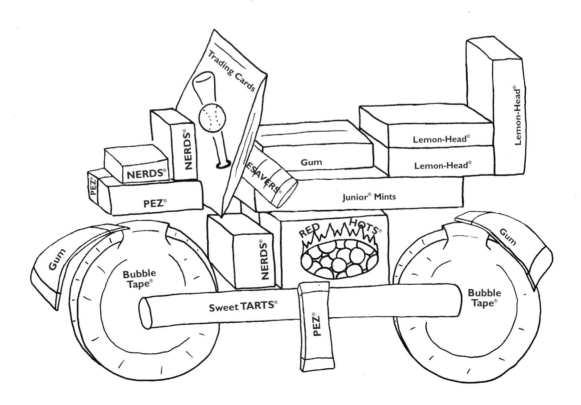

Midnight Snack Attack

Wagon wheel pasta and sauce

Candy Trains (see page 135, *Christmas Parties …What Do I Do?®*)

Cucumber "wheels" and ranch dressing

Nestlé® Baby Ruth® candy bars

Popsicle® Firecrackers™

PowerBars®

The Wright brothers invented the first working airplane in 1903. It was in the air for 12 seconds and flew 120 feet.

Video Recommendations

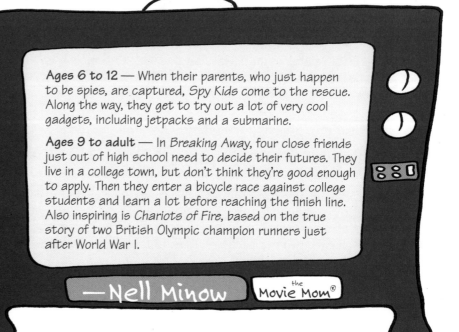

Ages 6 to 12 — When their parents, who just happen to be spies, are captured, *Spy Kids* come to the rescue. Along the way, they get to try out a lot of very cool gadgets, including jetpacks and a submarine.

Ages 9 to adult — In *Breaking Away*, four close friends just out of high school need to decide their futures. They live in a college town, but don't think they're good enough to apply. Then they enter a bicycle race against college students and learn a lot before reaching the finish line. Also inspiring is *Chariots of Fire*, based on the true story of two British Olympic champion runners just after World War I.

—Nell Minow — the Movie Mom®

Helicopter Eggs, Toast, and Bacon

Ingredients and Supplies

Makes 2	Spatula	Bread (one slice)
Knife	Hard-boiled egg	Two paper plates
Bacon (two strips)	Toaster	Two grapes
Frying pan	Butter	Two toothpicks

Directions

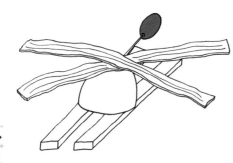

1. Cut the bacon slices in half lengthwise, so you have four long pieces. Fry it until crisp and set aside.

2. Meanwhile, peel and cut the hard-boiled egg in half, crosswise (not like deviled eggs).

3. Toast, butter, and cut the bread in half (not diagonally), then in half again lengthwise, so you have four long pieces. Lay two of the pieces on each paper plate (about ½ inch apart), for the helicopters' landing gear.

4. For the helicopters' bodies, put one-half the egg, sunny-side down, on each set of landing gear.

5. For the helicopters' propeller blades, set two pieces of the fried bacon (criss-cross) on top of each egg half.

6. Stick the grapes on the toothpicks, then stick the toothpicks in the egg halves, for the helicopters' tails.

Twenty Extra Fun Ideas

1. Take the boys to go-cart races.

2. Let them watch car races on TV or a video.

3. Set up an obstacle course for electric racecars.

4. Get on your knees and race Matchbox® cars through tunnels. (Use paper towel tubes.)

5. Spring for a demolition derby.

6. Help the kids make checkered flags.

7. Go to a park and help the boys shoot off rockets (available at hobby stores).

8. Go on a "field trip" to the airport.

9. Fold paper airplanes (sturdier from construction paper) and see whose is the fastest, or set up laundry baskets for an airplane throwing contest.

10. If it's legal where you live, light some fireworks. *Don't* leave the boys unsupervised!

11. Let the boys pretend they are on spaceships going to Mars or Jupiter.

12. Take them for a ride on a train.

13. Dust off your model train from the attic and let the kids set it up.

14. Strap on ice-skates or in-line skates and show the boys how it's done. (Don't forget safety gear!)

15. Have a bicycle race. (Don't forget helmets!)

16. Hold a foot race to see who is the fastest runner.

17. Take the kids snow or water skiing.

18. Rent paddleboats for more fun than you'd think.

19. Give the children fabric for Superman capes—tell them to tuck the fabric into their shirts at the neck.

20. Teach the boys helicopter jump rope: One boy spins a jump rope in a circle, low and parallel to the ground, and others jump over it.

Full Speed Ahead Invitation

Rubber cement
Seven pieces of each:
- 6 x 11-inch green construction paper,
- 6 x 11-inch cardboard,
- 3 x 11-inch black construction paper, and
- 3½ x 6-inch green construction paper

White-out
Pen
Seven heavy books
Roll of Lifesavers® (14 candies)
Seven of each:
 small rubberbands,
 sticks of gum
  (still wrapped),
 Smarties®, and
 peppermint candies
  (with twisted
  wrappers)

Outdoor Car Races

Pillow (only one)
Sleeping bags
 (one per boy)
Whistle
Optional: Checkered flag

Fill 'em Up Drink

Ginger ale
New plastic gas can
Clear plastic cups

Pilot-Tested Airplane Food

Scissors
Plain paper
Pen
Chairs (one per boy)
Sticky notes
TV dinners (one per boy)
Soda pop (assorted)
Plastic cups
Ice
Bags of peanuts
 (one per boy)
Cocktail napkins
Plastic silverware
Option 1: TV set
Option 2: TV trays

Don't forget the
camera and film

Wacky Airplane Ride

None

Capture the Socks

Socks (one pair per boy)

Candy Motorcycle

Two Bubble Tape®
 bubble gums (any flavor)
Glue gun
Two 1.8-ounce rolls
 SweetTARTS®
 (any flavor)
Three 0.8-ounce boxes
 RED HOTS®
Three boxes NERDS®
 (snack size, any flavor)
1.84-ounce box
 Junior® Mints
Three 0.29-ounce PEZ®
 fruit candies
Small pack sport
 (trading) cards
Two packs gum
 (five-stick, any flavor)
Three 0.8-ounce boxes
 Lemon-Head® candies
Knife
Two 1.14-ounce rolls
 LIFESAVERS®
 (any flavor)
Two sticks gum
 (any flavor)

Helicopter Eggs, Toast, and Bacon

Knife
Bacon (two strips)
Frying pan
Spatula
Hard-boiled egg
Toaster
Butter
Bread (one slice)
Two paper plates
Two grapes
Two toothpicks

Midnight Snack Attack

Wagon wheel pasta
 and sauce
Candy Trains (see
 page 135, *Christmas
 Parties …What Do I
 Do?*®)
Cucumber "wheels"
 and ranch dressing
Nestle® Baby Ruth®
 candy bars
Popsicle® Firecrackers™
PowerBars®

CHAPTER ELEVEN

Pack it up and head to Africa for a Safari your child's friends have only seen in the movies. You'll hunt for panthers with your Binocular Cameras, fight off pythons, and even outsmart poisonous darts and pesky giant ants while canoeing down the Congo River! You'll get to eat Snake Sandwich for dinner, and wash it down with Swamp Juice. Yum! After a Flashlight Tour searching for every imaginable animal, you'll try your hand at Nighttime Doodles in the dark. And what else could you serve for breakfast but Gorilla Bread and Quicksand Toast!

Jungle Safari Invitation

Supplies

Pencil

Card stock

Scissors

Plain white paper

Markers (assorted)

X-acto® knife

Glue

Pen

Optional: Tape

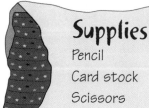

Directions

1. For each invitation, trace the following pattern pieces onto card stock and cut out: one alligator (pattern piece #1) and one invitation (pattern piece #2).

2. Trace the following pattern piece onto white paper and cut out: envelope (pattern piece #3). Set aside

3. Color the alligator, parrot and leaves (on the invitation), and monkey and branch (on the envelope) with the markers.

4. Carefully cut two slits in the invitation with the x-acto® knife, using the two lines to the left of the parrot.

5. Insert the tabs below the alligator's legs into the slits through the front of the invitation, with the colored side of the alligator facing forward. Underneath the invitation, fold the tabs back to make the alligator stand up, glue them in place.

6. Fill in the details on the invitation with the pen.

7. To make the envelope, fold back the side tabs, fold up the bottom flap, and fold down the top flap.

8. Fold the alligator flat against the invitation, then insert all into the envelope and glue it closed. Hand deliver.

Optional: Use tape in place of glue.

Pattern #1

Jungle Safari Slumber Party

Take a trip with me to Africa!

Party Given By: _____

Special Occasion: _____

Day and Date: _____

Drop-off Time: _____

Pick-up Time: _____

Address and Directions: _____

_____

Phone Number: _____

Please call and tell me if you can join the Safari!

Pattern #2

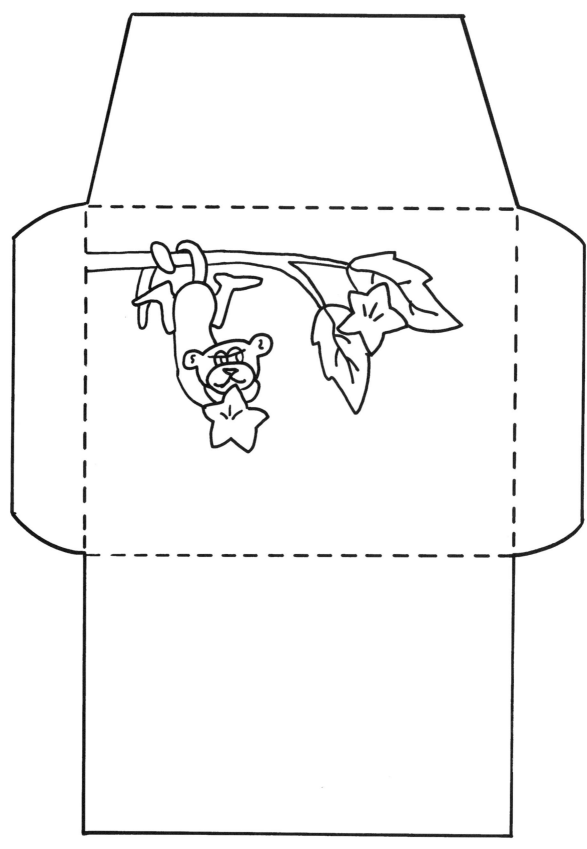

Pattern #3

Binocular Camera

Supplies

Makes one
Glue gun
Two toilet paper tubes

Paper hole puncher
24-inch piece
brown yarn

Button
Optional: Markers
(assorted colors)

Directions

1. Glue the toilet paper tubes together, side by side, to make the binoculars.

2. Punch a hole in each toilet paper tube at the top, close to one end, to attach the yarn (strap).

3. To attach the "strap," knot one end of yarn and thread through one hole, from inside the tube out. Thread the other end through the other hole, from outside the tube in, and knot.

4. Glue the button onto the right side of the binoculars for the camera button that you'll push to take a picture.

Tip: Don't use paint to decorate the binoculars because they won't be dry in time to use them for the Panther Hunt that follows.

Optional: Decorate your binoculars with markers.

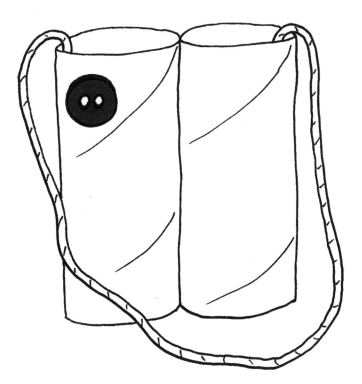

Where did you go on safari?

"I went 'gaming' (not hunting) in Zimbabwe, just north of South Africa."

—Tine Norseth
Oslo, Norway

What were your most memorable animal sightings while on safari?

"We were on a boat on Lake Victoria, watching the sunset, when this huge hippopotamus opened its entire mouth just 2 feet away from us! I'm sure its mouth was just 6 feet wide, but it felt like 15 feet to me. It was the scariest thing I had ever seen. Elephants are also scary up close. We were on foot when we came upon a herd of them. One was so irritated that he started backing up, with his ears flapping, which meant he was going to attack. Lucky for us, he backed up against a small tree, bending it over backwards. When the tree smacked him in the behind, he ran the other way!"

—Tine Norseth
Oslo, Norway

Panther Hunt
Snakes, Ants, and Natives, Oh, My!

What is your best idea for Slumber Party favor?

"A flashlight, with the child's name written on it with puff paint."

—Teri Bavley
Prairie Village, Kansas

Gorillas are not just the largest apes in Africa, they are the largest living primates, the "family" that also claims humans. There are eastern and western lowland gorillas, who have short fur, and mountain gorillas, made famous by Dian Fossey's book, *Gorilla's in the Mist*, and the movie by the same name. Their fur is longer because they live in higher altitudes than the "lowlanders."

Supplies

Safari hat (for the guide)
Chairs (one per child, plus one extra)
Plastic ivy or rope (vines)
Foam rubber mattress pad in wading pool with water (swamp)

Plastic ants
Blue tissue paper (river)
Narrow board (canoe)

Several brooms (oars)
G.I. Joe™ or Ken® dolls (natives)
Plastic dryer vent (snake)
Two ladders (trees)
Stuffed cat (panther)
Binocular Cameras (see page 139)

Optional: Anything you can use for the things in the story

Directions

1. Before the party, read the story on page 141, aloud once or twice so you'll be a good guide.

2. Using all the supplies except the chairs (Jeep®) and Binocular Cameras, set up the jungle in your basement, garage, or yard, even at a neighbor's. Follow the order in the story. (The G.I. Joe™ and Ken® dolls should only be wearing shorts or swimming trunks to look like natives.)

3. Set up the chairs like seats in a Jeep®, putting one where the driver's seat would go.

4. Have the children get in the Jeep® with their Binocular Cameras and tell them:

We are going on a jungle safari along the Congo River, deep in Africa. If we are successful, we will be rich! We must try to keep together because it is very dangerous out there. Follow me, do as I do, and keep an eye out for each other and other living creatures!

5. Pretend to start driving, then stand up and pick up your chair at the same time, holding it to your underside. Make sure the children do the same. Then lead them into the jungle, staying in the Jeep® "formation." When you get to the jungle, sit down again, and begin reading and acting out the story on the next page, reminding the children to follow along:

Climb out of the Jeep®. We have to walk from here. Clap your hands softly and say this as we go, because it will help us stay together: "Going on a panther hunt. Going on a panther hunt. Going on a panther hunt." First, we have to walk through a hot, steamy swamp with lots of vines hanging down in front of us. Push the vines aside! Push, push, push, push! Good! We are through the vines...

Repeat after me: "Going on a panther hunt. Going on a panther hunt. Going on a panther hunt." Now we have to walk through the swamp. Lift those legs really high! Oh, the mud is squishy. Squish, squish, squish, squish! Well, we made it through the swamp...

"Going on a panther hunt. Going on a panther hunt. Going on a panther hunt." But look over there. I see a huge anthill. Oh, no! The ants are after us! Run! Brush the ants off of you! Quick! Brush them off! Brush, brush, brush, brush. Keep on running! Run, run, run, run. Okay, we can slow down. It's safe now...

"Going on a panther hunt. Going on a panther hunt. Going on a panther hunt." Now we're at the river. We'll go the rest of the way by canoe. Grab the oars, climb in, and let's row together. First to the left, and then to the right. Row, row, row, row. Row, row, row, row. The river is quiet. I think it is too quiet. Look around. Do you see anything? Oh, no! There are natives over there with blow guns. They're going to shoot poisonous darts at us! Row faster! Row, row, row, row, row, row, row! Oh, good. We escaped...

"Going on a panther hunt. Going on a panther hunt. Going on a panther hunt." We're getting pretty deep in the jungle now. Oh, dear! What's that? Dangling from that tree? It's a snake! A big fat snake. Someone, push him in the river with your oar. Quick before he strangles one of us! Oh, thanks! You're so brave! I hate snakes. But he's in the water now...

"Going on a panther hunt. Going on a panther hunt. Going on a panther hunt." I'd keep your eyes open for panthers now. Oh, my! Look what's in the top of that tree! It is a panther! Quick! Take out your Binocular Cameras and shoot him. Ready? One, two, three... Oops! He didn't like that! He's chasing us! Hurry! Turn the canoe around! Turn, turn, turn, turn! Now really row. Row, row, row, row. Row for your life! Row, row, row, row, row, row, row! The panther is swimming. He's still after us! The snake! He's slithering next to the canoe! The blow guns! The natives are shooting darts at us again! Row, row, row, row, row, row, row...

Shhhh! "Going on a panther hunt. Going on a panther hunt. Going on a panther hunt." This is where we get out and walk back through the jungle. But we're going to have to run. Run, run, run, run. The ants again! Brush them off! Keep running! Run, run, run, run, run, run, run! We lost the snake but the panther is still behind us. Now we're back at the swamp. Lift those legs really high. We have to run through the squishy mud. Squish, squish, squish, squish, squish, squish, squish...

"Going on a panther hunt. Going on a panther hung. Going on a panther hunt." Oh, no! The panther is still behind us. He's so fast. Here we are at the vines. Push them aside. Quick! Push, push, push, push, push, push, push... Now let's jump in the Jeep® and go, but first we have to turn it around. Turn, turn, turn, turn. Let's get back to base camp....

Wow! That was great! Is everyone okay? Did everyone get a picture of the panther? Good! A nature magazine will buy them and we'll all be rich! Rich, rich, rich, rich, rich!

—*Kathryn Totten,* storyteller/author

What was your most memorable animal sighting while on safari?

"My most memorable sighting was of a pride of ten lionesses gathered to rest and sun themselves in the early morning after a night of hunting. They were beautiful, strong, and serene at the same time. Even though our guide assured us that the animals were accustomed to human visitors (as long as we stayed seated in our vehicle), I felt a distinct twinge of apprehension the closer we got, letting me know that these animals were to be respected."

—Ann E. Byrnes (a.k.a. Ann E. Dorbin) Author of *Single Women - Alive and Well!* and *Saving the Bay: People Working for the Future of the Chesapeake*

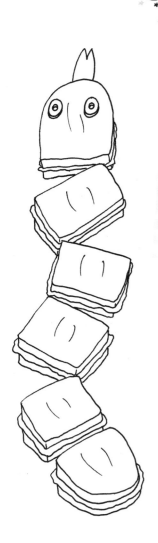

Snake Sandwich

Ingredients and Supplies

Bread knife
Two baguettes
(long thin French bread)
Leaf lettuce
Cookie sheet
Lunchmeat (assorted)
Small knife
Mayonnaise

Green olive (pimento stuffed)
Pickle spear
Optional: Sub sandwich
dressing, mustard, vinegar,
salt and pepper, cheese and
tomato slices, pickle and black
olive slices, shredded lettuce,
diced green pepper and
onion, and bowls

Directions

1. Slice the baguettes lengthwise, then into enough "sandwiches" for all the children.

2. Lay leaf lettuce on the cookie sheet and arrange the "sandwiches" into one long snake on top of the lettuce. You will have four heel "sandwiches." Make sure one is at the head of the snake and the other is at the tail. (Slice off the rounded ends of the other two heels and toss.)

3. Insert the assorted lunchmeat into the "sandwiches."

4. With the knife, dab one small glob of mayonnaise on each side of the snake's "head." Slice the green olive in half and attach the halves, cut sides out, to the globs of mayonnaise, for the snake's eyes.

5. Cut the snake's tongue from the pickle spear, then prick a hole in the snake's head between the eyes, just big enough to stick the tongue in, then do just that!

Optional: Add any of the ingredients or set them out in bowls for the children to garnish their own Snake Sandwiches.

Swamp Juice

Ingredients and Supplies

Green Kool-Aid®
Long-handled spoon

Clean large tub
(galvanized steel)
Sugar

Water
Paper cups
with handles

Directions

1. Follow the directions on the Kool-Aid® package and use the long-handled spoon to mix in the clean large tub with the called-for amounts of sugar and water.

2. Let the kids scoop some tasty Swamp Juice out of the tub with their cups.

Note: You may be tempted to add ice to the tub, but keep in mind what temperature swamp water must be!

Kool-Aid® (first called Kool-Ade) has been around since 1927. Author Wilhelminia Ripple discovered its birthplace when her son Mark went to college in Hastings, Nebraska, where the library is named for Edwin Perkins, who made Kool-Aid® in 1927 from his soft drink syrup, Fruit Smack. Both the Perkins Library and the town's museum keep a display on Nebraska's official soft drink, plus the town holds a Kool-Aid® Days Festival every summer.

My Grandfather's Jungle Safari Adventure

"Grandpa, my friends are here."

"Huh?"

"Grandpa, wake up. My friends want to hear your story."

"Huh? What story?"

"You know, Grandpa. The story about the jungle safari."

"Oh, yes. The jungle safari story. Well now, sit down here. I remember that trip like it was yesterday. But, you have to promise me, don't be SCARED!"

"We won't Grandpa. Tell us the story."

"I was a pilot as a young man. I was flying out of South Africa with a package that would make me rich. Diamonds. If only..."

"Grandpa, get to the part about the crash."

"Well, I was flying over the Congo River when the engines started to quit. I was losing altitude. I looked for some place, any place to land. All I could see were trees. I was flying over the jungle. There wasn't a speck of flat ground anywhere. Then I was in the trees! The plane wedged in the branches a hundred feet off the ground."

"Were you hurt?"

"Well, I had a cut on my head. I had to stop the bleeding with my bag of diamonds, but I didn't have any broken bones, so as soon as I could, I climbed out of the plane."

"In the trees?"

"The tallest trees you can imagine. I started down. It was very hot and humid. I was dripping wet. The birds were calling loudly because I had made such a mess of their trees. There were birds of every color. Dazzling yellows. Electric blues. Shimmering greens."

"Did you catch them?"

"No, I didn't try to catch them. I just kept climbing down. Then I put my foot down on something that didn't feel like a tree branch. When I looked down, I was stepping on a huge snake!"

"Gross!"

"It was as thick as my arm, and it wound around and around the branches so I couldn't tell how long it was. It started to wind around my leg. The more I pulled, the tighter it gripped me."

"Grandpa, it could have killed you!"

"Well, it might have killed me. But there were monkeys. Suddenly dozens of chattering monkeys came swinging through the branches and the snake was distracted, just long enough for me to pull myself free. I jumped to the ground quick as lightning!"

"You were so brave."

"I suppose I was, at that. But then I needed to find my way out of the jungle. I looked around. I knew if I found the river, I could follow it out."

"Was it a big river?"

"The river was so big, for it had been raining a lot more than usual that year. Now I needed some kind of boat. I gathered some fallen tree trunks and tied them together with jungle vines. I remembered my knots from the Boy Scouts, you see. Came in very handy."

"So you floated down the river, all by yourself?"

"I wasn't really all by myself. The river was full of living things. Once, a crocodile swam up right beside my raft and looked me over. I think he was deciding if I'd be a big enough lunch for him. I scrunched up in the middle of the raft and sat very, very still. Good thing I wasn't on his menu that day."

"What did YOU have for lunch, Grandpa?"

"Well, I was a pretty fair fisherman, you see. I just reached into the river whenever I got hungry and grabbed a big fat fish!"

"Is that all you ate?"

"Oh, no. Sometimes I pulled the raft over and climbed up the trees to pick fruit. I watched the monkeys. I learned from them, you see. But one time, I was trudging toward a stand of promising fruit trees when I stepped into a slippery mess. I found myself stuck in it. It was quicksand."

"Oh, no! What did you do?"

"Well, first thing to do when you're in quicksand is NOT to panic. Hold very still so you won't sink too fast. So I stayed as still as I could, just looking around with my eyeballs. There was a tree branch hanging close to me. I stretched as far as I could but I couldn't get my hand around it. I was sinking faster. I thought I was finished."

"What did you do?"

"Do? There was nothing to do."

"But, Grandpa..."

"Well, I had a little help, you see. A boy, wearing nothing but a little apron, came out of the trees. He got that branch and lifted it over to me. I climbed out, thanks to him. He took me home to his village for supper. We ate snake, as I recall."

"Not snake! You didn't really eat snake?"

continued

My Grandfather's Jungle Adventure *(continued)*

"I did and lived to tell you about it. I also ate some kind of roots. Very tasty. I stayed in the village for a month or so. They showed me how to paint black designs on my skin to keep the nasty mosquitoes off. Lovely tattoos, really, but not permanent, sorry to say."

"Did you want to stay there, Grandpa?"

"Well, after a bit, I began to think about getting on home. They helped me make my raft stronger. We worked on it a little every day, no hurry. Then one day, I got on the raft and floated away. Before long, I drifted into the Atlantic Ocean and was spotted by a big ship. I was pulled aboard and cleaned up, then sent home."

"Grandpa, you lost your chance to get rich."

"Well, not really. I still had the diamonds, you see."

"Did you sell them all?"

"Well, most of them."

"Where are the ones you didn't sell?"

"You've seen that diamond ring on your grandmother's finger, right?"

"Sure, Grandpa, but you could have made more money."

"Yes, but then I wouldn't have you, now would I?"

"Thanks, Grandpa!"

"Now get outta here and let me get back to my nap."

—*Kathryn Totten,* storyteller/author

Flashlight Tour

Supplies

Flashlight (one per child)
Stuffed animals (a herd)
Optional: Paper and pencil

Directions

1. On the invitation, ask each child to bring a working flashlight, unless you have a bunch still "on alert" from Y2K!

2. Set up lots of stuffed animals (borrowed, if necessary) throughout your house.

3. When it is dark outside, turn off the lights inside and guide the children with their flashlights through your house to search for animals.

Optional: Write down each animal's name after it's found. If there is more than one tiger, for example, let the children who find them give them descriptive names.

Variation: Set up the animals in your backyard.

Age Adjustment: Younger children may get scared of the dark, so be prepared to play this with a few lights on or some night-lights.

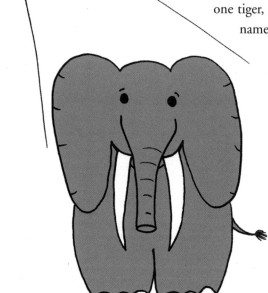

ighttime Doodles

Save this game of skill for after dark

Supplies

Scissors
Fourteen index
  cards
Pen

Two large notepads
Two pencils
Small notepad
Pencil sharpener

Optional:
Watch with a light
and second hand

The flashlight was invented in 1898 through the combined efforts of Joshua Lionel Cowen, owner of the American Eveready Battery Company, and one of his salesmen, Conrad Hubert.

Directions

1. Before the party, cut the index cards in half. Write the following items on them, one item per card:

Safari	Zebra	Gorilla	Safari Guide
Quicksand	Watering Hole	Jeep®	Binoculars
Jungle	Tent	Backpack	Safari Hat
Rainforest	Camera	Campfire	Monkey
Snake	Elephant	Swinging Vine	Hippopotamus
Bug	Lion	Flashlight	Peacock
Giraffe	Tiger	Walkie-talkie	Ostrich

2. Divide your guests into two teams. Give each team a notepad and pencil.

3. Put the index cards in a pile upside-down between the two teams.

4. Pick a team to start. The first person from that team takes a card from the pile and reads it to himself without letting anyone else, even on his team, see the card.

5. Tell him to return the card to the bottom of the pile, upside down, and pick up his team's notepad and pencil.

6. Then turn off the lights and give him 30 seconds to draw a picture of the item on his card.

7. Turn the lights back on and have him show his team (only) his drawing. They get 30 seconds to guess the item. If they are right, they get 1 point.

8. If they're wrong, the other team gets 30 seconds to guess the item. They get 1 point if they are right. Keep score on the small notepad.

9. Now let a player from the second team take his turn at Nighttime Doodles. Go back and forth until everyone has had a turn.

10. Take time out to sharpen the pencils when needed. The team with the most points wins.

Optional: For extra fun, and to be fair, use a watch with a light and second hand to time the players and teams.

Variation: For nighttime fun anytime, play this game without the Safari Party theme.

Tell us about your favorite Slumber Party?

"My favorite Slumber Party was a jungle sleepover."

—Katie Day, age 10
Littleton, Colorado

145

Midnight Snack Attack

Animal crackers

Fudge-striped cookies (like zebras)

Salted peanuts in the shell

Chocolate-covered frozen bananas

Banana splits in plastic "safari" boats

Quicksand cups— crushed vanilla wafer cookies, pudding, and gummy worms

You're hungry, it's late, there's no food in sight. Tell us your secret on how you get a snack?

"I sneak into the kitchen and make cinnamon toast."

—Todd Davidson, age 8 Burlington, Wyoming

Video Recommendations

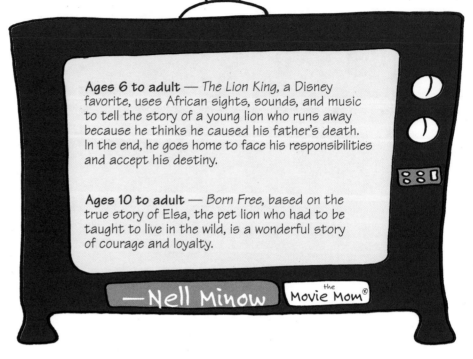

Ages 6 to adult — *The Lion King*, a Disney favorite, uses African sights, sounds, and music to tell the story of a young lion who runs away because he thinks he caused his father's death. In the end, he goes home to face his responsibilities and accept his destiny.

Ages 10 to adult — *Born Free*, based on the true story of Elsa, the pet lion who had to be taught to live in the wild, is a wonderful story of courage and loyalty.

—Nell Minow the Movie Mom®

Gorilla Bread and Quicksand Toast

A breakfast that will capture kids' cravings

Ingredients and Supplies

Banana bread (homemade or store-bought)

Bread knife

Ovenproof plate
Powdered sugar
Toaster
Sliced bread

Knife
Butter
Plate
Cinnamon sugar

Directions

1. Cut your homemade or store-bought banana bread into ½-inch slices and lay on an ovenproof plate. Sprinkle with powdered sugar and put in oven on warm. You now have Gorilla Bread.

2. Meanwhile, toast the sliced bread. Spread with butter, lay on a plate, then sprinkle with cinnamon sugar to make Quicksand Toast.

3. Serve both breads while warm.

Twenty Extra Fun Ideas

1. Tell your guests to come in safari garb, then take a group photo.

2. Make masks and claws from poster board for your guests to wear.

3. Have everyone bring his favorite stuffed animal.

4. Dress up like a lion or tiger to greet your guests at the door.

5. Give the kids face paint to paint faces on each other.

6. Let girls paint their fingernails and toenails like tigers, zebras, or giraffes.

7. Help everyone make rain sticks. (Search the Internet for instructions.)

8. Play snake with a jump rope: Two people hold the ends, wiggling the rope on the ground, while another person tries to jump over the "snake" without stepping on it.

9. Let the prize for a game be "resting" in a hammock.

10. Hold a contest to name a "new" safari drink.

11. Ask the children where the word "safari" comes from? (Have the answer.)

12. Ask the children what animals they would see on a safari?

13. Play hangman using only safari animals for the words.

14. Give each guest a turn pretending to be an animal while everyone else guesses what he is.

15. Set up plastic animals for your guests to drive toy Jeeps® around.

16. Tell a safari story with everyone adding one or two sentences.

17. Go through the alphabet naming things you would take or see on a safari.

18. Dance to jungle music.

19. Play musical chairs to jungle music.

20. Sing animal songs. (Not "Old McDonald"!)

Where did you go on safari?

"I went on safari at the Mala Mala Game Reserve in Kruger National Park in South Africa for three days, going on two safaris each day, one in the early morning and one in the afternoon and evening, where we watched the animals in their nocturnal activities."

—Ann E. Byrnes (a.k.a. Ann E. Dorbin) Author of *Single Women - Alive and Well!* and *Saving the Bay: People Working for the Future of the Chesapeake*

Jungle Safari Party Invitation

Pencil
Card stock
Scissors
Plain white paper
Markers (assorted)
X-acto® knife
Glue
Pen
Optional: Tape

Binocular Camera

Glue gun
Two toilet paper tubes
Paper hole puncher
24-inch piece brown yarn
Button
Optional: Markers
  (assorted colors)

Panther Hunt
Snakes, Ants, and Natives, Oh, My!

Safari hat (for the guide)
Chairs (one per child, plus one extra)
Plastic ivy or rope (vines)
Foam rubber mattress pad in wading pool with water (swamp)
Plastic ants
Blue tissue paper (river)
Narrow board (canoe)
Several brooms (oars)
G.I. Joe™ or Ken® dolls (natives)
Plastic dryer vent (snake)
Two ladders (trees)
Stuffed cat (panther)
Binocular Cameras (see page 139)
Optional: Anything you can use for the things in the story

Don't forget the camera and film

Snake Sandwich

Bread knife
Two baguettes (long thin French bread)
Leaf lettuce
Cookie sheet
Lunchmeat (assorted)
Small knife
Mayonnaise
Green olive (pimento stuffed)
Pickle spear
Optional: Sub sandwich dressing, mustard, vinegar, salt and pepper, cheese and tomato slices, pickle and black olive slices, shredded lettuce, diced green pepper and onion, and bowls

Swamp Juice

Green Kool-Aid®
Long-handled spoon
Clean large tub (galvanized steel)
Sugar
Water
Paper cups with handles

Flashlight Tour

Flashlight (one per child)
Stuffed animals (a herd)
Optional: Paper and pencil

Nighttime Doodles

Scissors
Fourteen index cards
Pen
Two large notepads
Two pencils
Small notepad
Pencil sharpener
Optional: Watch with a light and second hand

Gorilla Bread and Quicks and Toast

Banana bread (homemade or store-bought)
Bread knife
Ovenproof plate
Powdered sugar
Toaster
Sliced bread
Knife
Butter
Plate
Cinnamon sugar

Midnight Snack Attack

Animal crackers
Fudge-striped cookies (like zebras)
Salted peanuts in the shell
Chocolate-covered frozen bananas
Banana splits in plastic "safari" boats
Quicksand cups— crushed vanilla wafer cookies, pudding, and gummy worms

CHAPTER TWELVE

INSIDE OUT, UPSIDE DOWN, AND BACKWARDS

Throw a party that breaks all the rules, where kids get to do everything the wrong way for once! ~~Start~~ End with My Mixed-Up Babysitting Job, then serve an Upside Down Spaghetti dinner right in the middle of a brand new white tablecloth! Say "no" when you mean "yes," "good-bye" when you mean "hello," and "so long" to watching movies sitting right side up or from beginning to end. Run upside down races and backwards treasure hunts that will keep your guests feeling inside out for days to come, especially after eating Inside Out Eggs for breakfast. You'll be the talk of the town when the party is ~~long over~~ just beginning!

Upside Down Name Bug Invitation

Order of Inside Out, Upside Down, and Backwards Party

Start with My Mixed Up Babysitting Job

Have dinner (Upside Down Spaghetti with Fun Mixed Up Juice)

Read "A Backwards Day"

Find the Magic Key

Do Make A Treasure

Watch videos with Midnight Snack Attack

Sleep

Eat breakfast (Inside Out Egg in Toast)

Play Backwards Name Game

Brush teeth, get dressed, and pack

Say hello!

Supplies

Makes 12

Twelve pieces 5½ x 3¾-inch construction paper (any color)

Pencil

Markers or colored pencils

Glue stick

Twelve 4 x 5½-inch notecards

Copy paper

Scissors

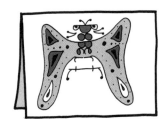

Directions

1. Fold one piece construction paper in half widthwise, crease, then unfold.

2. Print one child's name heavily with the pencil, with the bottom of the letters on the fold line.

3. Fold the paper again, with the writing on the inside. Using the side of the pencil, rub firmly. This will transfer your writing to the blank side of the paper, only upside down.

4. Open the paper and go over the upside down name with the pencil to darken it.

5. Draw a bug with wings, a head, antennae, and legs, using the names for the body, similar to the illustration. Color the bug with markers or colored pencils.

6. Glue the construction paper to the front of a notecard.

7. Repeat steps #1 to #6 for all the invitations.

8. Make twelve copies of the invitation. Cut them to fit inside the notecards, then glue in place.

9. Fill in the details and deliver.

¡ytraP Party!

Please come to my Inside Out, Upside Down, and Backwards Slumber Party.
We will walk, talk, and eat all the wrong ways!

Party Given By: _____

Special Occasion: _____

Day and Date: _____

Drop-off Time: _____

Pick-up Time: _____

Address and Directions: _____

_____

Phone Number: _____

Please call and let me know if you can come.
Be sure to wear your clothes Inside Out,
Upside Down, or Backwards!

My Mixed Up Babysitting Job

Supplies

None

Directions

1. Before the party, be sure to practice the sound effects in step #2 and read the story aloud in step #3.

2. Before reading the story in step #3 to the children, instruct them to make the following sound effects when the corresponding words in **bold** are read:

PHONE	ring ring ring
STRANGE	oooooooooo! (an eerie sound)
RULES	(clap once)
JUNIOR	Junior! Junior! Junior!
LAUGH	hee hee hee

3. Then read the story below to the children. Be sure to stop and wait for them to make the appropriate sound effect when you read a word in **bold.** You may have to help them get started:

The **PHONE** rang. It was Mr. Johnson who lives up on the corner. He said, "Can you babysit tonight? I will pay you twenty dollars."

I didn't have any other plans and I really wanted the twenty dollars, so I said, "Sure, I'll be right over." Little did I know I was in for a **STRANGE** night.

I knew it was going to be a **STRANGE** night as soon as I read his list of rules:

1. Do not let **JUNIOR** go to bed before 7 p.m..
2. If he **LAUGHS** when we leave, give him his Teddy bear to cuddle.
3. **JUNIOR** must eat all of his candy before he gets any vegetables.
4. Whatever you do, do not read **JUNIOR** a bedtime story...

Now those were **STRANGE** rules!

Mr. Johnson took me to **JUNIOR'S** room to get acquainted. **JUNIOR** was sitting quietly on the floor, playing with his toy **PHONE.** There was a large toy box in one corner, a chest of drawers, a closet door, and a little bed. Everything was neat and clean. **JUNIOR LAUGHED** and waved at me.

That's a little **STRANGE,** I thought, but this should be easy. Then Mr. and Mrs. Johnson left and the world turned upside down!

JUNIOR stopped playing with his **PHONE.** "Time for bed," he said, and he put on his pajamas. I remembered the **RULE** about not going to bed before 7 p.m. Since it was only 5 p.m., I took **JUNIOR** by the hand and led him out of his room.

When we walked into the living room and **JUNIOR** did not see his parents, he said, "Mommy and Daddy are gone." Then **JUNIOR** started to giggle and **LAUGH** really hard and roll on the

floor. Tears were streaming down his face. I thought that was a pretty **STRANGE** reaction, and I was kind of worried.

So I ran to **JUNIOR'S** toy box and found his Teddy bear. When I handed it to him, he quieted down and sucked his thumb. That was a good **RULE,** I decided.

Just then, the **PHONE** rang. "Is everything okay?" It was Mr. Johnson.

"Yes," I said, and he hung up. That was **STRANGE,** I thought.

At 6 p.m., I went to the kitchen to get **JUNIOR** his dinner. There was a plate already made up for him in the refrigerator, and one for me, too. Both plates had a variety of chocolates, jelly beans, and candy corn in neat little piles. What a **STRANGE** dinner, I said to myself.

There was a bowl of cut-up carrots, cucumbers, and celery in the refrigerator, too. **JUNIOR** grabbed for them. Remembering the **RULES,** I suggested he try some of the food on his plate first. He **LAUGHED** a little, but **JUNIOR** knew I meant it.

At first, I really liked the idea of eating nothing but candy for dinner, but after I ate most of the chocolates and candy corn, I felt kind of sick. After **JUNIOR** cleaned up most of his plate, I put out the bowl of vegetables. I felt kind of sneaky letting him eat them, though, since he hadn't finished all of his candy.

At 6:30 p.m., **JUNIOR** crawled onto his bed. I knew I'd better keep him awake until 7 p.m. It was one of the **RULES** of the house. I tried to get **JUNIOR** to play with his toy **PHONE,**
continued

My Mixed Up Babysitting Job (continued)

but he just sucked his thumb and looked sleepy. As a last resort, I pulled a book of bedtime stories out of **JUNIOR'S** toy box to read to him. I had forgotten that **RULE.**

I began reading a story about an enchanted forest when I noticed **STRANGE** shadows forming on the walls. They looked like branches of tall trees, swaying in the breeze. When it started to rain in the story, the room got darker and a light mist began to fall from the ceiling. Something smelled **STRANGE,** too. It smelled like a campfire.

I got sort of nervous. I thought I heard the **PHONE** ring in the distance. I started to **LAUGH.** I kept on reading. **JUNIOR** jumped off the bed and ran to his closet door. When he opened it, to my surprise, I saw a dragon inside! The dragon smiled and **LAUGHED,** and a little puff of smoke came out of his mouth. But for some reason, this didn't seem **STRANGE** to me.

JUNIOR climbed onto the dragon's back and rode him all over the bedroom. The dragon's tail kept knocking at the chest of drawers, actually scooping toys out of the toy box whenever he went by. It was so **STRANGE.** Soon toys were scattered all over the floor, all of **JUNIOR'S** clothes were spilled from the drawers, and the wallpaper was singed from the dragon's fiery breath!

Then I remembered the **RULE,** I quickly finished the story. When I got to the part where the dragon went to sleep in his cave for a hundred years, **STRANGE** enough, the dragon went back to the closet and closed the door. **JUNIOR** climbed back onto his bed. Holding his Teddy bear, he closed his eyes and went to sleep. His room was totally trashed.

Before I had a chance to clean it up, Mr. and Mrs. Johnson came back home. They walked into the bedroom and saw the mess. I didn't know what else to do, so I **LAUGHED.**

"You read **JUNIOR** the dragon story, right?" asked Mr. Johnson, shaking his head. Mrs. Johnson stared at the mess and smiled. I thought that was really **STRANGE.**

"Yes, I did," I admitted. "But **JUNIOR** didn't go to sleep before 7 p.m.."

"Good job," said Mr. Johnson, walking me to the door and **LAUGHING.** He handed me the twenty dollars, but I wasn't sure I should take it. After all, I didn't keep the **RULES.** Mr. Johnson insisted that I take the money and thanked me again.

As I walked home, a light mist began to fall and I thought I smelled dragon breath. No way, I said to myself. That dragon is asleep for a hundred years. But I kept looking in the shadows, just to be sure, and **LAUGHED** a little, too.

As soon as I got home, I heard the **PHONE** ring. I didn't dare answer it, though. I didn't need money that bad!

—*Kathryn Totten,* storyteller/author

Upside Down Spaghetti

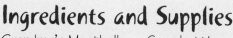

Ingredients and Supplies

Grandma's Meatballs (recipe on page 153)
Spaghetti noodles
Large pot
Strainer

Spaghetti sauce (store bought)
Garlic bread
White, new, plastic tablecloth
Bread knife

Weird utensils, such as chopsticks, spatulas, and tongs (one per child)
Optional: Frozen meatballs

Directions

1. Make the meatballs and set them aside. You will want them warm, not hot.

2. While you cook the spaghetti noodles in a large pot of water, heat up the sauce and garlic bread. Meanwhile, lay out the tablecloth on the table.

3. Drain the noodles when they're done, and slice the garlic bread into serving size pieces.

4. Then lay the meatballs directly onto the center of the tablecloth. Spoon the noodles over the meatballs, then pour the sauce over the noodles.

5. Place the bread slices around the Upside Down Spaghetti and lay the weird utensils out.

6. Let the kids choose a utensil to eat with and let them enjoy!

7. Wrap up the leftovers in the tablecloth and throw all out except the utensils.

Optional: Heat and serve frozen meatballs .

Note: This is a fun dinner to serve for April Fool's Day.

Grandma's Meatballs

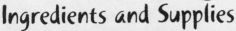

Serve with Upside Down Spaghetti

Ingredients and Supplies

Makes approximately 2 dozen
2 pounds ground beef
Six eggs
¾ cup grated parmesan cheese
1½ cups Italian bread crumbs
Crushed garlic (two cloves)
2 teaspoons salt

Pepper (squirt)   Frying pan
Fresh parsley   Olive oil
(squirt)   Spatula
¼ cup water

Directions

1. Dump the ground beef onto a clean counter and form a well in the center. Crack the eggs into the well along with the cheese, bread crumbs, garlic, salt, pepper, parsley, and water.

3. Knead all of the ingredients together with your hands until well blended.

4. Form the mixture into 2-inch round balls.

5. Fry the meatballs in olive oil until brown.

It's 2 a.m., you are exhausted, and there are still children awake— what drastic measures do you take?

"I shut everything down by recruiting teenagers for 'reinforcement,' making deals to reimburse them at a later date."

—Barbara Young
Lost Creek, West Virginia

Fun Mixed Up Juice

Wait 'til the party to stir this up

Ingredients and Supplies

Makes 8
Four assorted fruit juices
(2 cups each)

2-quart plastic pitcher with lid
Crushed ice
Eight 8-ounce cups

Directions

1. Have the kids pour the fruit juices into the plastic pitcher.

2. Place the lid on, making sure it fits snugly.

3. Let the kids take turns turning the pitcher upside down until the juices are all mixed up.

4. Place crushed ice into the cups and pour in the juice.

Tip: You might want to do this outside or over a floor that mops up easily!

153

Backwards Day

Bob and his sister, Bobbi, were walking home from the movie theater when the sky suddenly turned dark. A cold wind began to blow behind them, as if it were pushing them. With a flash of lightning, a pounding rain began.

Just ahead, there was a huge evergreen tree with branches that spread wide and hung down to the ground. The wind pushed harder and the tree branches swayed. As Bob and Bobbi ran toward the tree, the branches parted and they ran under the tree where they would be dry.

In the shelter of the tree, the sounds of the storm were not as loud. And rather than scary, the shadows made this place seem magical. Bob and Bobbi sat down and leaned against the tree trunk, and against each other for warmth.

Then they noticed that also leaning against the tree were two wooden boxes with hinged lids and metal clasps. On top of one box was written "Ibbob." On the other was the name "Bob."

"This must be mine!" laughed Bob. "But I've never seen it before."

"Don't open it," began Bobbi, sure the two boxes belonged to someone else. They looked valuable. But it was too late. Bob had already opened the box he thought was his.

"What does this note say?" Bob asked. "I mean, I can read it, but I can't understand it: THESE NEED WILL YOU."

Bobbi read the note, which was written in beautiful, old-fashioned handwriting on parchment paper. She tried to make sense of it, but couldn't.

Bob showed her the other things he found in the box. There was a small hourglass, a hand mirror, and a man's gold ring with a red stone. He slipped the ring on his finger. "Aaah!" he cried.

"What is it?" Bobbi asked, with her eyes wide open.

"I felt a little shock, or a tingle, that's all. I'm okay. Open your box." Bob picked up the box marked "Ibbob" and gave it to Bobbi.

"That isn't my name," she protested. "This says 'Ibbob...'"

But Bob was reading the note again: "YOU WILL NEED THESE...that's what it says! The words are just backwards. And that box is yours, Ibbob. That's 'Bobbi' with the letters backwards!"

"But what about 'Bob'?" asked Bobbi. "Oh, 'Bob' is the same backwards or forwards! How did you know?"

"It was the ring," said Bob. "When I put it on, the note suddenly made sense."

So Bobbi was convinced to open the other box, the one that said "Ibbob." She found a delicate pearl ring and slipped it on. "Ooch!" she said. But it didn't really hurt; it just surprised her when she felt its power.

Then when Bobbi looked in the hand mirror, she saw not her own reflection but the image of a house. "We have to go there," she said, showing it to Bob. "I just know it!"

Bob pushed the tree branches apart and looked out. The rain had stopped and there was a break in the clouds. Right in front of them stood a two-story stone house, covered with vines. All the shutters were closed. "Look, Bobbi, there's the house!"

Bobbi shoved the mirror into the "Ibbod" box, latched it closed, and tucked it under her arm. "Come on," she said to Bob, let's go. And she ran so fast that Bob could barely keep up.

She tried to open the front door, but it was bolted from the inside. Bob tried it, too, just in case. "We have to get in," Bobbi said as she explored the outside of the house.

She came to an old wooden cellar door. When she pulled on its handles, it gave a little, but it was too heavy for her alone. Bob tried, too, but he practically fell backwards from pulling so hard.

So they decided to try it together, one on each side, and they opened it up, as simple as that. There was a ladder going down into absolute darkness. "You have to walk backwards," Bobbi said, as if that was obvious.

"Wish I had a flashlight or something," said Bob as he stepped backwards into the blackness. Bobbi followed and, at that moment, a glowing light surrounded both of them. On the walls of the cellar were hanging rows and rows of old oil lamps, all lit up.

"How did you do that?" Bobbi gasped.

"I don't know, but my ring was tingling just now..." Bob stepped off the last rung of the ladder onto the dirt floor and helped his sister.

"What are we doing here?" she wondered aloud. All at once, a sheet of paper floated down in front of them, as if out of nowhere. Bob picked it up.

"KEY THE FIND MUST YOU." he read. "YOU MUST FIND THE KEY. What key?"

A Backwards Day (continued)

Bobbi opened the "Ibbob" box and took out the hand mirror. In it she saw a room with a fireplace and an old Persian rug on the floor. "The key's hidden in this room, upstairs. Let's go," she said. She took an oil lamp from the wall, studied the cellar, and found a narrow, steep stairway. Bob was right behind her.

At the top of the stairway, they entered a hall. There were doors on the left and doors on the right. Bob tried the ones on the right, Bobbi tried the ones on the left, but none of the doors would open.

Then the hallway split, appearing to go around a large room. Bob went to the right and tried the door. It opened, but there was a great gust of wind from inside the room that slammed the door shut before he could get in.

Bob went back and found Bobbi on the left side of the room where she had found a door, opened it, and got out of the way just in time before the wind slammed it shut, too. "How can there be wind in the middle of a house?" she asked Bob. She slumped on the floor, discouraged.

"I think this is the right room," said Bob. "But how are we ever going to get inside?"

He tripped on Bobbi's box, and it fell open. The mirror slid out onto the floor. Absent-mindedly, he picked it up, then nearly dropped it when he saw the message written on the face of the mirror: ONCE AT BOTH.

"BOTH AT ONCE," he read aloud. "Hey, we have to open both doors at once. You stay here and I'll go to the other side."

Bob helped his sister up and ran around to the other side of the room.

"I'll count," shouted Bobbi. "One, two, three!" Each of them opened their doors and the wind gushed past them. Then it became completely still.

They walked into a library with bookshelves on every wall, but the books were gone. The room was dusty and smelled stale. The oil lamp flickered. They walked around the room, searching, for what they hadn't a clue.

Bobbi came to a portrait hanging on the wall. "This is strange," she said. "This painting is upside down." When she touched it, she felt the familiar tingle of her ring. "This is something..." She started to take the painting off the wall and Bob reached over to help her.

"I wonder who this man is?" said Bob, as they leaned the painting against the wall. "Look at his clothes. Look at his hair. He looks like some kind of scientist...."

"I think it's him," said Bobbi, "the man who put the boxes under the tree. He wrote the notes. He must need the key!"

She ran her hands along the back of the painting and pulled out a small black velvet bag with a drawstring. She opened it, but it was empty. She put her hand inside to be sure, but there was nothing. "Phooey!" she said, tossing the bag on the floor.

"Bobbi, we have to think," said Bob. He opened her box and looked again at the mirror. There was no message.. He turned the ring back and forth on his finger. There was no tingle. He picked up the small hourglass. "YOU WILL NEED THESE, the note said," he remembered.

For a moment, they looked at each other, then at the same time they grabbed for the hourglass. Bobbi turned it over. They sat silently watching the sand slip down. They focused on the sand. They heard nothing, saw nothing.

They did not feel the coldness of the room, nor the hardness of the floor they were sitting on. There was nothing, nothing but the sand. Finally, the last grains slid down.

Bob looked up. Bobbi picked up the black velvet bag. Without knowing why, she turned it inside out. She reached inside it, and her hand closed on a key. Bobbi smiled as she placed it in Bob's hand.

"We found it!" they both said. Bob stood up and, without knowing why, walked out of the library, down the front stairs, and to the front door of the house. He put the key in the lock and turned it. Suddenly, his ring surged with power and he knew why they were here. "Now the man can come home," he said to Bobbi, who had followed him.

He opened the door and looked outside. The clouds were gone. The sun was shining. Before closing the door, he looked at the nameplate: MERLIN.

Bobbi read the name, too. "I know who that is," she said. "Merlin the Wizard, the scientist, the one who lives backwards. I read about him."

"Could he be the man in the painting? He looked like a wizard," said Bob, looking up toward the library.

"Why do you suppose he needed us?" wondered Bobbi.

"Maybe we need him," said Bob.

They walked back up to the library to get Bobbi's box and hang up the painting, right side up, on the library wall. When Bobbi picked up her little hourglass from the floor, she noticed tiny writing on it, going around one end.

"Look at this, Bob," she said, showing it to him. "THINK TO TIME TAKE...take time to think. I'm keeping this hourglass. This could come in handy. I'm keeping the box, the mirror, and the ring. I think Merlin meant them as gifts."

"Let's go back to the tree and get my box," said Bob. "I left it behind and we might have had an easier time with its treasures!" They locked the front door of the two-story stone house, leaving the key under a rock nearby.

"Will he find the key?" asked Bob.

Bobbi nodded. "He will, if he really is Merlin the Wizard."

—*Kathryn Totten, storyteller/author*

Magic Key

Supplies

Pen
Three strips paper
Medium-size box
  (with lock and key)

Candy rings (one per child)

Different candies (one per child)
Tennis balls
Two hand mirrors
Twelve assorted keys
Laundry basket

In 1900, Johann Hurlinger walked on his hands from Vienna, Austria, to Paris, France. It took him fifty-five days to travel 870 miles.

When the party's over, what do you do with things left behind, such as a sock, a toothbrush, a Teddy bear, even underwear?

"I put all 'leftovers' in a bag and ask each child the next time I see him if anything is his. But my children often know what belongs to what friend, so I call the parents."

—Barbara Taylor
Citrus Heights,
California

Directions

1. Write the following "backwards" sentence on one strip of paper and put it in the box with all the candy: TEAM LOSING THE WITH CANDY THIS SHARE. Lock the box and hide it in a cold oven without letting the kids see you.

2. Write the following "backwards" sentences on the remaining two strips of paper (one sentence on each side and set aside until the game is finished: TIMES AT HOT :CLUE and BOX HIDDEN THE FIND MUST YOU.

3. Divide your guests into two teams and have them line up, the children behind each other.

4. Put the tennis balls, mirrors, and all the keys (including the one that locked the box) in the laundry basket. Put the basket on the opposite side of the room from the children.

5. Explain that a member from each team will run to the basket, backwards, and take out a ball and a mirror. He then turns around and uses the mirror to look back at his team while bending over and rolling the ball between his legs to the next person on his team. That person catches the ball and rolls it back to the first person while he is still facing backwards.

6. The first person then catches the ball and puts the ball and mirror back into the basket, takes out a key, then runs backwards to his team and tags the next person. (You will explain later what the key is for.)

7. The next player runs backwards to the basket and takes his turn the same way as the first person, and so on until all the keys are gone from the basket.

8. Now give each team one of the strips of paper you put aside, with the "backwards" sentences, and tell them to figure out what their strips of paper say and "do as they say."

9. When the box is found, round up everyone and let the team that found the box try its keys to see if they have the Magic Key, the one that will unlock the box. Let each child try the key or keys he got from the basket.

10. If the first team does not have the Magic Key, the other team gets to try its keys.

11. When a team opens the box, it must read the note inside and "do as it says"!

Note: When gathering keys for this game, be sure only one key will unlock the box.

Make A Treasure

Supplies

One of the following per child:

Hand mirror

Small wooden box

Small sand timer

Small rock

Newspaper

Paint markers (assorted colors, found at craft stores)

Directions

1. Choose one item for each child according to availability, price, and/or gender.

2. Lay out newspaper and paint markers, then let the kids decorate their "treasures."

The Chinese language is written from right to left, as is Hebrew. English is written from left to right.

Video Recommendations

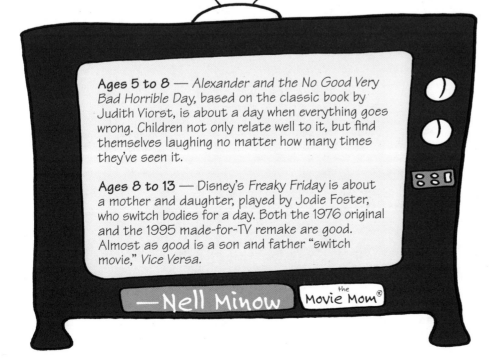

Ages 5 to 8 — *Alexander and the No Good Very Bad Horrible Day*, based on the classic book by Judith Viorst, is about a day when everything goes wrong. Children not only relate well to it, but find themselves laughing no matter how many times they've seen it.

Ages 8 to 13 — Disney's *Freaky Friday* is about a mother and daughter, played by Jodie Foster, who switch bodies for a day. Both the 1976 original and the 1995 made-for-TV remake are good. Almost as good is a son and father "switch movie," *Vice Versa*.

—Nell Minow *the Movie Mom*®

Midnight Snack Attack

Pineapple upside down cake

Backwards sandwiches (meat, bread, meat)

Scoops of ice cream with cones on top

Kellogg's™ Frosted Mini-Wheats®

Jelly filled donuts

Pizza Hut® Stuffed Crust Pizza—"the pizza you just have to eat backwards"

How many somersaults can you do in one minute? The record is seventy-five.

Inside Out Egg in Toast

Ingredients and Supplies

Makes one
Cooking spray
2½ to 3-inch round cookie cutter
Slice of bread
1 teaspoon butter
Frying pan with lid
Egg
Spatula

Directions

1. Spray the cookie cutter with the cooking spray.
2. Cut out the center of the bread with the cookie cutter and discard.
3. Melt the butter in the frying pan over low to medium heat.
4. Lay the bread in the pan and lightly fry both sides.
5. Crack the egg into the center of the bread, then place the lid on the pan to cook the egg until it's done to the child's liking.

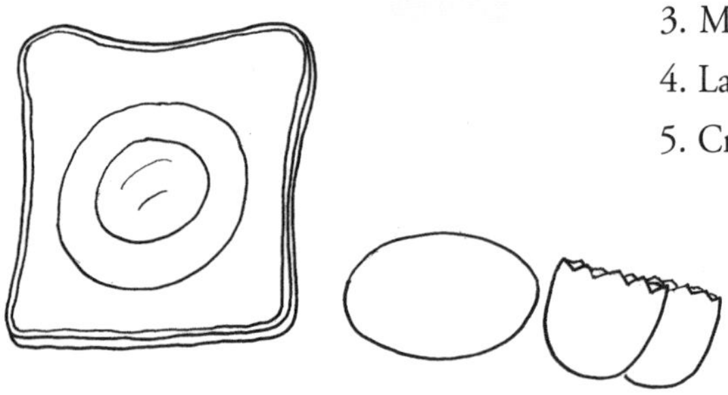

Tip: The Egg in Toast can be lifted by hand and eaten without silverware.

Note: You may cook the egg over-easy by eliminating step #4 and flipping the bread and egg together.

Backwards Name Game

Supplies

None

Directions

1. Have all the children sit in a circle.
2. One player will start by saying his first and last names backwards. Example: "My name is Ripple Nick" instead of "My name is Nick Ripple."
3. The player to his left repeats the first person's name, saying it backwards, and adds his name to the list. Example: "His name is Ripple Nick. My name is Peters Tom."
4. Continue playing until you get back to the first player. Any players who don't repeat the backwards names correctly are out. They can help to judge the players still in the game.
5. The player who lasts the longest is the winner.

Age Adjustment: Make this game more difficult for older kids by having the first player add what he likes for dessert. Example: "My name is Ripple Nick and I like pudding for dessert." He could also add what he likes for dinner (after dessert, of course). Example: "My name is Ripple Nick and I like pudding for dessert and macaroni and cheese for dinner."

Twenty Extra Fun Ideas

1. Wrap any favors or gifts with the paper inside out and bows on the bottom.

2. Hang the pictures in your house upside down.

3. Say "good-bye" to your guests when they come to the door.

4. Lead your guests into the party by walking them backwards.

5. Talk backwards—starting with your name.

6. Say "no" when you mean "yes," and "yes" when you mean "no."

7. Instruct everyone to sleep first, then play games.

8. Tell your guests to turn their sleeping bags inside out, then crawl in headfirst.

9. See who can stand on his head or walk on his hands the longest.

10. Play the wheelbarrow race.

11. Hold a somersault contest.

12. Invite your guests to watch a movie upside down. (They'll get dizzy, so just for a while.)

13. Show a DVD, rather than a video, so you can play the movie scenes backwards.

14. Ask the kids what they want to be when they're babies (rather than when they're grown up).

15. Tell a story beginning with "they lived happily ever after" and ending with "once upon a time."

16. Sing the song B-I-N-G-O, but spell it O-G-N-I-B.

17. Show your guests how to write their names backwards, letters reversed, then read them in a mirror.

18. Set the table "under the table."

19. Serve breakfast for dinner and dinner for breakfast.

20. Say "hello" to your guests when they leave.

Bud Badyna runs marathons backwards, usually finishing in the top 50%. His brother, Troy, follows him on his bicycle to watch for hazards.

You're hungry, it's late, there's no food in sight. Tell us your secret on how you get a snack?

"I jump up on the kitchen counter to find the chips I hid."

—Corina Nazzaro, age 11
Littleton, Colorado

159

Upside Down Name Bug Invitation

Twelve pieces
  5½ x 3¾-inch
  construction paper
  (any color)
Pencil
Markers or
  colored pencils
Glue stick
Twelve 4 x 5½-inch
  notecards
Copy paper
Scissors

My Mixed Up Babysitting Job

None

Upside Down Spaghetti

Grandma's meatballs
  (recipe on page 153)
Spaghetti noodles
Large pot
Strainer
Spaghetti sauce
  (store bought)
Garlic bread
White, new, plastic
  tablecloth
Bread knife
Weird utensils, such
  as chopsticks,
  spatulas, and tongs
  (one per child)
Optional: Frozen
  meatballs

Grandma's Meatballs

2 pounds ground beef
Six eggs
¾ cup grated
  parmesan cheese
1½ cups Italian
  bread crumbs
Crushed garlic (two cloves)
2 teaspoons salt
Pepper (squirt)
Fresh parsley (squirt)
¼ cup water
Frying pan
Olive oil
Spatula

Fun Mixed Up Juice

Four assorted fruit juices
  (2 cups each)
2-quart plastic pitcher
  with lid
Crushed ice
Eight 8-ounce cups

Magic Key

Pen
Three strips paper
Medium-size box
  (with lock and key)
Candy rings
  (one per child)
Different candies
  (one per child)
Tennis balls
Two hand mirrors
Twelve assorted keys
Laundry basket

Make A Treasure

One of the following
  per child:
Hand mirror
Small wooden box
Small sand timer
Small rock

Newspaper
Paint markers

Midnight Snack Attack

Pineapple upside
  down cake
Backwards sandwiches
  (meat, bread, meat)
Scoops of ice cream
  with cones on top
Kellogg's™ Frosted
  Mini-Wheats®
Jelly filled donuts
Pizza Hut® Stuffed
  Crust Pizza—"the
  pizza you just have
  to eat backwards"

Inside Out Egg in Toast

Cooking spray
2½ to 3-inch round
  cookie cutter
Slice of bread
1 teaspoon butter
Frying pan with lid
Egg
Spatula

Backwards Name Game

None

Don't forget the camera and film

CHAPTER THIRTEEN

DOUBLE TROUBLE

Double the fun with this simple yet sensational party, designed for twins but great for anyone! Give your guests the chance and challenge to be a twin for the night. Treat them to a hilarious story complete with Painted Harmonicas they play on cue. Dish out second helpings of Jake and Jack's Double Cheeseburgers and Harley and Farley's Double Layered Cheese Fries, then join the group to guffaw and giggle as four of their friends play Rise and Shine with Criss and Cross. You'll have to tuck them in twice after delighting them with a double feature and doubling their snacks, but it will be worth all the trouble!

Double Trouble Invitation

Supplies

Makes 12

Scissors

Three 9 x 12-inch pieces construction paper

Pencil

Twelve 9 x 12-inch pieces construction paper (contrasting color)

Glue stick

Copy paper

Pen

Twelve 9 x 11-inch pieces plain wrapping paper

Twenty-four stickers

Directions

1. Cut the three pieces of construction paper in fourths to make twelve 4½ x 6-inch pieces. Fold each piece in half to 4½ x 3 inches.

2. Trace a boy (pattern piece #1) or a girl (pattern piece #2) onto each piece, one hand on the fold. Cut out without cutting apart the hands. You now have twelve sets of twins.

3. Fold the contrasting pieces of construction paper in half, then in half again, to make twelve notecards.

4. Glue one set of twins on the front of each card, the heads toward the fold.

5. Make twelve copies of the invitation on page 163.

6. Fill in the details, then glue in place.

7. Wrap each invitation with wrapping paper, sealing with two stickers, of course!

Note: Try to coordinate the stickers with the theme of the party.

Pattern #1

Pattern #2

Double Trouble Slumber Party!

Dear _____

Your twin for the party will be _____

Please come to my party dressed as twins!

Party Given By:_____

Special Occasion: _____

Day and Date: _____

Drop-off Time: _____

Pick-up Time: _____

Address and Directions: _____

Phone Number: _____

Please call and let me know if you can come!

Painted Harmonica

Play these during the "Everything is Double" story

Supplies

Paint markers (assorted colors, found at craft stores)

Harmonicas (one per child, found at party stores)

Directions

1. Have the children paint designs on their harmonicas, keeping the paint away from the mouthpieces.

2. Tell them they can play their harmonicas, on cue, when you are reading the "Everything is Double" story on page 164.

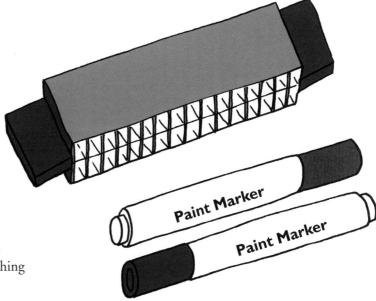

Everything is Double

It was a hot afternoon. Jake was sitting on his front porch playing his harmonica while his dog, Harley, kept the beat by wagging his tail. Jake wasn't being lazy—he just didn't have any work to do. He didn't have much money either. He raised a few sheep and sold the wool, and did a little blacksmithing now and then, often trading for various items.

Just last week, the fellow up the road paid Jake with an empty flour barrel for shoeing his horse. He sure could have used some flour in that barrel. He only had one sack of beans in the house for himself, and just one bare bone for Harley. He had planted a small garden, but the rain didn't come and the garden dried up. Which was a good thing since there was a hole in the roof! Jake had one chicken in the yard, but she hadn't laid an egg for a couple of weeks.

Still, they were happy. Happy, but hungry. Jake's stomach growled. He put his harmonica in his shirt pocket. "Harley," he said with a sigh, "I'm going to find me that chicken and fix us a stew." Harley wagged his tail faster and got up to help. It didn't take them long to find the chicken. She was perched in the barn, squawking loud enough to wake the dead.

"There you are, Lizzy, what's all the noise about?" asked Jake, as he climbed the ladder to the loft. "You'd think you knew what I was up to." When Jake got high enough, he could see why Lizzy was squawking. She had laid an egg! "Well, I'll be!" Jake exclaimed. "I'd much rather have an egg than chicken stew any day of the week." He reached out to grab the egg, but the chicken fluttered and knocked the egg into, of all things, the empty flour barrel below.

"Aw, Lizzy, now the egg's probably cracked," complained Jake as he climbed down the ladder. "Well, I'll just have to scrape it out of the flour barrel and cook it," he thought. "Come on, Harley." He went to the kitchen and found a clean pot and spatula. Harley wagged his tail all the way behind him then all the way back to the barn. Jake reached deep into the flour barrel, and found not one egg, but two. He gave out a whoop and holler, "Lizzy, you have been busy!"

Harley jumped up to see what Jake had in his hands, putting his front paws on the flour bin. He barked twice, as if to say, "Let me see! Let me see!" But he scraped his collar on the edge of the barrel, and it was so worn out that it broke and fell into the barrel. That made Harley whimper a bit since he'd had that collar since he was just a pup.

"Simmer down, Harley," said Jake. "I'm sure we can fix your collar." He carefully set the eggs down in the pan and reached into the barrel to get the collar. To his surprise, he found not one collar, but two, and just alike, both worn and broken. "Well, lookee here, Harley," he said. "Something strange is going on."

He put the pan with the eggs and the spatula into the barrel, padding them with a wool blanket so the eggs wouldn't crack, even though he knew they had to be special eggs to have survived their fall in the first place. "Come on, Harley. We need to check this out." He then picked up the barrel and carried it into the house, with Harley following at his heels.

Jake's stomach growled again so he lit the stove and reached into the barrel to get the pan and eggs. But he found not one pan and two eggs, but two pans and four eggs! He found not one spatula and one wool blanket, but two spatulas and two wool blankets! "Harley," he declared, "this flour barrel is doubling everything, or maybe I'm just crazy with hunger!"

To test his idea, Jake heaved his last sack of beans into the barrel and pulled out two sacks. He tossed in Harley's last bare bone and pulled out two bones! "Here you go, Harley, eat up!" Jake suddenly remembered the eggs and quickly scrambled them for an early supper. They tasted better than any eggs he'd ever had, even his mother's, even his grandmother's!

Happy and no longer hungry, Jake went to work. "There are lots of things around here I need more of," he said to Harley. He ran out to the barn and grabbed Lizzy, the chicken. Soon he had a yard full of clucking chickens,

Everything is Double *(continued)*

laying eggs everywhere. Harley herded a sheep into the house and before you know it, Jake had more than just a few sheep. He had a whole flock grazing on the hillside in the sunset. "Harley," he said, "when I sell all of the wool from all of those sheep, we will have enough money to buy anything we need."

The next morning, Jake took the one roofing nail he had and the one shingle and doubled them until he had enough to fix the hole in the roof. Clouds started to form overhead so he decided he'd better double his pair of boots and overalls just in case it rained and he wanted some dry clothes to wear. "Hey, Harley," he called, "what can I double for you today? Another bone or two?"

When Harley heard his name, he came running. He jumped up so Jake could rub his ears, but somehow he jumped right into the flour barrel. "Harley!" Jake called. "Don't worry, I'll pull you out!" He had just gotten Harley out of the barrel and given him a big hug when they both heard barking from inside the barrel. Jake pulled out another dog, exactly like Harley. "Hey, I guess I'll call you Farley," Jake said to the new dog.

Both dogs jumped up on Jake to lick his face, but knocked him backwards into the barrel. "Help, Harley and Farley, get me

out!" Jake yelled. Each dog took a boot in his jaws and pulled Jake out. But wait, there were two more boots sticking out of the barrel, kicking in the air. Jake and the dogs pulled out another man, who looked exactly like Jake. "Well, I'll be," said Jake. "I always wanted a brother. How about I call you Jack?" The twins shook hands and sat by the fire that night while it rained outside, talking as if they had old times to catch up on.

In the morning, they got busy. They used the barrel to double what lumber, paint, and tools Jake had around the place and built a new house and barn for Jack. That took more than a day, of course. They planted a garden now that the drought was over and sheared the sheep, making a pile of money from the wool. They decided not to try to double money, though, as that might make them greedy.

They lacked for nothing with their two houses, two barns, and two dogs, everything just alike except for an empty flour barrel in one barn. They kept it covered with a tarp, unless they needed it to double something. Every evening, unless it was raining, Jake and Jack sat on one of their porches. They played their harmonicas, and looked at the stars, while Harley and Farley kept the beat by wagging their tails.

—*Kathryn Totten,* storyteller/author

Double Delight Drink

This layered drink looks fantastic!

Ingredients and Supplies

Makes one

½ cup grenadine

12-ounce clear glass

Spoon

½ cup milk

Plastic wrap

Optional: 12-ounce plastic cup

Directions

1. Pour grenadine into glass.

2. Hold spoon inside glass above grenadine. Slowly pour milk over spoon.

3. Store in fridge until ready to use, but cover with plastic wrap.

Tip: Use a tall thin glass for the best look.

Note: You can make this drink days ahead!

Optional: Use a 12-ounce clear plastic cup if glass is not available.

Variation: You can increase or decrease the grenadine and milk, just be sure the amounts are equal.

Did you know that twins account for only 2% of all births? And although identical twins are 100% the same genetically, they actually have unique fingerprints.

Jake and Jack's Double Cheeseburgers

Ingredients and Supplies

Makes one
Frying pan or grill
Two hamburger patties
Spatula
Two pieces American
   cheese

Hamburger bun
Paper plate
Ketchup
Mustard
Knife
Pickles

Lettuce
Onion slices
Tomato slices
Serving plate

Directions

1. Fry or grill hamburger patties, melt cheese slices on top, then put it on an open hamburger bun on the paper plate.

2. Have the ketchup and mustard on the table with the knife for spreading, along with pickles, lettuce, onion, and tomato slices on the serving plate.

3. Tell the children to garnish their double cheeseburgers with two of everything— two squirts of ketchup, two dollops of mustard, two pickles, and so on.

Note: Serve with Harley and Farley's Double Layered Cheese Fries on page 167 and Double Delight Drink on page 165.

Harley and Farley's Double-Layered Cheese Fries

Ingredients and Supplies

Makes 6
Frying pan
½ pound bacon
Spatula
Paper towels
Knife

Three large potatoes
Deep fryer with oil
Slotted spoon
Oven safe platter
Shredded cheddar
cheese

These are yummy for the tummy

Shredded Monterey
jack cheese
Ranch dressing
*Optional: Frozen
French fries*

What is your best piece of advice for having a Slumber Party for twins?

"Make sure everything is ready—do the prep work and organize things ahead of time. Have games lined up."

—Linda Robinson
Castlerock, Colorado
Mother of 4 year old twins

Directions

1. Fry the ½ pound bacon, lay on paper towels to drain, then set aside.

2. Slice the potatoes into French fries.

3. Fry the French fries in the deep fryer.

4. Lay the cooked French fries onto the oven safe platter. Blot excess oil with a paper towel.

5. Sprinkle both cheeses over the French fries, then crumple the ½ pound bacon on top.

6. Bake in 350° oven until the cheese is melted. Serve with ranch dressing.

Note: Serve with Jake and Jack's Double Cheeseburgers on page 166 and Double Delight on page 165.

Variation: Rather than slicing and frying French fries, bake frozen ones in the oven.

Rise and Shine with Criss and Cross

A play that's hilarious to watch

What's your best tip for having a Slumber Party for twins?

"Make sure you have plenty of room. Let each twin pick out some stuff—do everything as evenly as possible so they don't resent each other! We always had two cakes at our party—one for each twin!"

—Peggy Masek Parker, Colorado Identical twin sister to Karen

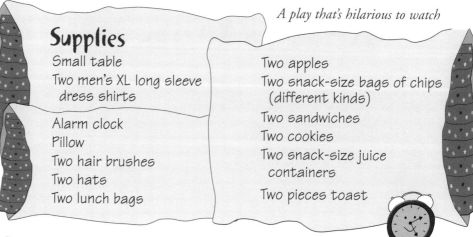

Supplies

Small table
Two men's XL long sleeve dress shirts

Alarm clock
Pillow
Two hair brushes
Two hats
Two lunch bags

Two apples
Two snack-size bags of chips (different kinds)
Two sandwiches
Two cookies
Two snack-size juice containers
Two pieces toast

Directions

1. Place all the supplies on the table except the shirts.

2. Choose two pair of children to act out the story of twins below. Have each pair stand on opposite sides of the table.

3. Dress each pair in a shirt. Have one child stand directly behind the other, the one in front with his arms down to his sides and the one in back with his arms through the shirtsleeves. Button the shirts down the back.

4. The pairs may move around, but should always keep the children in back hidden from the audience, except for their hands. They are to perform all the actions of the story while the children in front are to make appropriate facial expressions, including looking at each other.

5. Introduce one pair as Criss, the cheerful twin, and the other pair as Cross, the grumpy one.

6. Read the story below, pausing to let the pairs act out the story and the audience giggle and guffaw!

Rise and Shine with Criss and Cross

Criss and Cross were sleeping peacefully when suddenly the alarm clock rang. RRRRRING! Criss woke right up and turned off the alarm clock. Cross just kept on sleeping. Criss yawned and looked across the room at Cross. Criss tossed a pillow at Cross, cheerfully calling, "Rise and Shine!"

Cross opened one eye, looked at Criss, and snarled, "Leave me alone!" But Cross was awake now, like it or not, so he forced open his other eye. Criss was smiling at him. He scowled back and kept that face through most of their morning routine.

They both rubbed their eyes, stretched their arms, then scratched their heads, mussing up their hair more than it was already. They looked and pointed at each other. Criss laughed and Cross growled, "Your hair looks terrible!"

Criss and Cross each reached for a hair brush. It wasn't easy taming their wild-looking hair. First they brushed it all forward. They inspected each other. Criss smiled. Cross frowned. No, they shook their heads, that didn't look right. They brushed their hair back. They shook their heads to see if their hair would fall into place. Nope, this was going to be a bad hair day.

Yet Criss was whistling while Cross was mumbling as they reached for hats to cover their hair. After a couple of tries, they got their hats on. One glance at each other and they said, "Let's trade." So they tossed their hats to each other. Criss put on Cross's hat. Cross put on Criss's hat. That's better, they agreed, Criss grinning, Cross grousing.

Rise and Shine with Criss and Cross (continued)

The twins grabbed lunch bags to pack their lunches for school. Criss said, "I want an apple in my lunch," as he popped one in his bag. Cross scowled and said, "Apples, apples, apples! Don't you ever get tired of apples?" But Cross threw an apple in his bag, too.

The twins each picked up a bag of chips, but Cross, of course, didn't like the kind he had! Somehow, Criss knew that, so they looked at each other and said, "Let's trade." They tossed their chips to each other. Criss put Cross's chips in his bag, happy as could be. Cross stuffed Criss's chips in his bag, huffing and puffing. He continued the agonizing chore of packing his bag with a sandwich, a cookie, and some juice, while Criss did the same as if it were fun and games. Then it was time for breakfast, so they set their lunches on the table and reached for their toast.

Every morning Criss ate cinnamon toast. "This is really good," he said, taking a big bite. Every morning Cross ate plain toast. "I can't stand toast," he said, nibbling his piece around the edges. They looked at each other and said, "Let's trade." Criss gave his toast to Cross. Cross gave his toast to Criss. But when they started eating again, Criss was suddenly cross, frowning, and Cross was actually smiling! "Hey, " said Cross to Criss, "I could pretend to be you, and you could pretend to be me!"

Criss thought about that idea for about a second. It made him smile right along with Cross. "How about you just pretend to be me," said Criss to Cross. They both nodded a big yes, shook hands, and declared, "This is going to be a fine, fun day!" Criss picked up one lunch bag, and Cross picked up the other. "Let's trade," they almost shouted in unison, then handed each other their lunches, walking off to school, arm in arm, both grinning from ear to ear.

—*Kathryn Totten*, storyteller/author

Alarm Clock Race

Play this in a large room after the children have put on their pajamas

Supplies

Two alarm clocks with snooze buttons (same amount of snooze time)

Directions

1. Show the children how the snooze buttons work on the alarm clocks and how to turn off the alarms. Then tell them to get their pillows and the clothes they wore to the party.

2. Meanwhile, make sure the time and alarms are set to the same time on both clocks, with the alarms due to go off in approximately 15 to 20 minutes. Do not let the children know you are setting the alarms.

3. Divide your guests into two teams called A and B, or Criss and Cross—if you played Rise and Shine with Criss and Cross on page 168.

4. Put the alarm clocks on the floor in different parts of the room and have each team lie next to a clock, on their pillows, pretending to be asleep, with their clothes next to them.

5. Explain that when the alarms go off, someone on each team needs to hit their snooze button. They pretend to sleep until the alarm goes off again, then someone needs to turn it off.

6. They quickly get dressed and carry their pajamas, pillows, and the alarm clock to a designated spot, such as the kitchen. First team there wins!

Tip: Have extra pillows in case some children forgot to bring them.

Double vision (diplopia) can affect anyone, but most cases occur when the person is looking side to side, not straight ahead.

Midnight Snack Attack

Double Stuf® Oreo® cookies

Twice-baked potatoes

Wrigley's Doublemint® gum

Frozen twin pops

Tombstone® Double Top® pizza

Smucker's® Goober Grape peanut butter and jelly sanwiches

Can your immediate family handle having a Slumber Party for twins, or do you get an outside helper?

"Our immediate family can take care of it. Once you can handle twins, extra kids are a piece of cake!"

—Peggy Masek
Parker, Colorado

"My husband and I can handle it. It's fun!"

—Linda Robinson
Castle Rock, Colorado
Mother of 4 year old
twins

Video Recommendations

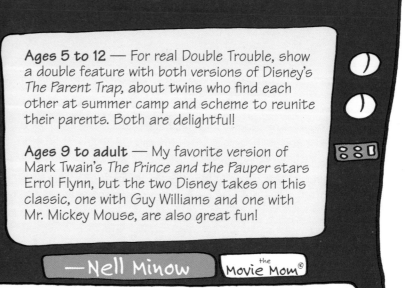

Ages 5 to 12 — For real Double Trouble, show a double feature with both versions of Disney's *The Parent Trap*, about twins who find each other at summer camp and scheme to reunite their parents. Both are delightful!

Ages 9 to adult — My favorite version of Mark Twain's *The Prince and the Pauper* stars Errol Flynn, but the two Disney takes on this classic, one with Guy Williams and one with Mr. Mickey Mouse, are also great fun!

—Nell Minow   the Movie Mom®

Double Vision Breakfast Face

Ingredients and Supplies

Makes one

Knife

One-half banana

Small bowl

Lemon juice

Two pieces link sausage

Two eggs

Two frying pans

Spatula

One piece bread

Toaster

Large flat paper plate

Butter

Two small cups orange juice or milk

Directions

1. Slice the one-half banana in half lengthwise, then put it in the small bowl with the lemon juice. (This keeps the banana from turning brown.)

2. Cook the sausage in one pan, and the eggs "sunny-side up" in the other.

3. While the bread is toasting, lay out the face on the plate using the eggs for eyes, the sausage links for the nose, and the banana slices for the mouth.

3. Butter and cut the toast in half diagonally, then set one half to the right of the nose and one to the left for cheeks.

4. Serve with two small cups of orange juice or milk.

Tip: Paper bathroom cups are the perfect size for the drinks.

Note: Be sure to cook the egg yolks all the way through according to government standards.

Double Scribble Pencil

Supplies

Makes one

Glue gun

Two colored pencils
(full size, different colors)

25 inches ½" ribbon

Small notepad

Directions

1. Glue the two pencils together, with both points down.

2. Glue one end of ribbon to the top, then wind around the pencils toward the points, leaving enough gaps to see the pencils.

3. When you get down to the shaven, sharpened part, wind the ribbon back toward the top. Glue the end at the top to secure.

4. Try out the Double Scribble Pencil on the notepad.

Tip: Let each child choose two different colored pencils from a box of colored pencils.

Age Adjustment: Younger children will need an adult to supervise the gluing.

Twenty Extra Fun Ideas

1. Rent a double-decker bus.

2. Start your party off at a double-header baseball game.

3. Ask your guests if they've seen any double overtime games?

4. Reserve some tennis courts and play doubles, of course!

5. Let the kids play basketball, but allow double dribbling.

6. Teach the group to play double-Dutch jump rope.

7. Lead the kids in a double-time march (180 steps per minute).

8. Let the children pick someone to shadow for the night.

9. Pair up your guests and handcuff them together to eat. (Use handcuffs sold as party favors.)

10. Give prizes to the double-jointed kids.

11. Get out your game of Trouble®—better yet, borrow another one so there will be Double Trouble!

12. Play the card game Concentration, otherwise known as Match.

13. Dust off your Old Maid deck of cards for old-fashioned fun.

14. Have several decks of cards so your guests can pair off and play War.

15. Sort through pennies to find two minted the same year. Let your guests keep any pairs they find.

16. See who can scrunch up the biggest double chin. Be sensitive to any over-weight kids—only play this if that is not an issue.

17. Let the children dream about going on double dates when they are older—to the prom, for example.

18. Buy some men's or ladies' double-breasted suits at a thrift store for your guests to try on.

19. Set out some chips and dip and encourage the children to double-dip! (They are going to share germs anyway at a Slumber Party.)

20. Go out for double-dip ice cream cones.

Double Trouble Invitation

Scissors
Three 9 x 12-inch pieces
  construction paper
Pencil
Twelve 9 x 12-inch pieces
  construction paper
  (contrasting color)
Glue stick
Copy paper
Pen
Twelve 9 x 11-inch pieces
  plain wrapping paper
Twenty-four stickers

Painted Harmonicas

Paint markers
  (assorted colors,
  found at craft stores)
Harmonicas
  (one per child, found
  at party stores)

Double Delight Drink

½ cup grenadine
12-ounce clear glass
Spoon
½ cup milk
Plastic wrap
*Optional: !2-ounce
  plastic cup*

Jake and Jack's Double Cheeseburgers

Frying pan or grill
Two hamburger patties
Spatula
Two pieces American
  cheese
Hamburger bun
Paper plate
Ketchup
Mustard
Knife
Pickles
Lettuce
Onion slices
Tomato slices
Serving plate

Harley and Farley's Double Layered Cheese Fries

Frying pan
½ pound bacon
Spatula
Paper towels
Knife
Three large potatoes
Deep fryer with oil
Slotted spoon
Oven safe platter
Shredded cheddar cheese
Shredded Monterey jack
  cheese
Ranch dressing
*Optional: Frozen French
  fries*

Rise and Shine with Criss and Cross

Small table
Two men's XL long sleeve
  dress shirts
Alarm clock
Pillow
Two hair brushes
Two hats
Two lunch bags
Two apples
Two snack-size bags of
  chips (different kinds)
Two sandwiches
Two cookies
Two snack-size juice
  containers
Two pieces toast

Alarm Clock Race

Two alarm clocks with
  snooze buttons
  (same amount of
  snooze time)

Don't forget the camera and film

Double Vision Breakfast Face

Knife
One-half banana
Small bowl
Lemon juice
Two pieces link sausage
Two eggs
Two frying pans
Spatula
One piece bread
Toaster
Large flat paper plate
Butter
Two small cups
  orange juice or milk

Midnight Snack Attack

Double Stuf® Oreo®
  cookies
Twice-baked potatoes
Wrigley's Doublemint®
  gum
Frozen twin pops
Tombstone® Double Top®
  pizza
Smucker's® Goober
  Grape peanut butter
  and jelly sanwiches

Double Scribble Pencil

Glue gun
Two colored pencils
  (full size, different
  colors)
25 inches ½" ribbon
Small notepad

CHAPTER FOURTEEN

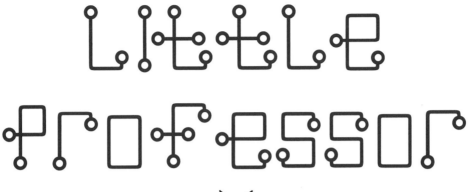

Introduce your guests to an amazing world of wonder where they get to be Little Professors, complete with their own Wire-Rimmed Glasses they wear all night. They'll figure out just how much baking soda and vinegar it takes to float a ping-pong ball, then eat Professor's Pizza Pillows for dinner, washed down with a Secret Formula Drink. After an "inventful" story, they get to make Air-Cushioned Pajamas, pillow helmets, and high-density slippers, followed by the Sleepwalking Obstacle Course. For a Midnight Snack Attack, feed them square hardboiled eggs or teach them to make candy structures. Instruct them to "shave" in the morning then travel down the assembly line to make Einstein's Contraption Breakfast before heading back to reality...

Order of Little Professor Party

Make Wire-Rimmed Glasses (wear the whole party)

Eat dinner (Professor's Pizza Pillows and Secret Formula Drink)

Do Ping-Pong Experiment

Read "The Sleepwalker Inventions"

Play Air-cushioned Pajamas Contest

Get on pajamas and lay out sleeping bags

Play Sleepwalker Obstacle Course

Watch videos with Midnight Snack Attack

Sleep

Do The Clean-Shaven Professor

Eat Einstein's Contraption Breakfast

Brush teeth, get dressed, and pack

Say good-bye!

Albert Einstein created the formula $E=mc^2$.

Smart-y Sleeping Professor Invitation

Supplies

Makes one

Empty check box (3¼ x 6½ x 1½-inch)

9 x 11-inch piece blue felt

Glue gun

Three 3¼ x 6½-inch pieces paper (coordinating)

Paper towel

2-inch square piece brown felt

Black permanent marker

Gold-wrapped chocolate coin

4½ x 6½-inch piece brown felt

Computer

Printer paper

Sharp scissors

Pen

Smarties® candies

Optional: Different box such as an empty bar of soap box

Directions

1. Wrap the top of the check box with the blue felt. Glue to secure.

2. Glue the three pieces of paper to: the bottom of the box, the inside of the bottom, and the inside of the top.

3. Roll up the paper towel to form a professor's body, then glue to the top of the check box, (bed).

4. Fold the 2-inch square piece brown felt in half, glue it closed, then above the professor's body, for a pillow.

5. Using the permanent marker, draw wire-rimmed glasses and some hair on the gold-wrapped chocolate coin, for the head. Glue onto the pillow.

6. Glue the 4½ x 6½-inch piece brown felt over the body and the sides of the box top for a blanket.

7. Type the following in italics font (12-point), print, cut out, and glue across the bottom of the blanket: *What's the formula for a fun party? E = MC²*

8. Type the following in large font (such as 48), print, cut out, and glue to the inside of the box top: *Eat more candy!*

9. Type the invitation on page 175 into a 3¼ x 6½-inch text box, fill in the details, print, cut out, and glue to the inside of the box bottom.

10. Fill the box with the Smarties® and hand deliver.

Note: Instead of using the computer hand write all.

Optional: If you use a different box, you will need to adjust the sizes of the felt and paper, plus how you wrap it, and whether or not you glue down the saying in step #8 and the invitation in step #9, or just insert them in the box.

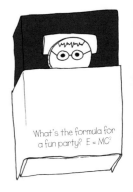

What's the formula for a fun party? $E = MC^2$

$E=MC^2$

Be a smarty! Come to my party!
Little Professor Slumber Party

Party Given By: _____

Special Occasion: _____

Day and Date: _____

Drop-off Time: _____

Pick-up Time: _____

Address and Directions: _____

Phone Number: _____

THINK if you can come and TELEPHONE me!

Wire-Rimmed Glasses

Supplies

Makes one
Three black pipe cleaners

3-inch piece black pipe cleaner
Scissors

Directions

1. Bend two pipe cleaners into circles for the eyeglass lenses.

2. Attach the 3-inch piece between the two circles for the nose bridge.

3. Cut the remaining pipe cleaner in half and attach one piece to each side of the glasses for ear stems. Bend them around your ears.

4. Wear these Little Professor glasses during the party.

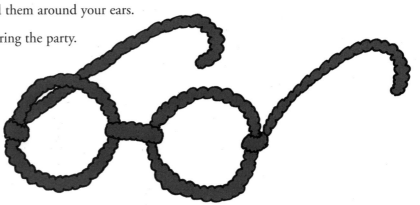

College students refer to their instructors as "professor" or "prof," never "teacher" or "teach."

Professor's Pizza Pillows

Ingredients and Supplies

Totino's® Pizza Rolls® (six per child)
Cookie sheet

Spatula
Paper plates
(one per child)

Directions

1. Bake the pizza rolls according to the package directions.

2. Scoop onto the paper plates and serve.

Age Adjustment: Younger kids may eat less and older kids more.

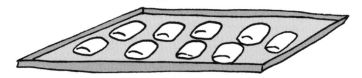

Secret Formula Drink

Ingredients and Supplies

Paint markers (assorted colors, found at craft stores)

Large test tube, 25 x 150*
(one per child, found at science stores)

Orange sherbet (about ¼ cup per child)

¼-cup measuring cup
Rubber bands (one per child)
Clear glass cup (10-ounce or larger, one per child)
1-cup measuring cup
Sprite® (approx. 1 cup per child)
Spoons (one per child)

Directions

1. Before the party, write the children's names on the test tubes.

2. Let the orange sherbet soften, almost to the melting stage. Put sherbet into test tubes.

3. "Rubber band" the test tubes to the glass cups with the children's names facing out.

4. Right before serving, pour approximately one cup of Sprite® into each glass and top off the test tubes. The test tubes will bubble. (Do not pour the Sprite® ahead of time.)

5. Let the kids pour the contents of their test tubes into their glasses and stir up their Secret Formulas before drinking them.

6. Have them keep their test tubes on their glasses so they can reuse them all night. Let them take their test tubes home.

* To order test tubes, call Oakbrook Publishing House (toll-free) 1-888-738-1733 or go to www.whatdoidobooks.com.

Ping-Pong Experiment

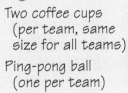

Supplies

Masking tape
Large table
TV trays (one per team)
Small box baking soda
(one per team)

1-teaspoon measuring
spoon (one per team)
16-ounce bottle white
vinegar (one per team)
Roll of paper towels
(one per team)

Two coffee cups
(per team, same
size for all teams)
Ping-pong ball
(one per team)

Directions

1. With masking tape, mark a starting line on the floor about 10 to 15 feet from the large table. Set up the TV trays behind the line.

2. Divide the kids into teams of three to five, and line them up beside the trays.

3. Put the baking soda, measuring spoons, vinegar, paper towels, coffee cups, and ping-pong balls on the TV trays next to the teams.

4. Explain that this is an experiment. They will pour baking soda and vinegar into a cup with the ping-pong ball to see which team can get the ball to float out of the cup first. They will need to think as a team and scientifically guess how much solution to use. The only thing you will tell them is that their cups need to be tilted or their balls will not float out. They should figure out how many folded paper towels to use to tilt their cups.

5. On "Go," one team member from each team runs down to the large table with the coffee cup and paper towels. He puts the cup on the table, not too close to the edge, on however many folded paper towels he wants.

6. He runs back to his team and the next player runs with the ping-pong ball and drops it into the cup.

7. After he gets back, the next player runs with the measuring spoon filled with baking soda, leaving the box with his team. If his team wants to add more baking soda, they must do it one scoop at a time using other players.

8. When they have finished with the baking soda, the next player pours the vinegar into the cup.

9. The first team to get the ball to float out of the cup wins.

10. If a team tries and fails, they can try again using their second coffee cup.

Tip: It will take about 1 tablespoon baking soda and ½ cup vinegar to get this to work, depending on the size of the cups.

Note: If the cup is not tipped, the ball only floats on top of the mixture and will not float out.

Variation: If you have a small group, let them play three times and then time them to get their best time.

The Sleepwalker Invention

The alarm clock didn't ring—it whistled, precisely at 6:30 a.m. The Little Professor was gently ejected from his bed, landing upright with his feet sliding into his slippers. The automatic bed-maker tugged his sheets and quilt into place. The Little Professor reached for his wire-rimmed glasses, then stepped onto the conveyor. It carried him down the hall, around the corner, and into the kitchen. When it stopped a foot away from his chair, he stepped off, grabbed a napkin and spoon, and sat down.

The juice dispenser in the refrigerator door squirted chilled grape juice into a frosted glass. A robotic hand placed it on the table. The cereal dispenser on the counter slid a bowl under its chute. It filled the bowl with the Little Professor's own invention, "smart food" cereal. Then the robotic hand put the bowl under the milk dispenser in the refrigerator door for just the right amount of milk before placing it on the table right in front of the Little Professor.

He started eating, chewing each spoonful six times before swallowing, then dabbing the corners of his mouth with his napkin. He always ate this way.

At 6:48 a.m. the Little Professor's phone in his pajama top pocket vibrated. He clicked it, and held it a few inches away from his ear. He knew at this time of the morning that the voice on the other end would be frantic.

"I've got a big bruise on my leg, Norton!"

"Professor. You are supposed to call me Professor."

"I woke up in my dog's house, with my head in his food bowl. Do you hear me, Norton?"

"I hear you, Max."

"I must have kicked something. That's why I have a bruise. It's dangerous. Seriously."

"I agree."

"Norton, you HAVE to help me."

"I will."

"When, Norton? When?"

"As soon as you call me Professor."

"Sorry. I just forgot. Help me, okay? Please, Professor?"

Norton, also known as the Little Professor, met his scruffy, rumpled, and bruised best friend, Max, in his science lab in his shed a half hour later. He examined the bruise and applied an ice pack.

"Stick out your tongue," demanded the Little Professor. Max obeyed. "Now balance on one leg, touch your nose, and whistle."

Max tried his best on every test, but his balance was off and his vision a little blurred.

"You are sleep-deprived," said the Little Professor, "because you sleepwalk. You hurt yourself almost every time. It could get you into trouble…"

"What are you going to do about it, Norton? I mean, Professor?"

"I have an idea."

Max watched in awe while the Little Professor started inventing. In a short while, he was finished.

"Call your mom, Max. Ask her if you can spend the night."

That day, Norton (the Little Professor) and Max walked downtown and climbed the stairs of the bank building all the way to the top, then they came home and swam in the backyard pool for hours and hours. They wanted to go skateboarding, but Max was still a little dizzy.

"You have to be good and tired, so you will sleep tonight," explained the Little Professor.

After dinner, the boys took their sleeping bags out to the lab in the shed. The Little Professor smoothed his out neatly. Max tossed his carelessly on the floor. They read some comic books and played cards. Finally, Max declared that he was sleepy.

"Then we have to prepare you for the night," said the Little Professor. He inflated the air-cushioned pajamas he had invented that morning and Max put them on. The Little Professor helped Max slide into the newly-invented high-density foam slippers and strapped the pillow helmet, also invented that morning, onto Max's head. "All of these will protect you from getting injured should you go sleepwalking."

Max got into his sleeping bag and was snoring softly within minutes. Norton sat up with his feet tucked inside his sleeping bag. He intended to stay awake and watch Max all night. Just to be sure, in case he fell asleep, he had stretched coils of wires around the room, which were connected to an alarm system. This would wake him up if Max started to sleepwalk.

The Sleepwalker Invention *(continued)*

Suddenly, the Little Professor jerked awake at the sound of his alarm system. Max was almost out the door before Norton could climb out of his sleeping bag, which he had snuggled into. He followed his friend, trying not to wake him. His goal was to keep him from getting hurt.

The Little Professor cringed as he watched Max walk under a low tree limb, thumping his head against it. The pillow helmet cushioned the blow and Max kept walking in his sleep. Norton grabbed the back of Max's pajamas to keep up with him.

Then out of nowhere it seemed, they both went splash! Max had walked right into the swimming pool, pulling Norton in with him. Max floated effortlessly, supported by his inflated pajamas. The Little Professor swam to the edge of the pool and pulled his friend out. He was amazed that Max was still asleep! They were both dripping wet, but Max was off again so Norton followed.

A gentle breeze helped to dry their pajamas. The Little Professor watched Max bounce off a fence then straight into a light pole. The inflated pajamas protected him again, and he kept sleeping through dogs barking and cats meowing. The two friends covered the whole neighborhood.

"Max, aren't you getting tired?" Max's unconscious mind must have heard the weariness in his friend's voice, because he slowed down a little. Norton gently took his arm and guided him back toward the science lab. He hoped to get Max to stay put for a while.

They were just inside the door of the shed when Max bumped a shelf and knocked a couple of paint cans down. One of them hit him on the foot! Good thing he was wearing those high-density foam slippers, and the lids on the cans didn't pop off!

At last, Norton got Max settled back into his sleeping bag. Yawning and nodding, the Little Professor kept watch over him, listening to the sounds of the night. A car passed on a nearby street. A back door opened long enough to let a cat inside. Two distant voices spoke a moment, then ceased. Even the breeze was still.

Slowly, the Little Professor became aware of warmth on a patch of his sleeping bag where sunlight was streaming through the window. He rolled over and opened his eyes. The delicious taste of sleep lingered as he glanced toward the other sleeping bag. Max was beginning to wiggle, too. He sat up and smiled broadly.

"I feel great!" he said. "I can't remember a thing. Did I sleep-walk last night?

"You not only walked. You swam, you bounced off fences, and you prowled the whole neighborhood!"

"I did? But I feel like I slept for a week in a mound of feathers. I haven't felt this good for months and months."

The Little Professor sat up and stretched. A smile curled his upper lip. He reached for his glasses. Smoothing his sleeping bag gently with the palms of his hands, he became aware of an idea creeping into his mind. Another invention was beginning to take form.

Another day was well begun.

—Kathryn Totten, storyteller/author

Air-Cushioned Pajamas Contest

Supplies

Each team needs:

Sleeping bags
Deflated air mattress (individual
   size for pool)

Pillows
Pair of slippers
Bubble wrap
String

Scissors
Balloons

Directions

1. Divide the kids into teams. Give each team the supplies and a half hour to create Air-Cushioned Pajamas, a pillow helmet, and some high-density slippers like the Little Professor in "The Sleepwalker Inventions" on page 178.
   Caution: Explain that they must keep objects away from their faces.

2. Have the kids pretend to sleepwalk using their inventions. Take a vote to see whose inventions look the best and whose inventions work the best. The teams with the most votes gets to lay out their sleeping bags first.

Sleepwalker Obstacle Course

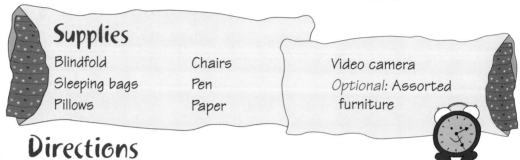

Supplies

Blindfold
Sleeping bags
Pillows

Chairs
Pen
Paper

Video camera
Optional: Assorted furniture

Directions

1. Divide the group into two teams. Ask who in the first team would like to try an obstacle course, then send him out with another adult to get blindfolded, preferably to a room in the house where he won't hear what is happening in the obstacle course room.

2. While he is gone, the other team quietly sets up an obstacle course for him using rolled-up sleeping bags to form a path, pillows to jump over, and chairs to wind around.

3. When they are finished, call the player back to the room.

4. On the word "Go," he puts his hands in front of him as if he is sleepwalking, and his team members call out instructions to direct him through the obstacle course. Give his team a point every time he bumps into something.

5. When he is through the course, choose a player from the second team and send him out of the room, letting the first team rearrange the obstacle course. Then call him back and let him be the sleepwalker, giving him points for things he touches.

6. Go through as many team members as time allows. The team with the lowest score wins.

7. Take videos of the sleepwalkers to show at breakfast.

Note: Limit the teams to about 10 minutes to set up each obstacle course.

Optional: Use assorted furniture in the room as part of the obstacle course.

Video Recommendations

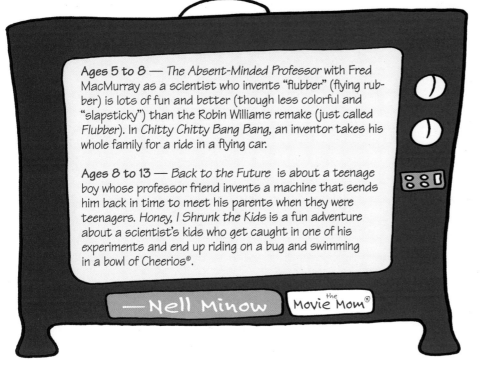

Ages 5 to 8 — *The Absent-Minded Professor* with Fred MacMurray as a scientist who invents "flubber" (flying rubber) is lots of fun and better (though less colorful and "slapsticky") than the Robin Williams remake (just called *Flubber*). In *Chitty Chitty Bang Bang*, an inventor takes his whole family for a ride in a flying car.

Ages 8 to 13 — *Back to the Future* is about a teenage boy whose professor friend invents a machine that sends him back in time to meet his parents when they were teenagers. *Honey, I Shrunk the Kids* is a fun adventure about a scientist's kids who get caught in one of his experiments and end up riding on a bug and swimming in a bowl of Cheerios®.

— Nell Minow   the Movie Mom®

Midnight Snack Attack

- Marshmallows cooked in microwave 1 to 1½ minutes (they will get large and be brown inside)

- Square hardboiled eggs (buy a square egg press at kitchen stores)

- Ice Cream in a Bag (see page 137, *Valentine School Parties...What Do I Do?®*)

- Rock candy

- Candy structure (build triangles and squares with gumdrops and pretzels, connect and make into 3-D designs)

- Spaghetti (brains)

In 1996, Eddie Murphy starred in the movie, *The Nutty Professor*, a remake of the 1963 original with Jerry Lewis.

The Clean-Shaven Professor

Supplies

Travel-size shaving cream (one per boy)

Large craft sticks (one per boy)

Clean washcloths (one per boy)

Zipper plastic bags (one per boy)

Directions

1. Before the party, put a can of shaving cream, a craft stick, and a washcloth in a zipper plastic bag for each boy. Label the bags with the boys' names.

2. In the morning, have the boys go to the bathroom with their "kits" to "shave" before breakfast. Tell them to squirt shaving cream onto their faces (away from their eyes) as if they had beards, then use their craft sticks to "shave."

3. When they're through, they should wet their washcloths and wipe off their faces.

Tip: Make sure the boys keep their mouths closed while shaving so they don't get shaving cream for breakfast!

Note: Let the boys take home their shaving kits as favors.

Einstein's Contraption breakfast

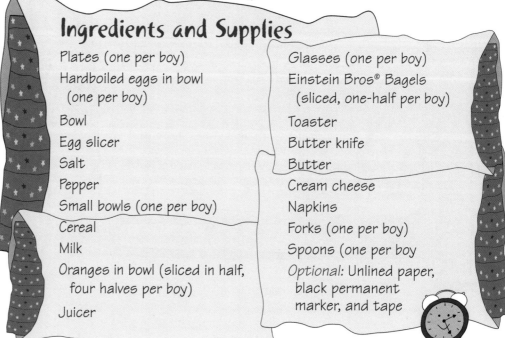

Ingredients and Supplies

Plates (one per boy)

Hardboiled eggs in bowl
(one per boy)

Bowl

Egg slicer

Salt

Pepper

Small bowls (one per boy)

Cereal

Milk

Oranges in bowl (sliced in half,
four halves per boy)

Juicer

Glasses (one per boy)

Einstein Bros® Bagels
(sliced, one-half per boy)

Toaster

Butter knife

Butter

Cream cheese

Napkins

Forks (one per boy)

Spoons (one per boy

Optional: Unlined paper,
black permanent
marker, and tape

When Einstein was 4 or 5, his father brought him a compass. The little boy, confined to his bed by a cold, was fascinated that the needle always pointed in the same direction. He played with it constantly for weeks, trying to figure out exactly what made it work.

Directions

1. Set up an assembly line in this order: plates, hardboiled eggs in bowl, bowl, egg slicer, salt, pepper, small bowls, cereal, milk, oranges in bowl, juicer, glasses, bagels, toaster, butter knife, butter, cream cheese, napkins, forks, and spoons.

2. Let the kids go through the line pretending they are on a conveyer belt. Tell them to work quickly and efficiently while making their breakfast with the ingredients and contraptions.

3. They will take a plate and an egg, peel the egg, put the egg shells into the empty bowl, slice the egg with the egg slicer, salt and pepper the egg, take a bowl, fill it with cereal and milk, take four-orange halves and juice them, pour the juice into a glass, toast a bagel half, and put butter or cream cheese on it. Then they take their napkins and spoons over to the table and eat.

Optional: Make a sign saying SMART FOOD and tape it onto the cereal box.

Twenty Extra Fun Ideas

1. Ask everyone what they think a professor does.

2. Talk about how many years it takes to become a professor.

3. Name ten things that are little.

4. Study things with a magnifying glass or microscope.

5. Make and color professors' degrees.

6. Make professor pointers with rolled-up newspaper and tape.

7. Play the game Mouse® Trap by Milton Bradley.

8. Go stargazing.

9. Draw and color brains, then have a contest to see whose is the best.

10. Do simple science experiments found on the Internet.

11. Search out a college professor to give a lecture or teach something.

12. Hire a "Mad Scientist" to come entertain the kids. (Look in your yellow pages under parties.)

13. Choose a scientific topic and have a debate about it.

14. Research a scientific topic on the Internet.

15. Build odd-shaped structures out of toothpicks and marshmallows.

16. See who can fold a piece of paper the most times.

17. Make your own crossword puzzle.

18. Create five questions you think should be on an IQ test.

19. Pose a question to the Little Professors (all the boys). Get the answer by having each boy say one word going around the circle.

20. Give the boys fake buckteeth to wear (found at costume or party stores) with their wire-rimmed glasses (to look like *The Nutty Professor*).

How would you entertain kids at a Slumber Party?

"I would show them my invention, Gideon Goose, the world's funniest talking goose. At least, that's what HE says.... 'We' would tell them about his friend, ALBERT, my 7-foot tall antique arcade machine I rescued from the scrap heap and rebuilt. ALBERT stands for Arcade Language-Based, Educatable, Responsive Tool...Gideon Goose and I would also tell the kids about my Van De Graaf Generator that makes 400,000 volts of static electricity! I'd ask the kids if they know what static electricity is and demonstrate it by giving each of them a big balloon to rub in their hair and stick on the wall, telling them to multiply that energy by thousands to get the feel for Van De Graaf's power! If there is a computer hooked up to the Internet, I'd take the kids to my web-site at www.ALBERTweb.com so they can see firsthand the kind of work I do every day. I get to learn constantly, make lots of gadgets, and teach kids how to make good decisions in life, like realizing that science is funtastic!"

—Todd Carpenter, "Professor Pockets" Poca, West Virginia

Smart-y Sleeping Professor Invitation

Empty check box
  (3¼ x 6½ x 1½-inch)
9 x 11-inch piece blue felt
Glue gun
Three 3¼ x 6½-inch pieces
  paper (coordinating)
Paper towel
2-inch square piece
  brown felt
Black permanent marker
Gold-wrapped chocolate
  coin
4½ x 6½-inch piece
  brown felt
Computer
Printer paper
Sharp scissors
Pen
Smarties® candies
Optional: Different box
  such as an empty bar
  of soap box

Wire-Rimmed Glasses

Three black pipe cleaners
3-inch piece black pipe
  cleaner
Scissors

Professor's Pizza Pillows

Totino's® Pizza Rolls®
  (six per child)
Cookie sheet
Spatula
Paper plates
  (one per child)

Secret Formula Drink

Paint markers (assorted
  colors, found at craft
  stores)
Large test tube, 25 x 150
  (one per child, found at
  science stores)
Orange sherbet (about
  ¼ cup per child)
¼-cup measuring cup
Rubber bands (one per child)
Clear glass cup (10-ounce
  or larger, one per child)
1-cup measuring cup
Sprite® (approx. 1 cup
  per child)
Spoons (one per child)

Ping-Pong Experiment

Masking tape
Large table
TV trays (one per team)
Small box baking soda (one
  per team)
1-teaspoon measuring
  spoon (one per team)
16-ounce bottle white
  vinegar (one per team)
Roll of paper towels
  (one per team)
Two coffee cups (per team,
  same size for all teams)
Ping-pong ball
  (one per team)

Don't forget the
camera and film

Air-Cushioned Pajamas Contest

Each team needs:
Sleeping bags
Deflated air mattress
  (individual size for pool)
Pillows
Pair of slippers
Bubble wrap
String
Scissors
Balloons

Sleepwalking Obstacle Course

Blindfold
Sleeping bags
Pillows
Chairs
Pen
Paper
Video camera
Optional: Assorted
  furniture

The Clean-Shaven Professor

Travel-size shaving cream
  (one per boy)
Large craft sticks
  (one per boy)
Clean washcloths
  (one per boy)
Zipper plastic bags
  (one per boy)

Midnight Snack Attack

Marshmallows
Square hardboiled eggs
Ice Cream in a bag
Rock candy
Candy structure
  (gumdrops and pretzels)
Spaghetti

Einstein's Contraption Breakfast

Plates (one per boy)
Hardboiled eggs in bowl
  (one per boy)
Bowl
Egg slicer
Salt
Pepper
Small bowls (one per boy)
Cereal
Milk
Oranges in bowl (sliced in
  half, four halves per boy)
Juicer
Glasses (one per boy)
Einstein Bros® Bagels
  (sliced, one-half per boy)
Toaster
Butter knife
Butter
Cream cheese
Napkins
Forks (one per boy)
Spoons (one per boy)
Optional: Unlined paper,
  black permanent marker,
  and tape

CHAPTER FIFTEEN

Dog Party

Why not invite friendly dogs and their owners to a Dog Slumber (nap) Party? Use your backyard if it's large enough or meet at a dog-friendly park. Start by letting the dogs get acquainted while the owners exchange tips and ideas. Play fun dog games like Tricks and Treats Show 'n' Tell. Then "let them (the dogs) eat cake" made from dog food and biscuits, while their owners snack from a Hot Dog Cart. Whether letting the dogs run, or taking them for walks, everyone will be ready to take a nap or rest in the shade. Or if you're truly courageous, one or two owners and their dogs can go back to your house to watch dog movies and spend the night. Whenever your party ends, be sure to have a favor or treat to keep the dog owners smiling and the dogs' tails wagging all the way home!

🐾og 🐾arty Invitation

What are important items to bring to a Slumber Party?

"My toy dog 'Patches' and my pillow."

— Matthew Radeck,
age 7
Germantown, Wisconsin

You're hungry, it's late, there's no food in sight. Tell us your secret on how you get a snack?

"Walk quietly to get past barking dogs and sleeping dads."

—Anonymous

Supplies

Makes one

Copy paper
Scissors
Glue stick
3 x 5-inch index card

Black permanent marker
Paper punch
12-inch piece curling ribbon
Bone-shaped dog biscuit

Directions

1. Make a copy of the invitation. Cut to fit, then glue onto the index card.

2. Fill in the details with the marker. If you want, your party can be given by you and your dog!

3. Punch a hole near the left edge of the index card. Curl the ribbon with the scissors and put it through the hole.

4. Tie the ribbon around a dog biscuit and walk your dog to deliver the invitation!

🐾og 🐾arty!

You and your dog are invited to a party.
We'll have a howling good time!

Party Given By: _____

Special Occasion: _____

Day and Date: _____

Time: _____

Address and Directions: _____

_____

_____

_____

Phone Number: _____

Please give us a bark back if you can come.

Dog Bonus

Have a Hot Dog Cart for the dog owners, complete with hot dogs in buns, condiments, chips, and drinks.

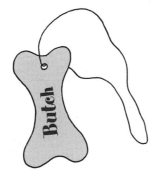

Make dog tags for the dog owners from construction paper and ribbon. Write the dogs' names on them and have the owners wear them around their necks.

Play Tricks and Treats Show 'n' Tell. Each owner has his dog do a trick, then they both get a treat.

Purchase inexpensive dog bowls and personalize with the dogs' names. Use for water during the party and send home as favors.

Make a dog cake by mixing equal amounts of canned dog food with crushed dry dog food and placing on a large plastic party tray. Save some crushed dry dog food to sprinkle around the sides of the cake and the top. "Garnish" with colored dog biscuits. Serve slices to each dog on doggie-themed paper plates.

Also for the owners, make Puppy Treats (see page 125 in *Valentine School Parties… What Do I Do?*®)

Keep in touch with old neighbor dogs or with puppies you've bred so you can have a doggie reunion party.

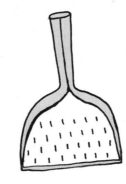

Don't forget to have a dog shovel for any messes during the party.

Have you had a Dog Party? Tell us about it.

"When my darling 'Annie' gave birth to seven beautiful Shelties, I became very attached while raising them for eight weeks. I knew when they left I would have a difficult time. I missed them so much that I decided when they turned "one," I would invite them all back for a birthday party. To be honest, this was one of the funniest parties I had ever been to. It was a little hectic, but all went great."

—Dinah Benedict
Woodstock, Illinois

What are your most memorable moments as Lassie's owner and trainer?

"'Lassie' was voted the eleventh greatest show ever out of fifty by TV Guide—a great honor since thousands were considered. I love that Lassie and I have brought so much joy to people! She has given me the chance to contribute, to help people. So much happens in a lifetime, it's hard to choose my most memorable moments. There were times of great emotion, for example, a producer crying when Lassie was washed down a river during the filming of *Lassie Come Home*, and a blind lady crying when Lassie kissed her at a convention. She said it was the best moment of her life! These are but a few of the thousands of rewards I have gotten from Lassie over the years…."

—Robert Weatherwax
Owner and Trainer
of Lassie

Dog Cheese Bones

Make these ahead and store in the fridge

Ingredients and Supplies

Makes 12

2 cups flour

1½ cups shredded cheddar cheese (room temperature)

Crushed garlic (two cloves)

½ cup vegetable oil

Food processor

¼ cup water

Rolling pin

Dog bone cookie cutter

Cookie sheet

Optional: Pencil, cardboard, scissors, and knife

Directions

1. Put the flour, cheese, garlic, oil, and water into the food processor. Mix until the dough is stiff. You may need to add ½ to 1 tablespoon more water.

2. Roll out the dough onto a floured board to ¼-inch thick. Cut into dog bones and bake at 400° for 10 to 15 minutes on a cookie sheet.

3. Cool completely before tossing to your doggie party guests.

Optional: If you don't have a dog bone cookie cutter, draw a bone shape on a piece of cardboard, cut it out, then for each treat, lay it on the rolled-out dough to cut around for each treat.

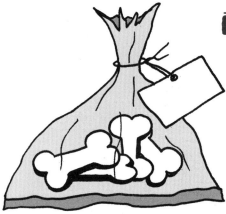

Video Recommendations

Ages 6 to adult — In *The Adventures of Milo and Otis*, a dog and a cat grow up together on a farm and become best friends. The narration by Dudley Moore is just right.

Ages 8 to 12 — *Homeward Bound: The Incredible Journey* is about two dogs and a cat separated from their family. They find their way home in this touching, exciting, and heartwarming classic.

All ages don't forget the classic Lassie movies.

— Nell Minow, the Movie Mom®

Labrador Retrievers are among the most popular breeds of dogs. They used to be just black, but yellow and chocolate ones are now common.

Although the Dalmatian most likely came from the European countries of Dalmatia and Croatia, its original roots may be in Ancient Egypt. The Gypsies are said to have spread this breed around the world, making it a very visible and popular one.

Final Thoughts

Time for you to Slumber (Party)... Time for me to rest!

Till next time
Willie

Index

Order Form

Become an expert the easy way! Order from the **What Do I Do?**® series.

CALL OUR TOLL FREE HOTLINE TO ORDER TODAY AT:

1-888-738-1733

Oakbrook Publishing House
P.O. Box 2463 • Littleton, CO 80161-2463
PHONE: (303) 738-1733 • **FAX:** (303) 797-1995
WEBSITE: http://www.whatdoidobooks.com
E-MAIL: oakbrook@whatdoidobooks.com

NAME: _____

ADDRESS: _____

CITY, STATE & ZIP CODE: _____ **PHONE: (** _____ **)** _____

Order 2 books and get a 10% discount, or order 3 or more books and get a 10% discount and free shipping.

BOOK TITLE	QUANTITY	PRICE	TOTAL
Christmas Parties...What Do I Do?® ISBN: 0-9649939-4-5	_____	$19.95 ea.	$ _____
Halloween School Parties ...What Do I Do?® ISBN: 0-9649939-8-8	_____	$19.95 ea.	$ _____
Slumber Parties...What Do I Do?® ISBN: 0-9649939-0-2	_____	$19.95 ea.	$ _____
Valentine Boxes...What Do I Do?® ISBN: 0-9649939-3-7	_____	$12.95 ea.	$ _____
Valentine School Parties...What Do I Do?® ISBN: 0-9649939-9-6	_____	$19.95 ea.	$ _____

100% fully guaranteed on all orders.

SUBTOTAL	$_____
DISCOUNT	$_____
SUBTOTAL	$_____
Colorado Res. Add 3.8% Sales Tax	$_____
Shipping & Handling (see below)	$_____
TOTAL	$_____

CHECK OR MONEY ORDER PAYABLE TO: Oakbrook Publishing House

CREDIT CARD: ☐ Visa   ☐ Master Card   ☐ Discover

CARD NUMBER _____ **EXP. DATE** _____

SIGNATURE _____

Canadian orders must be accompanied by a postal money order in U.S. funds.

SHIPPING AND HANDLING CHARGES ARE:
1st class $4.50, 4th class $2.50 (allow 7–10 days for 4th class mail), additional books add $1.50 each.
Free shipping is 4th class mail

SCHOOL SPECIAL
Purchase 5 books from the **What Do I Do**® series and get 1 book free.
Purchase 10 books and get 2 free and free shipping.
Get an order together, ask other parents, teachers, or friends
and get free books to be used in the school library or PTO room.